WONDROUS BRUTAL FICTIONS

WONDROUS BRUTAL FICTIONS

*Eight Buddhist Tales from
the Early Japanese Puppet Theater*

Translated, with an introduction, by
R. Keller Kimbrough

Columbia University Press   New York

Columbia University Press wishes to express its appreciation
for assistance given by the Pushkin Fund toward the cost of
publishing this book.

Columbia University Press
Publishers Since 1893
New York   Chichester, West Sussex
cup.columbia.edu

Copyright © 2013 Columbia University Press
All rights reserved

Library of Congress Cataloging-in-Publication Data
Wondrous brutal fictions : eight Buddhist tales from the early Japanese puppet
theater / translated, with an introduction, by R. Keller Kimbrough.
    pages cm
Includes bibliographical references.
ISBN 978-0-231-14658-6 (cloth : alk. paper)   ISBN 978-0-231-51833-8 (e-book)
1. Sekkyo joruri. 2. Buddhist literature, Japanese—Translations
into English. 3. Japanese drama—Edo period, 1600–1868—Translations
into English. 4. Puppet plays, Japanese—History and criticism.
I. Kimbrough, R. Keller, 1968– translator.
    PL768.J6W66   2012
    895.6′205160803—dc23   2012036924

Columbia University Press books are printed on
permanent and durable acid-free paper.
This book is printed on paper with recycled content.

Printed in the United States of America
c 10 9 8 7 6 5 4 3 2 1

COVER IMAGE: Detail of Funaki-*bon rakuchū rakugaizu* (ca. 1624–1644).
(Courtesy of the Tokyo National Museum)
COVER DESIGN: Noah Arlow

References to Web sites (URLs) were accurate at the time of writing. Neither the translator nor Columbia University Press is responsible for URLs that may have expired or changed since the manuscript was prepared.

For Peggy, who always loves a good story

Contents

Acknowledgments ix
Notes on the Translation xi

Introduction 1

Sanshō Dayū 23

Karukaya 60

Shintokumaru 96

Oguri 123

Sayohime 161

Aigo-no-waka 191

Amida's Riven Breast 216

Goō-no-hime 232

Appendix 1. Major Sekkyō Chanters 249
Appendix 2. Works in This Volume 253
Glossary 267
Bibliography 269

Acknowledgments

In his sixteenth-century commentary on the Lotus sutra, the priest Eishin of Sugaoji Temple recounts that the great fifth-century translator Kumārajīva once swore an oath in regard to the accuracy of his work: "If it is true that there are no mistakes in my sutra translations," the Central Asian monk is said to have declared, "then when my body is cremated after I die, my tongue alone will not burn." Indeed, when Kumārajīva died and his corpse was consigned to the flames, only his tongue is said to have survived.[1]

Not being Kumārajīva, I have refrained from making a similar vow. In the course of translating the following works, I have received extraordinary assistance from numerous institutions and individuals. In particular, I would like to thank the Japan Foundation for a generous research grant during the 2009/2010 academic year that allowed me to translate the majority of the works in this volume; the Nanzan Institute for Religion and Culture for a place to work in Japan; the University of Colorado Center for Asian Studies for a generous subvention to help defray the cost of including images; Haruo Shirane, Jennifer Crewe, and Columbia University Press for allowing my translations to see the light of day; the late Minobe Shigekatsu for his many insights and generous guidance; Bill Londo for reading and commenting on an early draft of *Karukaya*; Kelley Doore, for reading and commenting on early drafts of

Sayohime and *Aigo-no-waka*; the two anonymous reviewers for Columbia University Press for their many insights and suggestions; and my graduate students at the University of Colorado (2006–2011) with whom I first read many of the stories translated here: Molly Blair, Philip Christopher, Kelley Doore, Ian Ferguson, Alicia Foley, Preston From, Ben Grafstrom, Amanda Hotovec, Mackenzie Keegan, Sarah Keleher, Suneera Khurana, Lisa Kostelecky, Matt Levitas, Chris Lewis, Yuko Marshall, Hana Masters, Michael Meyer, Kazuko Osada, Atsuko Plampin, Aaron Proffitt, Nicole Russotto, Jesus Solis, Theo Takeda, Ayumi Tatsumoto, Eric Tischer, and Daniel Topal. Finally, I would like to thank my wife, Eiko, for her forbearance and tireless support. This book is dedicated to our daughter Peggy, a living *mōshigo* of the Kiyomizu Kannon.

NOTE

1. *Hokekyō jikidanshō* (Kyoto: Rinsen Shoten, 1979), 2:429–30.

Notes on the Translation

- Ages are given according to the Japanese count, by which a person is considered to be one year old at birth and to gain a year on the first day of every new year.
- I use the terms "temple" and "shrine" to distinguish between Buddhist and Shinto institutions, despite the ultimate futility of that task, because in medieval and early Edo-period Japan the two religious traditions were inextricably fused.
- The first five translations in this volume are divided into "parts" corresponding to the three booklets in which each of the works was published or transcribed, and the last three translations are divided into "acts" as in a *ko-jōruri* playbook.
- In Chinese sources, the bodhisattva Kannon is frequently depicted as female, but in Japan, Kannon is often male. Furthermore, in *Shintokumaru* and some other seventeenth-century Japanese sources, the living statue of Kannon at Kiyomizu Temple is explicitly identified as male.
- For explanations of the various manuscripts and woodblock-printed editions of the works translated here, see appendix 2.

The abbreviations for citations in the notes and appendices are as follows:

MJMS	Yokoyama Shigeru 横山重, ed. *Muromachi jidai monogatari shū*. 5 vols. Tokyo: Inoue shobō, 1962.
SKFS	Nakamura Yukihiko 中村幸彦 and Hino Tatsuo 日野龍夫, eds. *Shinpen kisho fukuseikai sōsho*. 46 vols. Kyoto: Rinsen shoten, 1989–1991.
SNKBT 90	Shinoda Jun'ichi 信多純一 and Sakaguchi Hiroyuki 阪口弘之, eds. *Ko-jōruri, sekkyō shū*. Shin Nihon koten bungaku taikei, vol. 90. Tokyo: Iwanami shoten, 1999.
SNKS *Sekkyō shū*	Muroki Yatarō 室木弥太郎, ed. *Sekkyō shū*. Shinchō Nihon koten shūsei. Tokyo: Shinchōsha, 1977.
SSS	Yokoyama Shigeru 横山重, ed. *Sekkyō shōhon shū*. 3 vols. Tokyo: Kadokawa shoten, 1968.
Tōyō bunko 243	Araki Shigeru 荒木繁 and Yamamoto Kichizō 山本吉左右, eds. *Sekkyō-bushi*. Tōyō bunko, vol. 243. Tokyo: Heibonsha, 1973.
TTZS 9 and 50	Tenri toshokan zenbon sōsho washo-no-bu henshū iinkai 天理図書館善本叢書和書之部編集委員会, ed. *Ko-jōruri shū*. Tenri toshokan zenbon sōsho washo-no-bu, vols. 9 and 50. Nara: Tenri daigaku shuppanbu, 1972, 1979.

WONDROUS BRUTAL FICTIONS

Introduction

In the first decades of the seventeenth century, Japan witnessed an urban revival of the medieval storytelling art of *sekkyō*, or *sekkyō-bushi*, a kind of lay Buddhist preaching about the workings of karma and the miraculous origins of celebrity Buddhist icons. The revival began sometime in the early 1600s when *sekkyō* began to be staged in theaters before large paying crowds. Old *sekkyō*, which is also known as *kado-sekkyō* or "street-corner *sekkyō*" in order to distinguish it from the later *sekkyō* performed at dedicated venues, apparently was chanted in the sixteenth century for small audiences of men, women, and children at bridges, crossroads, and the grounds of temples and shrines—at any place, that is, where people would naturally gather. Judging from their representations in early-seventeenth-century screen paintings of scenes in and around the Kyoto capital (*rakuchū rakugaizu*-type cityscapes), early *sekkyō* practitioners performed without any special props or sophisticated musical instruments. Standing under tall umbrellas—*ōkarakasa*, distinctive markers of their trade—they appear to have recited their tales to the simple rhythmic accompaniment of a *sasara*, a kind of notched bamboo scraper.[1]

Everything seems to have changed in the early seventeenth century, however, when the Osaka chanter Yoshichirō, later known as Osaka Yoshichirō, began using puppets in his *sekkyō* performances in the style of the incipient *jōruri* theater.² Although we know almost nothing about Yoshichirō's life, he was clearly a celebrity of sorts. He is the attributed chanter of the earliest extant *Sanshō Dayū* text, published around 1639 and translated here. It identifies him as Tenka-ichi Sekkyō Yoshichirō, "Yoshichirō, the Greatest Sekkyō Chanter Under Heaven," and he was granted the unusual posthumous honor of a cameo appearance in the *ko-jōruri* puppet play *Yoshitsune jigoku yaburi* (*Yoshitsune's Harrowing of Hell*, 1661).³ The scholar Shinoda Jun'ichi argues that in his heyday, Yoshichirō performed on the grounds of Shitennōji Temple in Osaka and that he was also the unattributed chanter of the 1631 *Sekkyō Karukaya*—the oldest dated *sekkyō* published in a woodblock-printed *shōhon* "true text" edition—as well as the fragmentary *Sekkyō Oguri*, published around 1634.⁴ Yoshichirō's influence on later *sekkyō* chanters was profound, for all of them seem to have followed him in adapting puppets to their own staged performances.

The early *jōruri* theater—now known as *ko-jōruri*, or "old jōruri," in order to distinguish it from the late-seventeenth-century *jōruri* of Chikamatsu Monzaemon and other later playwrights—seems to have emerged from the fifteenth- and sixteenth-century performance traditions of blind singers, raconteurs, and *ebisu-kaki* puppeteers.⁵ Near the end of the sixteenth century, *jōruri* chanters adopted the shamisen for musical accompaniment, and by the close of the Keichō era (1596–1615), full-blown puppet plays were being performed in makeshift theaters at festivals, shrines, and deserted riverbeds. Two of the earliest *ko-jōruri* compositions—*Amida no munewari* (*Amida's Riven Breast*) and *Goō-no-hime*, both of which are translated here—are known to have been performed in Kyoto, Kanazawa, and Kagoshima in 1614 and 1616.⁶ The popular author Asai Ryōi reported in 1659 that the two plays were formerly staged at the Fourth Avenue Riverbed in Kyoto,⁷ and there is visual evidence to support his claim. In figure 1—a scene from the Funaki screen paintings depicting scenes in and around the Kyoto capital in about 1614/1615—we can see actual staged performances of *Amida no munewari* and *Yamanaka Tokiwa* (*Lady Tokiwa at Yamanaka*) at adjoining theaters at the Fourth Avenue Riverbed.⁸ The audiences are composed of both men and women, some of whom appear to be crying. Although we can see *taiko* drums in the *yagura* watchtowers over the theater entrances, as well as puppets on the stage, the chanters and shamisen players are concealed from view.

As a living theatrical art, *sekkyō* would disappear by the mid-eighteenth century, absorbed into the burgeoning and evolving *jōruri* theater, but for several decades of the mid- to late seventeenth century, *sekkyō* and *ko-jōruri* stood shoulder to shoulder in the major urban centers of Edo, Kyoto, and

FIGURE 1
Staged performances of *Amida no munewari* and *Yamanaka Tokiwa* at the Fourth Avenue riverbed in Kyoto. From the Funaki-*bon rakuchū rakugaizu* screen paintings of circa 1624 to 1644. (Courtesy of the Tokyo National Museum)

Osaka as thriving, competing genres of puppet theater, each with its own repertoire and distinctive linguistic conventions. For example, in figure 2, a woodblock-printed drawing of an Edo street scene in Asai Ryōi's *Edo meishoki* (*Famous Places of Edo*), first published in 1662, we can see the *sekkyō* chanter Tenma Hachidayū's theater on the right, with a placard advertising a performance of the seminal *sekkyō Oguri*.[9] The placards on the theater at the left read "Tenka-ichi Ōsatsuma"—"The Great Satsuma, First Under Heaven," a reference to the *ko-jōruri* chanter Satsuma Jōun (1595–1672)—and they advertise a performance of the *ko-jōruri Takadachi*, which was closely based on the *kōwakamai* ballad-drama of the same name.[10] Similarly, Asai Ryōi's *Kyō suzume* (*Sparrow of the Capital*, 1665 [figure 3]) shows the Kyoto *sekkyō* chanter Higurashi Kodayū's theater directly across from the Kyoto theater of the *ko-jōruri* chanter Fujiwara Masanobu Kazusa-no-shōjō, otherwise known as Toraya Kidayū.

The performances of particular entertainers were legendary. There was a *sekkyō* chanter by the name of Sado Shichidayū, who was active in Osaka from around 1648 to 1658—a decade or so after Yoshichirō—and whose extant texts include the 1648 *Sekkyō Shintokumaru* (translated here) and the 1656 *Sekkyō Sanshō Dayū*. Shichidayū moved to Edo around 1661, where he was sometimes known as Osaka Shichidayū, sometimes as Tenka Musō Sado Shichidayū (The Universally Incomparable Sado Shichidayū), and sometimes as Tenka-ichi

FIGURE 2
Right, Edo theater of the *sekkyō* chanter Tenma Hachidayū (Iwami-no-jō), advertising a performance of *Oguri*; *left*, theater of the *ko-jōruri* chanter Satsuma Jōun ("Tenka-ichi Ōsatsuma"), advertising a performance of *Takadachi*. From *Edo meishoki* (1662), reproduced in *Seikyoku ruisan* (1839). (Author's collection)

Sekkyō Sado Shichidayū (Sado Shichidayū, the Greatest Sekkyō Chanter Under Heaven). The unknown author of a work entitled *Tenna shōishū* (*Funny Tales of the Tenna Era*, 1681–1684), which describes fires and other events in the early 1680s and seems to have been composed around 1684 to 1688, describes his performances as follows:

> From the moment the most famous *sekkyō* chanters chant their opening lines,[11] audiences are overwhelmed with grief and awe, penetrating their bodies to the core. Whatever kind of rapaciously cruel diamond deva king or wicked fiend a man might be, he will listen until his legs go stiff and his arms fall numb, shedding torrents of tears from his goggly eyes, oblivious to the shadows of the setting sun. Such are the performances of Osaka Shichidayū![12]

Introduction 5

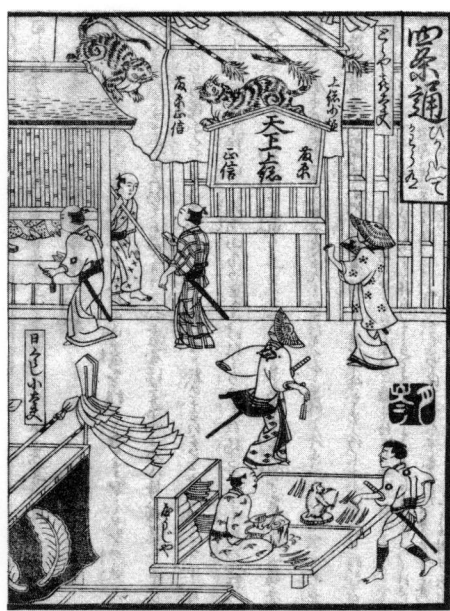

FIGURE 3
Top, Kyoto theater of the *ko-jōruri* chanter Toraya Kidayū (Fujiwara Masanobu Kazusa-no-shōjō); *lower left*, theater of the *sekkyō* chanter Higurashi Kodayū. From *Kyō suzume* (1665), reproduced in *Seikyoku ruisan* (1839). (Author's collection)

Although this description is hyperbolic, it is illuminating nonetheless. As we might imagine from the corpus of surviving *sekkyō* performance texts, famous for their formulaic and repeated attestations of their own emotional sway, Shichidayū and other *sekkyō* chanters spoke to the heart, describing the torture, mistreatment, and suffering of children and other pitiful protagonists as a way of engaging their audiences and keeping them in their seats.

THE THEATER IN PRINT

The rise of *sekkyō* and *ko-jōruri* in the seventeenth century was accompanied by a corresponding surge in theater-based publishing. From around the first years of the Kan'ei period (1624–1644), Kyoto publishers began producing what would soon come to be known as *shōhon* "true texts": woodblock-printed, purportedly faithful transcriptions of actual *sekkyō* and *ko-jōruri* performance manuscripts employed by professional chanters, with added illustrations and, in some cases, musical notation. The oldest dated text recognized as a *shōhon*

6   Introduction

FIGURE 4
A page from the 1625 *Takadachi* (1918 facsimile edition). (Author's collection)

today is a *ko-jōruri* adaptation of the medieval ballad-drama *Takadachi*—the play advertised at Satsuma Jōun's theater in figure 2—published by Katsubei of Teramachi, Kyoto, in the first month of 1625 (figure 4).[13] The work is simply titled *Takadachi godan* (Takadachi *in Five Acts*), and despite its contemporary classification as a *ko-jōruri shōhon*, it neither explicitly identifies itself as such nor claims to be the product of any particular chanter.[14] Published in fifty-one pages as a single *yokohon* "sideways" volume with basic hand-colored *tanroku*-type orange and green illustrations, it contains no punctuation and no musical notation. Nevertheless, it captures the unmistakable narrative style of *ko-jōruri* recitation and preserves the play in its original five acts.

Within the next fourteen years—by at least 1639—the term *shōhon* had come into popular use, as we can see from a reproduction of the first page of the no longer extant *ko-jōruri Yashima* in Ryūtei Tanehiko's *Yōshabako* (*Box of Scraps*, 1841 [figure 5]). Here, *Yashima* (or *Yashima michiyuki*) is identified as a *shōhon* by the famous female chanter Rokuji Namuemon of Yamashiro Province.[15] In subsequent decades, *shōhon* began to contain strong assertions of their own

FIGURE 5
Fragments of the lost 1631 *Yashima*, attributed to the chanter Rokuji Namuemon and reproduced in Ryūtei Tanehiko's *Yōshabako* (1841). (Author's collection)

authenticity—their status as true "true texts"—as evidenced, for example, in a *shōhon* edition of the *sekkyō Shintokumaru* attributed to the Osaka (and later Edo) chanter Sado Shichidayū and published by Urokogataya Magobei of Edo around the Kanbun era (1661–1673). In a short colophon on the final page of the book, the publisher avows that "the present published volume is transcribed without a single mistake from a *shōhon* derived directly from the chanter."[16] By the late seventeenth century, claims of this kind came to be commonplace in published playbooks, reinforcing the notion that *shōhon* true texts were really true to a particular performer.

The oldest dated *sekkyō shōhon* is the three-volume *Karukaya*, published by Jōruriya Kiemon—literally, "Kiemon, the *jōruri* bookseller"—in the fourth month of 1631 and translated here. Although no particular chanter is identified within the work (which is not surprising, given its early provenance), a majority of scholars assume that it was Osaka Yoshichirō, the chanter reputed to have been the first to adapt puppets to his *sekkyō* performances.[17] *Karukaya* also survives in a colorful, late-sixteenth-century illustrated manuscript (an *e-iri shahon*, now in the collection of the Suntory Museum), which is the oldest known *sekkyō* document of any kind. In addition to these two early texts, *Karukaya* is preserved in an edition published by Hangiya Hikoemon of Edo in the first years of the Kanbun era (ca. 1661) and in two undated *shōhon* produced by the Urokogataya publishing house of Edo in the late seventeenth or early eighteenth century and attributed to the chanters Tenma Magoshirō and Tenma Hachidayū. Theoretically, considering that the term *shōhon* is understood to designate a faithful transcription of a particular performance manuscript, each of these five *Karukaya* texts should represent the voice of an individual chanter.[18]

Because *sekkyō* chanters did not always see eye to eye, we can occasionally detect what appear to be the voices of particular performers. For instance, in *Karukaya*, after the monastic hero Karukaya sends his son Ishidōmaru away without telling him who he is and first entrusting him with a fake memorial marker that he claims to be the boy's dead father's, the various narrators reveal their own conflicting emotions. The chanter of the 1631 *shōhon* (Osaka Yoshichirō?) avoids commenting on the scene, but the unknown narrator of the late-sixteenth-century *Karukaya* seems to side with the father: "Alas, poor Ishidōmaru!" he exclaims. "Although he had met his living father, he did not recognize him as such. And even though Karukaya knew Ishidōmaru to be his son, he did not identify himself as the boy's father. The poor priest wanted to reveal himself, but fearing the vow that he had sworn at Shinkurodani, he refrained. The feelings in his heart were pitiful indeed!"[19] In contrast, the chanter of the circa 1661 *shōhon* (Tenma Hachidayū?) sides with the son, declaring, "Everyone curses Karukaya for driving away his son without telling him who he was. The poor boy! Unaware that he had been deceived, he hoisted the meaningless memorial marker onto his shoulder and hurried back to the Kamuro post station. The feelings in his heart were pitiful beyond description!"[20] Karukaya's moral conflict is the central theme of the story, dividing readers still today. Not even the two storytellers could agree.

Sekkyō and *ko-jōruri shōhon* can be difficult to tell apart. Whereas early *ko-jōruri* scripts tended to be published in two volumes, early *sekkyō* were published in three,[21] and in cases in which a play is known to have been performed as both *sekkyō* and *ko-jōruri*, scholars sometimes differentiate between the genres on the basis of volume-count alone. For example, the 1651 text of *Amida no munewari*, which is translated here, is classified as a *ko-jōruri shōhon* largely because it was published in two volumes—even though *Amida no munewari* is also known to have been performed as *sekkyō* by Tenma Hachidayū and to be thematically consistent with the *sekkyō* of its time.²² Over the course of the seventeenth century, as *sekkyō* became increasingly influenced by *ko-jōruri*, *sekkyō shōhon* began to take on the characteristics of *ko-jōruri* playbooks. From around 1658—the publication date of the *sekkyō Kumano no gongen ki* (*Record of the Kumano Deity*)—*sekkyō shōhon* came to be divided into six acts and to incorporate grand battle scenes in the manner of *ko-jōruri*.²³ The 1651 *Amida no munewari* is also divided into six acts and contains a battle scene in its third act, but considering that these features were to become standard aspects of *sekkyō* within only seven years of its publication, they cannot be taken as conclusive proof of the 1651 text's status as a *ko-jōruri shōhon*.²⁴

In light of the seventeenth-century history of *sekkyō*, the works translated in this volume are perhaps best understood as occupying points on a continuum between "pure" *sekkyō* and *ko-jōruri*, with *Karukaya* (1631), *Sanshō Dayū* (ca. 1639), and *Shintokumaru* (1648) representing a relatively older form of *sekkyō*; the six-act *Aigo-no-waka* (ca. 1670) representing the genre of *sekkyō-jōruri* (*sekkyō* under the heavier influence of *ko-jōruri*); and *Amida no munewari* (1651) and *Goō-no-hime* (1673) representing *ko-jōruri*. The undated *Oguri* and *Sayohime* manuscripts represent an early- to mid-seventeenth-century form of *sekkyō*, but as either illustrated transcriptions of *sekkyō* performances or novelistic adaptations of *sekkyō shōhon*. Muroki Yatarō identifies *Karukaya*, *Sanshō Dayū*, *Shintokumaru*, and *Oguri* as constituting the heart of *sekkyō*, and Yokoyama Shigeru is said to have agreed, except with the addition of *Aigo-no-waka*.²⁵ Of the eight works translated here, the Kyoto *sekkyō* chanter Higurashi Kodayū is reported to have staged puppet performances of six—every one except for the *ko-jōruri Amida no munewari* and *Goō-no-hime*—at a theater in Nagoya in 1665.²⁶

The stories themselves are timeless, originating in the murky depths of the medieval past. Seventeenth-century chanters shaped and recycled them as they pleased, but neither the original authors nor the circumstances of composition are known to us today. In performing their narratives, *sekkyō* chanters seem to have extemporized, filling out their tales with stock scenes and plot motifs, including long and formulaic oaths (in *Sanshō Dayū* and *Karukaya*), puzzling riddle-letters (in *Shintokumaru*, *Oguri*, and *Aigo-no-waka*), desperate child-supplication scenes (in *Shintokumaru*, *Sayohime*, and *Aigo-no-waka*), epiphanies at the sight of birds (in *Sanshō Dayū* and *Karukaya*), and many others. Repetition of this kind is recognized the world over as a characteristic of oral composition,[27] and it suggests that the seventeenth-century *sekkyō* repertoire may have been more akin to a store of interchangeable scenes and events than a collection of strictly disparate plays. *Sekkyō* stories also are united by their *michiyuki* travel sequences—frequently long, lyrical passages listing the names of places through which the characters pass, parts of which are repeated verbatim in the different works—which allow for a sense of movement within the stories and, like a drum solo in a modern musical performance, may have provided an opportunity for the chanter to demonstrate his verbal chops.

In discussing the *ko-jōruri* theater, Donald Keene questions whether the works in the genre might even be properly referred to as "plays," considering that they were declaimed by a single chanter who performed both the narration and all the different characters' voices. Keene makes the point that in their published forms, there is "little to differentiate the texts from prose fiction,"[28] which is certainly the case. This is also the reason why, in English translation, there is nothing to distinguish the pre-1658 *sekkyō shōhon* (*Sanshō Dayū*, *Karukaya*, and *Shintokumaru*) from the non-playbook manuscripts included here (*Oguri* and *Sayohime*). Moreover, lacking any kind of stage direction or paratextual description, the extant *shōhon* and illustrated manuscripts give little indication of what an actual performance may have been like in the seventeenth or early eighteenth century.

One of the most distinctive features of *sekkyō* and *ko-jōruri shōhon* are their inclusion of illustrations, which, as we can see in figure 4, were incorporated from the earliest of times. In the older playbooks (dating from 1625 through about 1651), simple woodblock-printed line drawings were daubed with patches of red, green, and sometimes orange and yellow paint, creating asymmetrically colorful images with a primitive, sloppy charm. In the second half of the seventeenth century publishers tended to dispense with color, leaving individual customers to embellish the pictures as they wished. The illustrations invariably depict imagined scenes within the narrated story rather than staged productions of those scenes. The alternative, which one never actually sees in *sekkyō* or *ko-jōruri shōhon*, would be something like figure 6, a representation of an unidentified *sekkyō* performance by the chanter Tenma Hachidayū in *Yakusha-e zukushi* (*Compendium of Actors' Images*, ca. 1688). We might therefore say that seventeenth-century *shōhon* true-text illustrations were true to the recited tale rather than to its theatrical performance.

FIGURE 6
An unidentified puppet performance by the Edo *sekkyō* chanter Tenma Hachidayū (Iwami-no-jō). From *Yakusha-e zukushi* (ca. 1688, 1920–1921 facsimile edition). (Author's collection)

But the images were not always true. Like *nara ehon*—manuscripts with colorful hand-painted illustrations, mass-produced in the sixteenth through the eighteenth century—*shōhon* sometimes betray a surprising inconsistency between text and illustration. In the case of *nara ehon*, including *Oguri* and *Sayohime* in this volume, irregularities of this sort are typically ascribed to the division of labor between illustrators and calligraphers.[29] In *Oguri*, for example, while the narrator tells us that the heroine Terute-no-hime has been set adrift on the waves inside a barred palanquin, the accompanying illustration simply shows her sitting in a boat (figure, p. 139). Likewise, in *Sayohime*, although the narrator says that the teenaged Sayohime has been placed on the upper tier of a three-tiered platform in order to be fed to a giant snake, the corresponding illustration shows only a single-tiered stand (figure, p. 184).

The text-illustration issue is similarly perplexing in the 1631 *Karukaya*. The chanter explains that after receiving the fake memorial marker from his father and returning to the Tamaya Inn to see his mother, "Ishidōmaru pushed open the creaky outer door [of the inn] and pulled aside a folding screen, only to discover his poor mother lying on her side, her head pointing north and her face turned to the west, just as she had been when she attained Pure Land rebirth."[30] But in the illustration the mother is seated upright, as if she had died that way.[31] Then when Ishidōmaru and his father (still unknown to the boy) set out for the cremation grounds with the mother's corpse, Ishidōmaru laments, "Here on Mount Kōya, I've got no one to turn to, so it's just me and this priest, and nobody else!"[32] Nevertheless, the illustration shows Ishidōmaru and his father carrying the funeral palanquin with two unidentified mourners at their side. The chanter of the circa 1661 *shōhon* explains that "Karukaya placed his wife's body in a funeral bier" and that "with Karukaya bearing the front shafts and Ishidōmaru bearing the rear, they carried her to the cremation grounds with the innkeeper and his wife."[33] Although seemingly mismatched to its own textual account, the 1631 illustration fits the story published in the 1661 text.

THEMES AND MOTIFS

The characters for the term *sekkyō* 説経 mean "sutra explanation," but as a dramatic and literary genre, *sekkyō* has little to do with Buddhist sutras, doctrine, or sectarian belief. Instead, the earlier texts tell of the general workings of karma, prayer, and the once-human origins of celebrity Buddhist icons, including the Branded Jizō Bodhisattva of Tango Province (*Sanshō Dayū*), the Parent and Child Jizō Bodhisattva of Zenkōji Temple in Shinano Province (*Karukaya*), the Shō Hachiman Bodhisattva of Sunomata Village in Mino Province (*Oguri emaki*), the goddess Benzaiten of Chikubushima Shrine in Ōmi Province (*Sayohime*), and the Great Sannō Deity of Hie Shrine near Kyoto (*Aigo-no-waka*). The chanter/narrator of the 1631 *Karukaya*, for example, begins with a traditional *sekkyō*-style introduction, declaring,

> I shall speak to you now about the origins of the Parent and Child Jizō Bodhisattva that is worshipped to the left of the Main Buddha Hall at

Zenkōji Temple in Shinano Province. Ask me about its past, and I will tell you that it was once a man by the name of Lord Shigeuji, chieftain of the Matsura League of Chikuzen Province in Great Tsukushi.[34]

As *sekkyō* became increasingly influenced by *ko-jōruri* in the mid- to late seventeenth century, this kind of distinctively religious framing device disappeared. The 1648 *Shintokumaru* lacks one entirely, and in *Aigo-no-waka* (1661 and ca. 1670), the only reference to the Great Sannō Deity occurs in the final passage of the play. What remained—without explanation—were the terrible tales of those who, in earlier renditions of their stories, became buddhas and deities as a result of their tribulations in the human realm.

Many of the protagonists of these stories are either children or adolescents, including some as young as five and seven years old. As in medieval and early Edo-period fiction in general, many of them are *mōshigo*, or "supplicated kids": children born in response to their parents' prayers to a particular buddha, deity, or bodhisattva. They are variously sold, cursed, beaten, abandoned, branded, tortured, and murdered but also loved, healed, consoled, and sometimes rescued and redeemed. Their revenge, when it comes, can be dreadfully sweet.

In *Sanshō Dayū*—a story made famous in the modern period by Mori Ōgai's 1915 short story and Mizoguchi Kenji's 1954 film of the same name—the thirteen- and fifteen-year-old Zushiōmaru and Anju-no-hime are kidnapped, separated from their mother, and sold into slavery. *Sayohime* and *Amida no munewari* contain similar plot motifs, but with a twist: in these stories, the children choose to sell *themselves* into bondage in order to raise money to commission Buddhist rites for their dead parents. The trope is slightly unusual in the world of medieval Japanese fiction, in which characters typically take monastic vows in order to dedicate their own lives to praying for the deceased. In the sixteenth-century British Library text of the *otogizōshi Tengu no dairi* (*The Palace of the Tengu*), for example, the thirteen-year-old Minamoto no Yoshitsune recalls hearing that "when a person takes monastic vows, nine generations of his ancestors will ascend to heaven" and that "even the family horses and oxen will attain buddhahood."[35] Likewise, in the *otogizōshi Chūjōhime no honji* (*Chūjōhime in Her Original Form*), the fourteen-year-old Chūjōhime rationalizes her decision to disobey her father and become a nun by concluding that her "true repayment of obligation" will be when she is reborn in Amida Buddha's Pure Land Paradise and leads both of her parents there.[36]

But self-enslavement stories also were popular in the sixteenth and seventeenth centuries, and they seem to be derived in part from imported Confucian filial piety tales that were adapted for Buddhist preaching on the miraculous powers of the Lotus sutra and the worldly benefits of the Pure Land cult. In the 1661 *Matsura Chōja* (*The Millionaire of Matsura*, a *sekkyō shōhon* version of the *Sayohime* story), the sixteen-year-old Sayohime reasons that she should sell herself to raise money because she has heard that other people do so, too.[37] In fact, there are numerous examples in Japanese and Chinese textual sources of filial children enslaving themselves for their parents' sake. The most famous may be Dong-yong of the Later Han period (25–220), a poor boy who is said to have sold himself in order to give his father a funeral. His story is recounted in multiple Chinese sources, including Guo Jujing's (fl. ca. 1295–1321) *Ershisi xiao shi* (*Verses on the Twenty-four Filial Exemplars*), which was imported to Japan in the late fourteenth century and served as the basis for the *otogizōshi Nijūshikō* (*Twenty-four Tales of Filial Piety*).[38]

In *Amida no munewari*, the siblings Teirei and Tenju lose their parents at the ages of five and seven. Then when the brother Teirei is ten years old, he proposes to his elder sister that they sell themselves as slaves. "Children of the world hold services for their parents' enlightenment," he explains, "as an act of religious charity, one of the six bodhisattva practices."[39] He refers to the *ropparamitsu*, the six religious practices on the bodhisattva path to enlightenment. One of these is the *dan haramitsu*, the "practice of charity," or, more narrowly construed, the practice of providing material support for monastics.[40] Thus, with his simple explanation, he articulates the doctrinal basis for the self-enslavement motif in a way that Sayohime never does.

In *Amida no munewari*, a rich man buys the children in order to feed Tenju's raw, "living liver" to his cursed, ailing son; in *Sayohime*, a wealthy village headman named Gonga buys Sayohime in order to feed her to a giant snake in a lake near his home. (The snake requires a virgin once a year, and it is Gonga's turn to procure a girl.) Marina Warner writes that "in myth and fairy tale, the metaphor of devouring often stands in for sex,"[41] and although her observation pertains to European literature, it might be equally applied to *sekkyō* and *ko-jōruri*. After all, one does not need a degree in Freudian psychology to see the significance of Gonga's desire to feed a sixteen-year-old maiden to a giant, ravenous snake. In *Amida no munewari*, the specter of Tenju's liver being consumed by the boy who will in fact become her husband is similarly sexually charged, at least insofar as it recalls Freud's theory of "cannibalistic pregenital sexual organization": an early phase in the development of human sexual instincts in which, to borrow Freud's explanation, "sexual activity has not yet been separated from the ingestion of food."[42]

Saitō Ken'ichi writes about children and the slave trade in medieval Japan, observing that while boys and girls were commonly sold from around the age of seven, they were generally permitted to sell themselves only after they turned fifteen.[43] Saitō avoids discussing the likely sale of young women as sexual objects—it is nicer not to think about such things—but Janet Goodwin ventures that some extant Kamakura-period documents "suggest a thriving underground trade in the bodies of women."[44] One can imagine that the possibility of sexual exploitation would have been frightening for any young woman facing the prospect of being sold. That unspoken anxiety seems to have been manifested obliquely in the terrible, suggestive fates that are said to await Tenju and Sayohime.

Tenju and Sayohime are eventually saved by their Buddhist devotion, but the religious messages of their tales are mixed. While the stories propound the salvific powers of Amida Buddha and the Lotus sutra, they simultaneously undermine those lessons by emphasizing the necessity of *dan haramitsu* practices of engaging religious professionals. This is most obvious in the *otogizōshi Chikubushima no honji* (*The Chikubushima Deity in Her Original Form*), an alternative and abridged version of the *Sayohime* story, which explains that before selling herself as a slave, Sayohime made it her daily practice to read the Lotus sutra for the sake of her father's enlightenment. Nevertheless, after hearing a priest declare that "we should make offerings for our parents' enlightenment, even if we have to sell ourselves to do so," she interrupts her readings of the Lotus sutra in order to sell herself to sponsor memorial services for her father.[45] The implication is clear: although Sayohime's sutra recitations may be enough to release the great snake from its reptilian form—emasculating the great phallic menace and transmuting it into a more congenial manifestation—they are insufficient by themselves to save her father in his own next-life incarnation.

The inconsistency results from *Chikubushima no honji*'s tendency toward religious inclusion—its rejection, that is, of exclusionary Buddhist practices in favor of a broad, Tendai-like acceptance of diversity in religious praxis and belief. The woodblock-printed text of ca. 1615–1624 concludes with the following passage, which is characteristic of many works of medieval Japanese fiction and drama in its advocacy of Confucian filial piety as a Buddhist practice and in its generally unbiased support of both the Lotus sutra and the *nenbutsu*, the ritual invocation of the name of Amida Buddha:

> It was true in the past, and it is true today that all those who are filial toward their parents will immediately receive a miraculous response.

Everyone who sees this story should take this lesson to heart. They should seek only to serve their parents as best as they can, day and night, in every possible way. As for those who read the Lotus sutra, they should read it with all their heart. And if there are those who do not read the Lotus sutra, then they should repeat the *nenbutsu* again and again, appealing for enlightenment in a future rebirth and never slacking in their efforts to be saved.[46]

In the diversity of its religious expression, combining Confucian and Buddhist elements into a loosely integrated whole, *Chikubushima no honji* and its related works suggest the composite nature of late medieval Japanese religious culture, which tended to constitute an amalgam of diverse and occasionally incompatible ingredients rather than an organized or internally consistent universe of practice and belief.[47]

In the frequently misogynistic world of medieval and early Edo-period fiction and drama, in which women are said to be women because of their sins in previous lives,[48] *sekkyō* and some *ko-jōruri* are remarkable for the strength of their female characters, including Sayohime, Tenju, Terute-no-hime (in *Oguri*), Anju-no-hime (in *Sanshō Dayū*), Otohime (in *Shintokumaru*), and Goō-no-hime (in *Goō-no-hime*). Scholars see their presence as indicative of the early role of female shamans and storytelling nuns in the formation of their tales.[49] Although such theories are compelling, they also are largely speculative. The fact remains, however, that the women of *sekkyō* tend to rival and often surpass their fathers, brothers, and husbands in loyalty, faith, and fortitude. And for whatever reason, they tend to suffer an unequal share of duress.

In 1678, Fujimoto Kizan wrote that "*jōruri* is a vulgar art, so well-to-do people should avoid chanting it, even as amateurs."[50] He seems to have a point, insofar as one of the hallmarks of *sekkyō* and *ko-jōruri* is their exceptional brutality. Like characters in some contemporary Hollywood "slash" and "splatter" films, their young heroines are routinely tortured to death in the course of sadistic interrogations, for no apparent reason other than the visceral gratification of voyeuristic audiences. The women's stories are replete with miracles of every sort, including divine revelations and supernatural substitutions, but the women are rarely saved when they need it most. Strangely, their all-powerful guardians tend to leave them to suffer and die. Indeed, Anju-no-hime is slowly tortured to death in *Sanshō Dayū*, even though the bodhisattva Jizō had previously saved her from disfigurement (by removing a burn from her face) and even though he saves her brother in his own time of need. Considering the internal logic of the story, in which miracles *do* occur, why, then, does Anju-no-hime have to die?

The answer may lie in *Goō-no-hime*, in which the seventeen-year-old Goō-no-hime is tortured to death, as was Anju-no-hime, during a merciless interrogation. In act 5, the young lady is arrested and brought before Kiyomori, who orders that she be tormented until she talks. Goō-no-hime's extended ordeal, which lasts for nearly two full acts, constitutes the climax of the play: seventeenth-century entertainment in its most basic, popular form. She is waterboarded with freezing and boiling water, has arrows screwed into her joints, is made to walk across a pinewood plank studded with nails, has her fingernails and toenails cut out, is buried up to her waist and tormented with snakes, is "bird-roasted" over fiery coals, and is slowly hanged by the neck from the branch of a tree so that she will choke but not die. In the *ko-jōruri Yoshiuji*, a vivacious young woman named Meigetsu is similarly tortured until she decides to bite off her tongue and expire.⁵¹

Works such as *Goō-no-hime*, *Yoshiuji*, and *Sanshō Dayū* play to a fundamental human fear of bodily destruction, but they are also concerned with celebrating psychological strength and the power of the human will: the ability of physically vulnerable women and children to defy the most brutal forms of coercion. What is particularly interesting about the torture scene in *Goō-no-hime* is Goō-no-hime's repeated assertion that because she is already suffering a particular punishment here, she will not have to suffer it in the next life; that she will be able to proceed directly to Amida's Pure Land instead (an event foreshadowed at the beginning of the play when Yoshitsune, at his father's grave, recites a passage from the Lotus sutra pertaining to buddhahood for women). Meigetsu says similar things in *Yoshiuji*, although not with the same clarity and consistency. Anju-no-hime makes no such statements in the 1639 *Sanshō Dayū* or any other extant rendition of her tale, but given the formulaic nature of these kinds of interrogation scenes, she is likely to have done so in some earlier version of her story.

Like Meigetsu in *Yoshiuji*, Goō-no-hime presses her palms together in her mind (because her hands are bound), recites the name of Amida Buddha, and then bites off her tongue and dies. Blossoms rain from the sky, and a host of twenty-five bodhisattvas come to carry her away to the Pure Land. Her salvation is a miracle—we are subsequently informed that Kiyomori, too, can see the wondrous signs—but we might also consider the cruel manner in which she dies to be a kind of miracle as well. Despite Pure Land Buddhist claims that all those who recite the *nenbutsu* may be reborn in the Pure Land after death, there are persistent, troubling assertions in medieval Japanese textual sources that Pure Land rebirth is not so easy.[52] For example, near the end of the Engyōbon text of *Heike monogatari* (*The Tale of the Heike*), the nun Kenreimon'in explains to Retired Emperor Go-Shirakawa that in her current life she has already experienced the six paths of non-enlightened existence—including, of course, the three evil paths of hell, animals, and hungry ghosts—and that because of this, she is finally ready to achieve Pure Land rebirth. Her current state is miserable, she admits, but she thinks of it as a blessing when she considers her future enlightenment.[53]

Likewise, the miracle of Goō-no-hime's death is that it allows Goō-no-hime to quickly expiate her karma—to suffer all that she needs to suffer in a very short space of time so that she will not have to suffer it in future lives. Like the famous Dragon Girl in the "Devadatta" chapter of the Lotus sutra, who does not instantly change into a buddha but, rather, passes through an intermediate process of transforming into a man, carrying out all the many bodhisattva practices, and then becoming a buddha,[54] Goō-no-hime endures a purificatory process that will allow her at its end to attain rebirth in Amida's Pure Land. The same is true for Meigetsu in *Yoshiuji*, although in that case audiences are not informed of her Pure Land rebirth, and for Anju-no-hime in *Sanshō Dayū*, even though the meaning of her anguish is left wholly unexplained. By refusing to save Anju-no-hime from her terrible demise, Jizō may be allowing her to suffer the painful steps that will permit her to attain immediate salvation.

Citing Martin Bridgstock's work on modern horror fiction, Michael Arnzen writes that "it is generally understood by critics that most horror films are essentially conservative in nature: They tend to re-establish the order (social, moral, or otherwise) that they symbolically deconstruct. As in conventional westerns, horror films typically have identifiable heroes, and good usually overcomes (the overt) evil."[55] The same is generally true of *Sanshō Dayū* and other *sekkyō*, in which good usually triumphs in the end. Anju-no-hime dies, but she is avenged. Likewise, *Goō-no-hime* concludes with Kiyomori's execution of Goō-no-hime's greedy aunt. As we can see in the figure on page 247, a demon swoops down from above and carries the aunt off to hell, putting her in her rightful place. The illustration is similar to figure 6—the image of an unidentified *sekkyō* performance by the Edo chanter Tenma Hachidayū—which shows the kind of supernatural scene that is typically associated with seventeenth-century puppet performances. But in *sekkyō* and *ko-jōruri*, not all miracles of the stage take such blatantly obvious forms.

NOTES

1. For English-language treatments of early *sekkyō*, see Susan Matisoff, "Holy Horrors: The Sermon-Ballads of Medieval and Early Modern Japan," in *Flowing Traces: Buddhism in the Literary and Visual Arts of Japan*, ed. James Sanford, William LaFleur, and Masatoshi Nagatomi (Princeton, N.J.: Princeton University Press, 1992), 234–61; and Nobuko Ishii, "Sekkyō-bushi," *Monumenta Nipponica* 44, no. 3 (1989): 283–307.

2. According to Fujimoto Kizan's *Shikidō ōkagami* of 1678, in *Shinpan Shikidō ōkagami*, ed. Shinpan Shikidō ōkagami kankōkai (Tokyo: Yagi shoten, 2006), 235.

3. The dead Yoshichirō is said to have composed a poem in praise of Suita no Tarōzaemon's looting of King Enma's court in the afterworld. See Kokusho kankōkai, ed., *Shin gunsho ruijū* (Tokyo: Daiichi shobō, 1976), 9:673.

4. Shinoda Jun'ichi, "Kinsei shoki no katarimono," in *Ko-jōruri, sekkyō shū*, SNKBT 90:568–70.

5. Shinoda, "Kinsei shoki no katarimono," 551–55. In English, see C. J. Dunn, *The Early Japanese Puppet Drama* (London: Luzac, 1966).

6. According to entries in *Mitsubo kikigaki*, *Tokiyoshi-kyō ki*, *Tokio-kyō ki*, and *Nanpo bunshū*, *Amida no munewari* was performed in Kyoto and Kanazawa in 1614, and *Goō-no-hime* was performed in Kanazawa and Kagoshima in 1614 and 1616. Cited in Shinoda, "Kinsei shoki no katarimono," 554; and Kuroki Kanzō, *Jōruri-shi* (Tokyo: Seijisha, 1943), 47–51.

7. Asakura Haruhiko, ed., *Tōkaidō meishoki 2*, Tōyō bunko (Tokyo: Heibonsha, 1979), 361:186.

8. The plays are labeled *Munewari ayatsuri* and *Yamanaka Tokiwa ayatsuri*, the term *ayatsuri* meaning "puppetry." The Funaki screens have been tentatively attributed to Iwasa Matabei (1578–1650). Regarding issues of date and attribution, see Sandy Kita, *The Last Tosa: Iwasa Katsumochi Matabei, Bridge to Ukiyo-e* (Honolulu: University of Hawai'i Press, 1999), 178; and Matthew Philip McKelway, *Capitalscapes: Folding Screens and Political Imagination in Late Medieval Kyoto* (Honolulu: University of Hawai'i Press, 2006), 259n.64.

9. Tenma Hachidayū, also known as Iwami-no-jō, was the dominant Edo *sekkyō* chanter of the mid- to late seventeenth century. See appendix 1.

10. The identification of "Tenka-ichi Ōsatsuma" with Satsuma Jōun is from Yasuda Fukiko, *Ko-jōruri: Tayū no zuryō to sono jidai* (Tokyo: Yagi shoten, 1998), 147–48. According to one source, Jōun moved to Edo in the first years of the Kan'ei period (ca. 1624). See Wakatsuki Yasuji, *Ningyō jōruri-shi kenkyū* (Tokyo: Sakurai shoten, 1943), 103–12; and Muroki Yatarō, *Zōtei katarimono (mai, sekkyō, ko-jōruri) no kenkyū* (Tokyo: Kazama shobō, 1981), 469.

11. Literally, from the moment they chant "*sate mo*," the standard opening phrase in *ko-jōruri*.

12. Quoted in Shinoda, "Kinsei shoki no katarimono," 577.

13. The single extant text (from the former Matsunoya bunko collection) was destroyed in a fire following the Great Kantō Earthquake of September 1923. Luckily, a close facsimile reproduction had been published by Yoneyamadō in 1918. For a discussion of the original Matsunoya bunko *shōhon* and its reproduction, see Yokoyama Shigeru, "Takadachi," in *Ko-jōruri shōhon shū* (Tokyo: Kadokawa shoten, 1964), 1:323b–29b.

14. Based on the image in *Edo meishoki*, Wakatsuki Yasuji suggests that Satsuma Jōun was the chanter. Nevertheless, *Kokyōgaeri no Edo-banashi* (1687) reports that Rokuji Namuemon also chanted *Takadachi*, so it is impossible to say who was the chanter of the 1625 *Takadachi*. See Wakatsuki, *Ningyō jōruri-shi kenkyū*, 108, 119.

15. *Shōhon* were not necessarily published in or near the year of their performance. As Muroki Yatarō observes, although women were banned from performing *jōruri* in 1629, Rokuji Namuemon's *Yashima* was published in 1639. See Muroki, *Zōtei katarimono no kenkyū*, 57.

16. The colophon is transcribed in Shigeo Sorimachi, *Catalogue of Japanese Illustrated Books and Manuscripts in the Spencer Collection of the New York Public Library* (Tokyo: Kōbunsō, 1978), cat. 322.

17. Yokoyama Shigeru, Muroki Yatarō, and Shinoda Jun'ichi all hold this view (see SSS 2:505b); Muroki Yatarō, "Kaisetsu," in SNKS *Sekkyō shū*, 411; and Shinoda, "Kinsei shoki no katarimono," 569.

18. In this case, the number of chanters may have been only three. Yokoyama Shigeru suggests that the circa 1661 text was originally attributed to Tenma Hachidayū and that the Tenma Magoshirō text was actually a re-release of the circa 1661 text with altered publisher's and chanter's attributions. See appendix 2.

19. SNKBT 90:299–300.

20. SSS 2:50a. Also see the similarly opposing passages in SNKBT 90: 307 and SSS 2:52a–b.

21. Shinoda, "Kinsei shoki no katarimono," 561. The 1625 *Takadachi* was produced in a single volume, but from around 1633 (Kan'ei 10, the publication date of the *ko-jōruri Tōdaiki*), *ko-jōruri shōhon* were generally published in two.

22. Shinoda Jun'ichi, "Amida no munewari," in *Nihon koten bungaku daijiten* (Tokyo: Iwanami shoten, 1983), 1:80d. See also Muroki, *Zōtei katarimono no kenkyū*, 24, 301.

23. Muroki, *Zōtei katarimono no kenkyū*, 298, and "Kaisetsu," 412.

24. Shinoda Jun'ichi argues that the publisher of the 1651 *Amida no munewari* actually used most of the printing blocks from an *Amida no munewari* text published around the Kan'ei period (1624–1644), in which case the battle scene and the six-act division of the text would significantly predate the transformations of around 1658 in *sekkyō shōhon*. See Shinoda, "Amida no munewari," 80–81.

25. Muroki, *Zōtei katarimono no kenkyū*, 298, and "Kaisetsu," 411; Ishii, "Sekkyō-bushi," 288.

26. According to *Biyō kejō jishi* (1782), cited in Muroki, *Zōtei katarimono no kenkyū*, 313.

27. Minobe Shigekatsu, for example, draws on Western theories of orality to comment on this phenomenon in medieval Japanese literature. See Minobe, "*Monokusa Tarō no kōshōteki shikumi shōkō*," in *Ronsan: Setsuwa to setsuwa bungaku*, ed. Mitani Eiichi et al. (Tokyo: Kasama shoin, 1979), 421–22.

28. Donald Keene, *World Within Walls: Japanese Literature of the Pre-modern Era, 1600–1867* (New York: Holt, Rinehart and Winston, 1976), 237–38.

29. The circumstances of *nara ehon* production are largely unknown. The late-seventeenth-century calligrapher Isome Tsuna is known to have painted her own *nara ehon* illustrations in addition to brushing the text, but she may have been the exception rather than the rule. See Ishikawa Tōru, *Nara ehon, emaki no tenkai* (Tokyo: Miyai shoten, 2009), 4–41.

30. SNKS *Sekkyō shū*, 68.

31. All fifteen images from the 1631 *Karukaya* are reproduced in TTZS 50: 3–106.

32. SNKS *Sekkyō shū*, 72.

33. SSS 2:52a. The circa 1661 text contains no corresponding illustration of the scene.

34. SNKS *Sekkyō shū*, 11.

35. Tsuji Eiko, *Zaigai Nihon emaki no kenkyū to shiryō* (Tokyo: Kasama shoin, 1999), 362b. *Otogizōshi* are short, usually anonymous works of fiction dating from around the Muromachi period (1336–1573).

36. Ōshima Tatehiko and Watari Kōichi, eds., *Muromachi monogatari sōshi shū*, Shinpen Nihon koten bungaku zenshū (Tokyo: Shōgakukan, 2002), 63:409; R. Keller Kimbrough, trans., "Chūjōhime," in *Traditional Japanese Literature: An Anthology, Beginnings to 1600*, ed. Haruo Shirane (New York: Columbia University Press, 2007), 1145.

37. SNKS *Sekkyō shū*, 352–53.

38. Tokuda Kazuo, *Otogizōshi kenkyū* (Tokyo: Miyai shoten, 1988), 342–44; Tokuda Kazuo, ed., *Otogizōshi jiten* (Tokyo: Tōkyōdō shuppan, 2002), 376b. Further examples of the self-enslavement motif include the *otogizōshi Hōmyō Dōji*, in which an eight-year-old Indian boy sells himself so that he might rescue his mother from begging, and two stories in the sixteenth-century Japanese Lotus sutra commentary *Jikidan innenshū* (*Straight Talk on Causes and Conditions*)—a kind of Tendai manual for preaching on the Lotus sutra—in which a ten-year-old Indian girl and an Indian boy sell themselves to passing traders in order to provide for their impoverished mothers. *Hōmyō Dōji* is typeset in MJMS 4:144–80. For the *Jikidan innenshū* episodes, see Abe Yasurō et al., eds., *Nikkō tenkaizō Jikidan innenshū: Honkoku to sakuin* (Osaka: Izumi shoin, 1998), 140, 307–8.

39. SNKBT 90:395.

40. The other five practices are those of rectitude, forbearance, exertion, meditation, and wisdom.

41. Marina Warner, *From the Beast to the Blonde: On Fairy Tales and Their Tellers* (New York: Farrar, Straus & Giroux, 1994), 259.

42. Sigmund Freud, *Three Essays on the Theory of Sexuality* (1905), trans. James Strachey, in *The Essentials of Psycho-Analysis*, ed. Anna Freud (Harmondsworth: Penguin, 1986), 337. See also "Instincts and Their Vicissitudes" (1915) in the same volume, esp. p. 215.

43. Saitō Ken'ichi, *Kodomo no chūsei-shi* (Tokyo: Yoshikawa kōbunkan, 2003), 100–101.

44. Janet R. Goodwin, *Selling Songs and Smiles: The Sex Trade in Heian and Kamakura Japan* (Honolulu: University of Hawai'i Press, 2007), 127.

45. SSS 3:489b.

46. SSS 3:493b–94a. Likewise, in the *otogizōshi Hōmyō Dōji*, the eight-year-old Hōmyō Dōji is said to have made it his daily exercise to recite the Lotus sutra in its entirety and to recite the *nenbutsu* one hundred times for the sake of his dead father and living mother. See MJMS 4:168.

47. Hank Glassman and Keller Kimbrough, "Editors' Introduction: Vernacular Buddhism and Medieval Japanese Literature," *Japanese Journal of Religious Studies* 36, no. 2 (2009): 201–8.

48. According to the 1627 text of the *otogizōshi Fuji no hitoana sōshi*. See R. Keller Kimbrough, *Preachers, Poets, Women, and the Way: Izumi Shikibu and the Buddhist Literature of Medieval Japan* (Ann Arbor: University of Michigan Center for Japanese Studies, 2008), 102.

49. Susan Matisoff, "*Oguri*: An Early Edo Tale of Suffering, Resurrection, Revenge, and Deification," *Monumenta Nipponica* 66, no. 1 (2011): 51–52; "Reflections of Terute: Searching for a Hidden Shaman-Entertainer," *Women and Performance: A Journal of Feminist Theory* 12, no. 1 (2001): 113–34; and "Holy Horrors," 258–59.

50. Shinpan Shikidō ōkagami kankōkai, ed., *Shinpan Shikidō ōkagami*, 235.

51. Although *Yoshiuji* survives today only in a manuscript dated the tenth month of 1651 and in a woodblock-printed *shōhon* published around 1661, according to the diary *Ryōgen'in-dono gyoki*, the Edo chanter Satsuma Jōun traveled to Kyoto and performed *Yoshiuji* at the palace in the tenth month of 1636, around the time of the publication of Osaka Yoshichirō's 1639 *Sanshō Dayū*. We therefore know that the two works are contemporaneous. See Yasuda, *Ko-jōruri*, 27–28.

52. The perils include imposter Pure Lands and the like. See R. Keller Kimbrough, "Tourists in Paradise: Writing the Pure Land in Medieval Japanese Fiction," *Japanese Journal of Religious Studies* 33, no. 2 (2006): 274–76.

53. Kitahara Yasuo and Ogawa Eiichi, eds., *Engyō-bon Heike monogatari: Honbun hen* (Tokyo: Benseisha, 1990), 2:519; Amy Christine Franks, "Another *Tale of the Heike*: An Examination of the Engyōbon *Heike monogatari*" (Ph.D. diss., Yale University, 2009), 274–75.

54. Burton Watson, trans., *The Lotus Sutra* (New York: Columbia University Press, 1993), 187–88.

55. Michael A. Arnzen, "Who's Laughing Now? . . . The Postmodern Splatter Film," *Journal of Popular Film & Television* 21, no. 4 (1994): 178. Arnzen cites Martin Bridgstock, "The Twilit Fringe—Anthropology and Modern Horror Fiction," *Journal of Popular Culture* 23, no. 3 (1989): 115–23.

Sanshō Dayū

PART 1

Ask me about the origins of the Branded Jizō of Tango Province, and I will tell you that he was once the guardian deity of the Japanese general Iwaki no Hangan Masauji of the province of Michinoku.[1] This Masauji had two children: a daughter named Anju-no-hime and a son named Zushiōmaru, who was also Masauji's heir. The daughter was five years old, and the son was three. They were adorable, and their parents doted on them constantly.

Times were good for Masauji and his family, but it seems that someone slandered him to the emperor, for the poor man was censured and banished to Anrakuji Temple in distant Tsukushi.[2] His heart was filled with endless grief. His wife was to be pitied, too, for although she had lived a life of splendor, whiling away the autumn nights in the light of the moon and excelling in the ways

---

Translated from the incomplete *Sanshō Dayū* of circa 1639, supplemented by *Sanshō Dayū monogatari* of circa 1670. For a detailed explanation, see appendix 2.

1. Michinoku was the northernmost province of old Japan. Tango lay to the southwest, just to the north of Kyoto and bordering the Sea of Japan.
2. Tsukushi is an old name for the southern island of Kyūshū.

of poetry and music, no one came to see her in her dispossessed state.[3] Nevertheless, she took consolation in her children. Time quickly passed, and soon it was eleven years since her husband's misfortune.

One day a pair of swallows fluttered down from unknown heights. Gathering twigs from the garden, they built a nest on a Chinese crossbeam. The mother bird laid twelve eggs. When the father bird went to gather food, the mother bird would stay and warm the eggs, and when the mother bird went to gather food, the father bird would stay and do the same. Thus they raised their little ones together. Zushiōmaru watched as the father and mother birds led their children to the branch of an orange tree. "Mother," he said, "what kind of birds are those?"

"Those are called *tsubame*," his mother explained, "because they fly from the Eternal Land.[4] They are also called *giba*. The male chirps *shi-shi-fu-shi-setsu* from volume five of the Lotus sutra. They are exceptionally kindhearted birds. That one there is the father, and this one here is the mother. Those little ones in between are their children."

"How strange," Zushiōmaru said. "Whether they fly in the sky or run on the ground, all creatures have a mother and a father, just like that! So why don't Anju-no-hime and I have a father? Was he cut down on the road for some argument or offense, as samurai sometimes are? And when is his death anniversary? I want to visit him at his grave."

"Well, it's like this, Zushiōmaru," the mother began. "Your father, Lord Iwaki, was slandered to the emperor and exiled to Anrakuji Temple in Tsukushi. It caused him terrible grief."

"And all this time I thought he was dead!" the boy cried. "But if he's still alive, then please let me and Anju-no-hime leave here for a while. We'll go to the capital and explain to the emperor that our dad did nothing wrong. That'll cheer him up, and I'll be made governor of the fifty-four districts of Michinoku!"[5]

---

3. According to the 1656 *Sekkyō Sanshō Dayū*, Masauji's wife fled with her children to the Shinobu estate in the Daté district in present-day Fukushima Prefecture. See SSS 1:29a.

4. The Eternal Land (Tokiwa no Kuni) is a mythical place without change. The connection between the name *tsubame* and the Eternal Land is unclear.

5. In the 1667 and 1713 *Sanshō Dayū*, Zushiōmaru simply proposes visiting his father in Tsukushi. See SSS 1:46b, 70b.

"Rather than sending you two off to the capital while I stay here and fret," the mother said, "we should all go together."[6] Reasoning that it would be easier to travel without too many retainers, she invited only the wet nurse Lady Uwataki to accompany them. They set out lightheartedly on the seventeenth day of the third month, but it was a journey they would later regret.

After thirty days on the road, the travelers came to Naoi Bay in Echigo Province. The sun had risen in the east and lit up the land, and now it was evening at last. "Uwataki, find us a place to stay," the mother said. Wandering among Naoi's thousand homes, Lady Uwataki repeatedly asked, "Will you take in travelers for the night?" But although she begged at 999 houses, no one offered them lodging.

Alas, those four poor travelers! Sitting down to rest, they lamented, "What mean, selfish people! The whole town lacks compassion. To think that there's no one here who will give us shelter for the night!"

A woman carrying buckets of brine approached from the road along the shore. "Traveling ladies," she said, having overheard the party's complaints, "you are absolutely right. The residents here are actually very kind, but because of one or two bad people, word has spread throughout the land that Naoi Bay in Echigo Province is the home of kidnappers and slave traders. The local steward took it as a personal affront. He figured that it was the innkeepers who were selling people, so he made it a crime for anyone to provide lodgings. What's more, he said that his punishment would extend to the three households on either side of the offender's. Just look at that placard! With warnings like that up around here, people aren't likely to give you shelter even if they wanted to. But look over there—at the edge of that dark forest, there's a broad bridge called 'Meeting and Parting Bridge.' Go and spend the night there, and then be on your way." Taking this as the instruction of their clan deity, the mother immediately led Lady Uwataki and her children to the bridge.

Now in all the past, there has been nothing so moving as the love between a parent and her child. Recalling how the north wind blows so cold, the mother had Lady Uwataki block it from the side while she herself guarded against frosty gusts from the south. Producing a single set of small-sleeved robes with a light and dark drum-crest design, she spread them on the ground between them and had her children lie down.

---

6. There is an apparent lacuna here, which I have remedied in the translation. In the 1667 text, the mother says, "If you are so determined, then I'll go with you!" See SSS 1:46b.

Naoi Bay was the home of a notorious slave trader by the name of Yamaoka Dayū. He excelled at abducting people, and he was in a vile mood because he had missed his chance that afternoon to offer shelter to the traveling ladies. He had meant to trick them and sell them in order to see himself through the spring. "They're only women," he thought, "so they couldn't have gotten very far." Strapping on his sandals and his leggings, he wondered whether he ought to search the road along the shore, or perhaps the Meeting and Parting Bridge. Then, picking up his walking stick, he hurried off toward the bridge.

At the bridge, Yamaoka Dayū found the four exhausted travelers sound asleep, dead to the world. Intending to give them a fright, he pounded on the bridge planks with his stick and declared, "Whether or not you travelers went to sleep here knowing it, this bridge was never blessed! That's why a giant snake slithers down from the mountains every night to tie the lover's knot with another great serpent that slithers up from below. They meet and part on this bridge every morning at dawn, which is why it's called the Meeting and Parting Bridge. Rumor has it that they grab people after dark and carry them off someplace. Those poor people!" And with that, he walked off without a care in the world.

The mother jumped up with a start. Seeing Yamaoka Dayū's figure in the moonlight, she took him to be in his fifties. She thought that he looked like a merciful man, and desperate not to lose this chance, she grabbed him by the sleeve and said, "Please, sir, if I were alone, I'd resign myself to the foxes, wolves, and shape-shifting monsters. But take a look at those children! That boy sleeping there is heir to the fifty-four districts of Michinoku. We're on our way to the capital to settle a strange dispute, and after we receive a deed from the emperor confirming our lands, we'll return home. I'll pay you handsomely then, so please put us up for the night!"

Hearing the mother's entreaty, Yamaoka Dayū knew that if he were to refuse now, she would beg him all the more. Then, when he finally agreed, she would be especially pleased. He therefore lied, saying, "Dear lady, I would be happy to give you lodging, but as you know, it's forbidden. Even though I'd like to, I can't take you in."

"Please, sir," the mother implored, "they may not compare, but Fei Changfang and Ding Lingwei lodged in the wings of cranes, and the reverend Bodhidharma sheltered among reeds.[7] As people say, 'Be kind to travelers and caring

---

7. Fei Changfang and Ding Lingwei are legendary Chinese Daoist figures. Bodhidharma was a sixth-century monk of Central Asian extraction; he is recognized today as the progenitor of the Chan/Zen school of Buddhism.

in life.' Ships anchor in coves, and villages raise foundlings. Where there are trees, there are birds, and where there's a harbor, there are boats drawing near. What's more, I hear that when strangers share shelter from a passing storm, it's because of karmic bonds from a previous life. Women are used to being discreet—they lie low for seven days every month—and we can certainly keep quiet tonight. So please give us lodging this one time!"

"I wasn't going to put you up," Yamaoka Dayū said, "but you're so persuasive that I suppose I will. But if we meet anyone on the road, then let me do the talking. You just keep quiet." Yamaoka Dayū led them to his home. Fortune was with him, but not with the mother, because they came to his street without encountering anyone on the way.

Yamaoka Dayū addressed his wife: "Hello, dear. I've offered lodging to those ladies from this afternoon. Bring some water to wash their feet, and show them inside to the inner room. Get some dinner for them, too."

"I thought you'd given up your evil ways," the wife snapped back, "but I guess not! So you want to give 'lodging' to those ladies for the night? If that's the case, then you'll have give me my leave!"

Yamaoka Dayū scowled. Glaring at his wife, he said, "What, so you're going to start preaching at me like some half-baked nun? It's the thirteenth anniversary of my parents' death this year, and I was going to put those people up as an act of mercy. But maybe that's too much for you."

"Well, I thought you were planning a purchase or a sale. But if you really do mean to give those people shelter as an act of kindness, then come on inside." After bringing water to wash their feet, the wife showed her husband's guests to the inner room. Then, she brought them food.

Later, in the dark of night, the wife covered her head with a cloth and made her way to where they slept. "Traveling ladies," she whispered, "I am the woman of the house. I have come to tell you something. You must be vexed at me for saying in the daytime that I couldn't give you lodging. I am a woman like you, so it's not that I couldn't take you in, but the truth is, my husband has manned a slave boat since the age of seven. He's a notorious slaver, and he's especially good at abducting people. I thought he might sell you in the mountains somewhere, and since I couldn't stand the thought of you cursing us for it later, I said that I couldn't take you in. But if it's true that he's invited you here as an act of mercy, then you can stay for five or ten days if you like. Just don't let up your guard! If I find out that he intends to sell you, I'll let you know. And in that case, don't flee to the north, but head south instead. The capital highway lies to the south. If my rough husband has the nerve to follow you there, then shout that he's a slaver and a kidnapper."

Yamaoka Dayū listened through the wall. "Meddling wife!" he thought. "But even with her warning, I'll trick them and sell them to see myself through the spring." And thinking such thoughts, he was unable to sleep.

Goodness being the weak thing that it is, and wickedness being strong, Yamaoka Dayū got up while his wife was dozing and approached the inner room. "Wake up, ladies," he said. "I am the master of the house. I've come to speak to you about something. Is this your first time traveling to the capital?" Their luck having run out, the women answered that it was. Yamaoka Dayū knew that if this was indeed their first time, then he would have no trouble selling them, either on land or at sea. "Traveling ladies," he said, "I have something else to ask. Will you go by land or sea?"

"By land or sea . . . which do you think would be easier?" the mother replied. Yamaoka Dayū knew that the land route was easy enough, but intending to frighten them, he said, "The road passes through places like 'Tumbling Nun' and 'Abandon Your Bowl,' which are so treacherous that parents sometimes die without their children even noticing, and where children sometimes die without their parents realizing it, either. There are also the forty-eight branches of the Kurobe River to consider . . . So, you should go by sea! I have a nice little vessel of my own. I'll row you out to the offing and flag down a ship to take you farther on. In any case, it's going to be dawn soon. And once morning comes, the house will be in a commotion, so let's sneak away now, quickly."

Alas, those four poor travelers! Not realizing that they were to be sold, they quietly crept out of Yamaoka Dayū's home. Slinking along the sides of houses, they made their way to the road along the shore. Yamaoka Dayū put them in a night boat, and declaring that there was no time to untie the hawser, he drew a sword from his waist and sliced it in two. Rejoicing in his heart at having escaped with his merchandise intact, he took to the oars. He marked each of his pulls with a powerful grunt, rowing some three leagues before it was light.

Staring out to sea, Yamaoka Dayū saw two boats in the mist. He shouted, "You boats there—are you merchant or fishing vessels?"

"This is Edo no Jirō here," a man called from one craft.

"And I'm Miyazaki no Saburō," a man shouted from the other. "Who's asking?"

"Yamaoka Dayū."

"Well, what a surprise! Got anything to sell?"

"You bet!" Yamaoka Dayū held up one open hand with his thumb folded forward to show he had four people on board.

"If you've got four, I'll give you five *kan* for the lot," Edo no Jirō shouted, quickly setting his price. Watching from his own boat, Miyazaki no Saburō said, "If he's offering five, I'll kick in an extra *kan* and make it six, since I've got a buyer lined up already." The two men argued back and forth, eventually taking to their swords.

Yamaoka Dayū leaped onto one of their boats. "Take it easy," he urged, "or else our birds might fly! And with these particular birds—grown ones and little ones, too—you both can turn a profit, which is why I'm going to split them up between you. Edo no Jirō can have the two ladies, and Miyazaki no Saburō can have the kids. I'll even give you a break and take just five *kan* for the bunch."

Yamaoka Dayū jumped back onto his own boat. "Hello, traveling ladies," he said. "What do you think all that quarreling was about? It was over you! Those two captains are my nephews, and since I'm their uncle, they were arguing over who should have the honor of giving you passage. But there's a simple solution. Since they're bound for the same harbor in the same town, we'll split you up between them so they can travel lighter. You two ladies will go in that boat there, and you two children will go in this boat here." Having thus sold his passengers for five *kan*, Yamaoka Dayū set out on his return.

Those poor divided travelers! Though they sailed side by side for some six hundred yards, at twelve hundred yards one of their vessels turned north, and the other one, south. Taking in the sight, the mother said, "Our two boats have certainly drifted apart! It doesn't even look like we're heading for the same harbor. Please row us back, captain, and then take us on more slowly."

"What?" the captain exclaimed. "I lost my chance this morning to buy the four of you together, so I'm in a bad mood already. You ladies are my property now. Get down in the bottom of the boat!"

"What's this, Uwataki?" the mother cried. "We've been bought and sold! That cruel Yamaoka Dayū! And you hateful captain! If we had to be purchased, then why couldn't it have been together? How awful to sell parents and children apart!"

Gazing toward Miyazaki no Saburō's boat, the mother shouted, "Listen, children! We've been bought and sold! Always treasure your lives! Oh, will you ever regain your place in the world? Anju-no-hime, there's an amulet of the bodhisattva Jizō hanging around your neck. He'll step in and take your place if you two are ever in danger, so wear it with faith! And Zushiōmaru, around your neck there's a lineage scroll showing your right to the Shida and Tamatsukuri districts. You can give it to Enma when you're dead and gone.[8] But don't lose it before then!" The mother continued shouting for as long as her voice would carry. When the boats had sailed farther apart and she could no longer be heard, she took a fan from her waist and waved it toward her children. But they only continued on their way.

"Oh, what grief!" the mother cried. "Though I set out this morning from Naoi Bay in Echigo Province, I'm denied the sight of my children by the white-crested waves, rising like frothy clouds of delusion! Even the legendary seabird longs for its young![9] Please, captain, row the boat back and let me see my children again!"

"Nonsense!" the captain bellowed. "It's a rule that once you take a vessel out, you don't turn around and go back in. Now get down in the bottom of the boat!"

Lady Uwataki announced that she understood. "A superior retainer serves no two masters," she declared, "and a virtuous wife takes no two husbands. I'll not be a warrior who pulls two bows!" She stood on a strut and produced a beaded rosary. Turning toward the west, she pressed her palms together and recited the *nenbutsu* ten times in a strong voice.[10] Then she threw herself into Naoi Bay, where she quickly joined the weeds at the bottom of the sea.

The mother cried, "Is this to be your end, my long-serving Uwataki? And what's to become of me?" With that, she broke down and wept. Later choking back her tears, she took out the set of small-sleeved robes with the light and dark drum-crest design and said, "Listen, captain, I know it's insufficient, but please take this in exchange for the sum that you paid this morning and let me go free. I am going to throw myself into the sea, too."

"What?" the captain exclaimed. "I may have lost one of you today, but I'm certainly not going to lose you both!" He beat her down with an oar, bound her to a strut, and then sold her on the island of Ezo.[11] When the buyer there discovered that she had no particular skills, he slashed the tendons in her wrists and ankles and set her to work chasing birds from a millet field. She lived on a single cup of grain a day.

---

8. King Enma is the ruler of the afterworld and the judge of the dead.
9. The *utōyasukata*, a fabled seabird of northern Japan, is said to weep tears of blood at the loss of its children.
10. The *nenbutsu* is the ritual invocation of Amida Buddha's name.
11. Ezo is an old name for the northern island of Hokkaidō.

The mother and Lady Uwataki (*right*) sail away from Anju-no-hime and Zushiōmaru (*left*). From *Sanshō Dayū* (ca. 1639 woodblock-printed edition). (Courtesy of Tenri University Library)

    Meanwhile, the two children were in a pitiful plight. Although they had been bought first by Miyazaki no Saburō for two-and-a-half *kan*, they were sold and resold until Sanshō Dayū of Yura Harbor in Tango Province reckoned a price and purchased them for thirteen *kan*. He was terrifically pleased. "What a pleasure to buy good slaves!" he thought. "As hereditary retainers, their descendants will serve my family for generations to come."
    One day Sanshō Dayū summoned the children and spoke. "Everyone serving in this house has a name," he said. "So what are you two called?" Anju-no-hime replied, "Well, sir, since we come from deep in the mountains and far away from here, we don't have any particular names. I'm just called 'big sister,' and my little brother is called 'little brother.' Please give us whatever names you like." Sanshō Dayū thought this was reasonable. "In that case," he said, "where do you come from? I'll give you names from around your home."
    "We're from the Shinobu estate in the Daté district," Anju-no-hime replied. "We set out lightheartedly from our home on the seventeenth day of third month,

but we were sold at Naoi Bay in Echigo Province. It's been very hard on us, sir, but when I concentrate, I can count seventy-five times that we've been sold since then. Our previous owners referred to us as 'the merchandise' or 'the goods,' rather than by any definite names. So please, sir, call us whatever you think best."

"If that's the case," the master said, "then we'll call you Shinobu, or 'fern,' after the Shinobu estate in the Daté district.[12] And since ferns go with *wasuregusa*, or 'forgetting grass,' we'll call your brother Wasuregusa, so that he'll forget his many hardships and serve me well. Now as for you, Shinobu, starting tomorrow I want you to fetch saltwater from the shore. And you, Wasuregusa, you are to help me by cutting three loads of brushwood every day."

Dawn broke in the fifth hour of the night,[13] whereupon the children received a sickle, a carrying pole, a tub, and a ladle. Taking up their tools, the poor brother and sister headed off to the mountains and the shore. Alas, little Anju-no-hime! Later pausing to rest, she threw down her tub and ladle and gazed up toward the mountains. "If I can't even scoop the saltwater that's here all around me," she sobbed, "then how could it be for my brother, who's never held a sickle before? Has he swung too close and cut his hand? Or has a storm moved in at the peak? It looks so cold up there. Oh, Zushiō!"

Elsewhere, Zushiōmaru sat on the edge of an outcrop and gazed down toward the shore. "If I can't even cut this brushwood that's here all around me," he wept, "then how could it be for my sister? I've heard that among the whitecaps, there are male and female waves. People say that you should let the male waves strike and then scoop from the gentler female waves. But Anju-no-hime doesn't know anything about that. Has the surf stolen her tub and ladle? Or has a storm moved in at the coast? It looks so cold down there. Oh, Anju!" Thus, in the mountains and on the shore, the two children passed the day in tears.

The local woodsmen were returning from the mountains with their brushwood when they saw Zushiōmaru. "That boy's from Sanshō Dayū's place," they said. "He's new, but if he goes home without any wood, that evil Sanshō Dayū and his son Saburō will beat him to death for sure. You know, helping others is a bodhisattva practice, so let's do a good deed and cut him some brushwood." The woodsmen cut a little bit each, and they soon provided Zushiōmaru with a full three loads. "Now bundle it up and take it away," they said.

"But sirs," Zushiōmaru replied, "I didn't cut it, and I can't carry it, either."

---

12. Written with a different character, *shinobu* can also mean "to tolerate" or "to endure."
13. The fifth hour of the night is approximately 3:00 to 5:00 A.M.

"Yes, that may be so," the woodsmen agreed. They all added a portion of the boy's wood to their own heavy loads and carried it as far as Short Asumi Beach. Since the distant past, people have spoken of "adding a little weight to a heavy burden," and the saying comes from this.

Poor Zushiōmaru carried his three loads of brushwood home. Seeing him come in, Saburō grabbed him with one hand, snatched his wood with the other, and trundled him off to see Sanshō Dayū. "Excuse me, sir," Saburō said. "Take a look at this brushwood that the boy cut."

Sanshō Dayū surveyed the wood. "Well," he said, "you told me you couldn't cut brushwood! But if that were true, then your ends wouldn't be aligned. Your pieces would be tied together in a jumble. But you've cut this wood beautifully, just like a local! If you're so talented, then three loads aren't nearly enough. I'll add seven to your three, for a total of ten. From now on, if you don't cut ten loads of brushwood every day, I'll have you and your sister killed!"

Zushiōmaru stepped out of the front gate to await his sister's return. He was a sad sight to see! And poor Anju-no-hime! Balancing her tub on her head, she returned to the house in a dreadful state, her hem soaked with brine and her sleeves drenched with tears.

Zushiōmaru clutched his sister's sleeves and whimpered. "Listen, Anju. I couldn't cut the brushwood today, so some woodsmen from the village cut it for me. They did it beautifully, but I was punished anyway. Sanshō Dayū added seven loads to my three, and now I have to cut ten. Anju, please go and beg him to make it three again!"

"Don't grieve like that, Zushiōmaru," Anju-no-hime said. "I couldn't scoop the surf today, either. And the waves took my tub and ladle! A fisherman kindly scooped the water for me. I got the job done this time, but I don't know if I can do it again tomorrow. Anyway, I hear that Sanshō Dayū has five sons and that the second one, Master Jirō, has a kind heart. We'll plead with him to put your quota back to three. So don't grieve like that, Zushiōmaru—you'll make me upset, too!" Together, the two siblings returned inside.

Word reached the evil Saburō that Anju-no-hime had helped her brother by having his brushwood assignment reduced to three loads. He approached his father and spoke: "Hello, sir. I was wondering whether the boy actually cut that brushwood yesterday, and then I heard that the villagers did it for him on a whim. I'll go have a word with them all." Cruel son that he was, Saburō's warning was terrible indeed. "There are two new children working at Sanshō Dayū's place," he proclaimed. "If anyone cuts brushwood or fetches saltwater for them, I'll punish him and his family and the seven adjoining households on either side of the street." Everyone said that Saburō was like a demon.

Alas, poor Zushiōmaru! Unaware of Saburō's injunction, he returned to where he had been the day before in the hope that someone would cut his wood for him again. The woodsmen saw him standing there. "None of us begrudges you the brushwood," they said, "but that evil Saburō gave us a warning, and now no one's likely to cut you any, even if he wanted to." They showed Zushiōmaru how to handle a sickle, saying, "Hold your tool this way, and cut like this." Then they walked on.

Poor Zushiōmaru! Telling himself that he would have to be brave, he took his sickle from his waist. There was a tree, and although he did not know what kind it was, he managed to chop it down. But because he did not know how to break it apart for brushwood, he began to pull it by its base. The hillside was densely overgrown, and feeling as if he were pulling at the wrong end of the trunk, he made little progress. "I'm doing what I'm supposed to," he complained, "but I can't even handle brushwood!" His frustration was natural.

"People live to be eighty, ninety, or a hundred years old," he thought. "I may be young, but if I can accept that my own allotted span is just thirteen years, then it shouldn't be hard to take my own life."[14] He untied the cord to his dagger, preparing to do himself in. "But then again," he thought, "my sister is at the beach, and if I kill myself here, it'll be awfully hard to let her go when I'm dead. I'll visit her where she's working and say good-bye." He put away his dagger, shouldered his sickle and carrying pole, and headed down the mountain toward the road along the shore.

Poor Anju-no-hime was scooping brine. The hem of her robe was soaked from the surf, and her sleeves were drenched with tears. Zushiōmaru took her by the arm and said, "Listen, Anju. I was going to kill myself, but then I thought how much I'd miss you in the next world, so I came here to say good-bye first. I'm going to take my own life!"

Anju-no-hime took in her brother's words. "You may be my little brother," she replied, "but you're a man, too, which is why you thought to die. I also was going to throw myself into the waves, and I'm so happy now that I decided to wait. If you really want to do it, then let's jump into the sea together!"

---

14. There is an inconsistency in the text. If Zushiōmaru was three years old at the time of his father's exile and if he waited eleven years before setting out to seek a pardon, he should be fourteen years old now.

The children filled their sleeves with pebbles and climbed onto a boulder that jutted over the froth. "Listen, Zushiōmaru," Anju-no-hime said. "We lost our mother at Naoi Bay in Echigo Province, but look in my face and pray to me now like you're praying to her. Then I'll look at you and pray like I'm praying to our father, Lord Iwaki, who was banished to Anrakuji Temple in Tsukushi."

The children were preparing to leap when a fellow servant by the name of Ise no Kohagi saw them and called out, "Hello, kids! You look like you're ready to do yourselves in. But you should always treasure your lives! As people say, live and you'll see Mount Hōrai.[15] Otherwise, how will you ever regain your place in the world? If you want to live, then let me tell you about myself. I wasn't born one of Sanshō Dayū's slaves, either. I'm from Uda in Yamato Province. My stepmother slandered me, and I was sold at Futami Bay in the province of Ise. In my grief, I cut a notch in my staff every time I was bought and sold. By counting the marks, I can tell that I've been purchased forty-two times. Anyway, this is my third year serving here. It isn't easy at first, but you'll get used to it after a while. If you can't cut brushwood, then I'll cut it for you. And if you can't scoop saltwater, I'll do that for you, too. But please, treasure your lives!"

"It's because we couldn't do our jobs that we were going to kill ourselves," Anju-no-hime replied. "If we could only do our work, then why would we want to die?"

"If that's how you feel," Kohagi said, "then from this day forward, you should think of yourselves as having an elder sister at Sanshō Dayū's place."

"And please think of us as your younger brother and sister!" the children exclaimed. Having thus sealed a sibling bond, Kohagi and the kids returned together to Sanshō Dayū's house.

PART 2

Time passed, and before Sanshō Dayū knew it, it was already the last day of the year. He beckoned his son Saburō and spoke: "Hello, Saburō! You know, those two children come from so deep in the mountains and far away from here that they've probably never even heard of New Year's. They won't stop sniveling! It's bound to ruin our luck for the next twelve months. Go build them a brushwood

---

15. In other words, good things come to those who survive. Mount Hōrai is a legendary island of Daoist immortals.

shack beside the third inner gate and let them see in the new year there." "Yes, sir," Saburō replied, and he did just that.

Passing the new year in their hovel, the children wept and complained in a way that was moving to hear! "Until last New Year's," Anju-no-hime moaned, "we may have been dispossessed, but at the Shinobu estate in the Daté district we had menservants and serving ladies who would dote on us and play games like 'smashing demons' and 'little foreign devils.'[16] But this year we're spending New Year's in a brushwood shack! I've heard that it's the custom in our land to shut people away like this when they're tainted or taboo, so maybe that's what they do to regular folks here in Tango. Oh, Zushiōmaru, I'm so cold! And hungry, too! Now listen, brother—we're never going to be any good at serving Sanshō Dayū. I hear that the First Mountain Rites in this province are on the sixteenth day of the new year.[17] If you go to the ceremony, then run away as soon as you're in the mountains! You don't have to say good-bye. Once you've gotten away and regained your place in the world, you can come back for me then."

Zushiōmaru pressed his hand to his sister's mouth. "Quiet, Anju!" he hushed. "Around here, the stones have ears and the walls can talk! Who knows what would happen if Sanshō Dayū or his sons heard you speaking like that. If you want to run away, then do it by yourself. I'm not going anywhere!"

"I could escape easily enough," Anju-no-hime snapped, "but I'm a girl, and I don't have a pedigree! But you've got the family lineage scroll, so you should get out and take your place." The children argued back and forth. "You run away!" they each insisted. "No, you run away!" "You go!" "I won't!"

Evil Saburō happened to be stalking little birds in the bushes, and he overheard the children's quarrel. He visited his father and spoke: "Hello, sir! Those two kids are urging each other to run away. They may even be escaping now."

"Bring them here!" Sanshō Dayū demanded. "Yes, sir," Saburō replied, and he sent a messenger to summon them from beside the third inner gate. Poor Anju-no-hime! "Didn't I tell you?" she exclaimed, misunderstanding the command. "The master is going to give us a New Year's present! We may be slaves, but don't forget how our serving men and women used to offer their proper

---

16. *Hama* and *kogi no ko* are two traditional New Year's games for children. *Hama*, or *hamayumi*, involves shooting small arrows at a straw target; *kogi no ko*, also known as *hago* or *hane*, is a kind of battledore and shuttlecock.

17. First Mountain Rites (*hatsuyama*, or *hatsuyama-iri*) is a New Year's ritual in which people who work in the mountains make offerings to the mountain gods.

New Year's greetings at the Shinobu estate in Daté." With that, they went to see the master.

Sanshō Dayū scowled. "I bought you two for seventeen *kan*," he said, glaring at the children. "But you haven't done seventeen *mon* worth of work for me yet,[18] and you're plotting an escape! Do you think I'd let you run away? I'm going to mark you so that wherever you go, everyone will know you're my slaves. How about it, Saburō?"

"I wonder what sort of brand we should give them," Saburō mumbled as he lowered some charcoal from a bin in the ceiling and hauled it to the courtyard. He took an arrow from his quiver, and after using a great fan to rouse the charcoal to a raging heat, he seized poor Anju-no-hime by her long black hair. Brutally twisting it around his fist, he pinned her to the ground with one knee.

"Please, Master Saburō!" Zushiōmaru begged. "Whether you're serious or fooling or just trying to scare us, if you really do brand her, it might kill her. And if she does survive, then when she waits on your wife and your sisters-in-law at moon-viewing or cherry-blossom parties, the women will all ask what a beautiful girl like her could have done to deserve being branded like that. And they won't talk about her crime—only about how cruel you were! You can brand me twice, sir, but please let my sister go!"

"I wonder what sort of brand would make a really good mark," Saburō mumbled. He fired the arrowhead until it glowed. Then, pressing it against Anju-no-hime's face, he drew a cross.[19] Zushiōmaru watched, and although he had remained calm until then, he panicked at the sight of his sister's mutilation and bolted.[20] "So, you're not as brave as you say!" Saburō taunted. "Now do you really think I'd let you get away?" He grabbed the boy by his topknot, dragged him back and pinned him to the ground with one knee.

Poor Anju-no-hime! Touching her hands to her burn, she said, "Please, Master Saburō! What you're doing is monstrous! I'm the one who told him to escape! He had only good things to say about our master! People say that the scar on a man's face is his to keep, even if it's bought,[21] but some scars are

---

18. One *kan* is equivalent to a thousand *mon*. In part 1, Sanshō Dayū is reported to have bought the children for thirteen, rather than seventeen, *kan*.

19. According to the 1667 and 1713 *Sanshō Dayū*, Saburō branded Anju-no-hime on her forehead. See SSS 1:54b, 80a.

20. According to the circa 1670 *Sanshō Dayū monogatari*, Zushiōmaru ran for the gate. See SSS 1:321a.

21. For warriors, a facial scar was regarded as a sign of valor.

Top, Zushiōmaru silences his sister as Saburō listens outside; *bottom*, Saburō brands Anju-no-hime, and Zushiōmaru tries to escape. From *Sanshō Dayū* (ca. 1639 woodblock-printed edition). (Courtesy of Tenri University Library)

different from others. Since this one's a mark of shame, please brand me two or three times and let my brother go!"

"I wonder what sort of brand would make a really good mark," Saburō mumbled as he pressed the arrowhead to Zushiōmaru's face. The metal made a sizzling sound. Sanshō Dayū took in the sight. "Your big mouths have gotten you into a hot spot this time, haven't they!" he quipped and then burst out laughing. "But when you're faced with death, it's whiners like you who won't even speak to save your own lives. Saburō, take them down to the road along the shore and put them under that big pine tub—the one that it takes eighty-five men to lift. They can spend New Year's there. And don't give them any food! Just let them starve." "Yes, sir," Saburō replied, and he did as he was told.

Passing New Year's under the pine tub, the children naturally wept and complained. Anju-no-hime clung to her brother and cried, "Oh, Zushiōmaru! I've heard that in our own province, it's a custom on the last day of the sixth month to jump through a ring of cogon grass for the summer purification ceremony. So what we're doing now must be a custom in Tango. But they haven't given us anything to eat! Do you think they mean to starve us? Oh, Zushiō!" The children held each other and wept bitter, anguished tears.

Among Sanshō Dayū's five sons, his second son, Jirō, was exceptionally kind. Every night he set aside a little of his own food and hid it in his sleeve. Avoiding his parents' and brothers' gaze, he took it to the road along the shore, where he bored a hole through the base of the pine tub and gave it to the children. Anju-no-hime and Zushiōmaru were terribly grateful.

Time passed, and before Sanshō Dayū knew it, it was already the sixteenth day of the new year. He beckoned his son Saburō and spoke: "Hello, Saburō! You know, a person's life seems like a fragile thing, but it's actually quite sturdy. Go and see if those children are still alive at the road along the shore." "Yes, sir," Saburō replied.

Saburō made his way to the shore, where he overturned the pine tub for a look underneath. The poor children were the color of dirt. Saburō led them to his father, who peered at them and said, "How nice that you're alive! Now get back to the mountains and the beach."

"We understand, sir," Anju-no-hime replied. "But please send us together. We'll go to the mountains or the beach, whichever you decide."

"Well, I suppose every group needs a laughingstock," Sanshō Dayū sneered. "If you insist on working in the mountains, then we'll have to give you a boy's haircut! How about it, Saburō?" "Yes, sir," Saburō replied. Alas, poor Anju-no-hime! Saburō seized her by her long black hair and cruelly twisted it around his fist. He sliced it off near the nape of her neck, and then sent her to the mountains looking like a boy. She and her brother grieved piteously.

Poor Zushiōmaru stared at his sister from behind. "People talk about the 'thirty-two signs of beauty,'" he said, "but you're so pretty, you've got forty-two! And they say that of the forty-two signs, a woman's hair is the most important. But yours is all gone now, so it breaks my heart to look at you, even from behind. And how much worse it must be for you!"

"Nice hair's for those who can afford it," Anju-no-hime countered, "and for us, it's a luxury we can do without. I'm just glad we could come to the mountains together."

The children followed an animal trail to a cleft in some boulders among patches of melting snow. Anju-no-hime took the Jizō amulet from around her neck and hung it on a pointed rock. Then she prayed: "Jizō Bodhisattva, our mother said that if we were ever in any danger, you would step in and take our place. But the gods and buddhas must have lost their power, because you haven't protected us at all! It's distressing."

Zushiōmaru peered at his sister's face. "Hey, Anju!" he cried. "The burn is gone!"

"It's true!" Anju-no-hime exclaimed. "And it's gone from your face, too!" Examining the amulet, they saw that the bodhisattva had taken their scars on his own brow. He had stood in for them after all. "But if Jizō has taken away our burns," Zushiōmaru reasoned, "then that evil Sanshō Dayū and Saburō are sure to brand us again! Oh, Jizō, please put back our marks so they won't burn us and hurt us again!"

"Once he's stood in for us, he's not going to undo it," Anju-no-hime scolded. "And anyway, it's a blessing that he won't. You should take this chance to run away. Once you've escaped and regained your place in the world, you can come back for me then."

"Didn't you learn your lesson?" Zushiōmaru cried. "Next time they'll kill us! If you want to run away, then do it by yourself! I'm not going anywhere."

"So you think we got branded because of my big mouth? When I told you to escape, if you had just agreed, do you think we would have been burned? If that's how you feel, then from now on you can forget you ever had a sister at Sanshō Dayū's place! And I'll forget I ever had a brother." Swearing on their sickles, the children clinked metal to metal and set off for the valley below.

Zushiōmaru looked at Anju-no-hime. "Grouchy sister!" he said. "If you really want me to run away, then I'll do it while you go back."

"So you'll escape then? That's wonderful! Let's share a cup to say good-bye." Because the children had nothing to eat or drink, they used oak leaves to scoop up the pure valley water. Calling it wine, Anju-no-hime drank a cup, after which she offered one to her brother.

"I'm going to give you the Jizō amulet that I wear around my neck," she said. "Now don't be rash even if you do manage to get away. I've heard that it's actually a sign of weakness. Wherever you escape to, if there's a village there, find a temple right away and ask a priest or a nun for help. People say that you can count on monastics. Run away, now, quickly! Looking at you makes me want to cry. No, wait, Zushiōmaru, listen! After it's snowed a little bit like this, put your straw sandals on backward and switch your staff from your right hand to your left. That way, when you climb a hill, it'll look like you were walking down it, and vice versa. Run away, now, fast!" The two children said good-bye. They thought that it would be for only a little while, but it was to be for a very long time indeed.

Alas, poor Anju-no-hime! "After today," she cried, "who can I talk to as I did with my brother?" Choking back her tears, she gathered some brushwood that others had cut, bundled it into a small load, and carried it on her head back to Sanshō Dayū's place. As it was the sixteenth day of the new year, the master had climbed the tower at the front of his estate, where he was taking in the view. Seeing Anju-no-hime's brushwood, he called out, "Well, you've cut better wood than your brother! And where is he?"

"This morning, sir, after I said I wanted to work in the mountains instead of at the beach, he said he wouldn't go with a stupid sister like me who had lost all her hair. He set out with the local woodsmen. Maybe he got lost if he's not back yet. What a pity! I'll go see if I can find him."

"You know, there are five kinds of tears," Sanshō Dayū began. "Surface tears, bitter tears, joyful tears, sorrowful tears, and lamenting tears. But yours aren't even real! You look like you're weeping for pleasure at having helped your brother make such a quick escape! Saburō, where do you think the boy went? Torture his sister and find out!"

"Yes, sir," Saburō replied. He bound Anju-no-hime to a twelve-rung ladder and plied her with the hot- and cold-water interrogation techniques.[22] But she refused to break, so he took out a triple-edged awl and twisted it into her kneecaps. Anju-no-hime wondered if she ought to confess, but steeling her heart against it, she said, "Please, let me say something."

"We're doing this to make her talk," Sanshō Dayū interrupted, "so if she's got something to say, let her say it."

"If my brother's back from the mountains," Anju-no-hime continued, "tell him I was tortured to death because of him! Then keep a close eye on him and make him serve you well."

"Saburō!" Sanshō Dayū snapped. "If the stupid girl is going to ignore our questions and speak out of line, then interrogate her until she can't speak anymore!"

Evil Saburō lowered some charcoal from the bin in the ceiling and hauled it to the courtyard. He used a great fan to rouse it to a raging heat, after which he grabbed poor Anju-no-hime by her remaining hair and dragged her across it. "If it's hot, then break!" he shouted. "Break! Break!" Saburō's punishment was

---

22. A method of simulating drowning by pouring water into the mouth and nose. The seventeen-year-old Goō-no-hime also is subjected to these and other torments in *Goō-no-hime*.

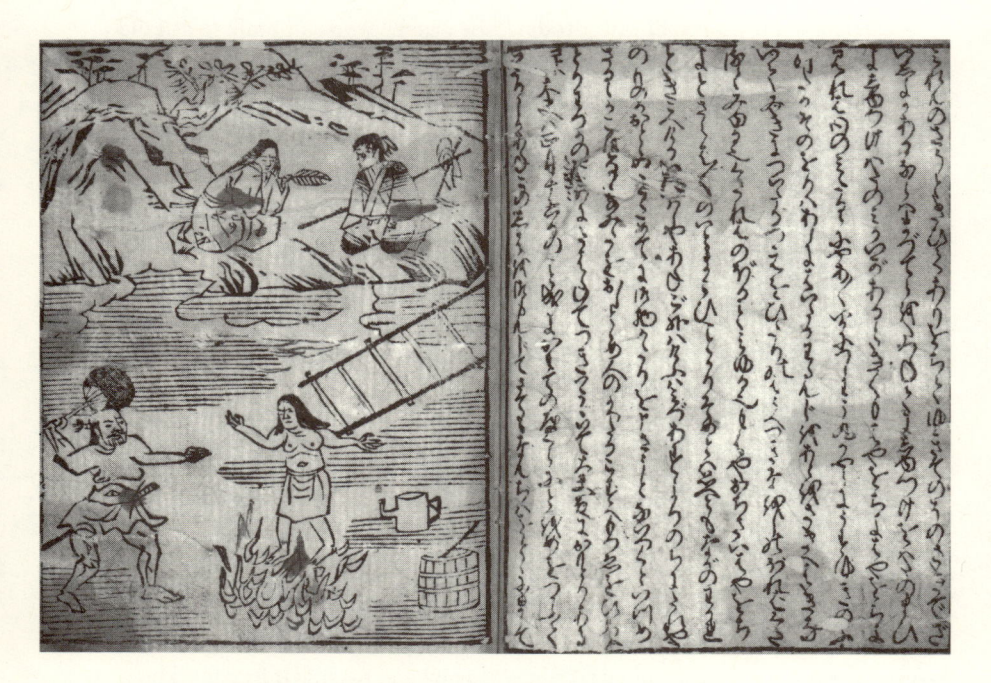

Top, Anju-no-hime and Zushiōmaru say good-bye; *bottom*, Saburō tortures Anju-no-hime to death. From *Sanshō Dayū* (ca. 1639 woodblock-printed edition). (Courtesy of Tenri University Library)

fierce and the girl's flesh was weak, so how could she have endured for long? It was thus that at the age of sixteen, toward noon on the sixteenth day of the new year, Anju-no-hime met her brutal end.

Sanshō Dayū saw that the girl was dead. "We were only trying to scare her," he said, "so she must have been frail. Go dump her body over there. As for the boy, he's too young to have gotten far. We'll chase him down." And Sanshō Dayū and his sons immediately set out with eighty-five retainers in four groups.

Alas, poor Zushiōmaru! Fearing that his sister was being whipped, beaten, or brutalized, he considered turning back. He sat down to rest on a mountain pass, but when he gazed in the direction from which he had come, he saw Sanshō Dayū approaching, followed by his five sons. "You deities of Suwa and Hachiman," he vowed, "there's no escape for me now. I'll untie my dagger and stick it in Sanshō Dayū's heart, even if it costs me my life!" But then he reconsidered. Hadn't his sister warned him against being rash? He made up his mind to flee for as long as he could, and he took to his heels and ran.

Suddenly Zushiōmaru encountered a villager. "Is there a settlement ahead?" he asked.

"Yes," the man replied, "Watari Village."

"Is there a temple there?"

"Certainly. It's a *kokubunji* provincial temple."[23]

"What's the principal image?"[24]

"Bishamon," the man replied.[25]

"Thank goodness!" Zushiōmaru thought. "Bishamon is a manifestation of Jizō, whose amulet is hanging around my neck!" He prayed for strength and hurried on his way.

Soon arriving at the temple, Zushiōmaru saw the intendant engaged in his midday practice. "Excuse me, master," he called out. "I am being pursued, and my life is in danger. Hide me, please!"

"But you're so young!" the priest exclaimed. "What crime could you have committed for that to be true? Tell me now and I'll see if I can help."

"I'll explain it to you if I live," Zushiōmaru implored, "but please, hide me first!"

"I suppose you're telling the truth," the priest said. He took an old leather hamper from a side room and bundled the boy inside. After tying it up tightly, front to back and side to side, he hung it from the rafters. Then, as if nothing had occurred, he resumed his midday practice.

Since it was still only the sixteenth day of the new year, Sanshō Dayū and his sons were able to follow Zushiōmaru's footsteps in the snow. They pursued him to the provincial temple, where Sanshō Dayū stood guard at the front gate tower while his five children went inside to see the intendant. "Hello, priest," they said. "A boy came in here a little while ago. Hand him over." Although the priest could hear perfectly well, he replied, "What's that you say? The spring nights are dull, and you want to invite me for a meal?"

---

23. One of the temples established throughout Japan by the eighth-century emperor Shōmu for the protection of the state.

24. The principal object of worship at a particular temple, typically a statue of a buddha or a bodhisattva.

25. Bishamon is a Buddhist guardian deity otherwise known as Bishamonten or simply Tamonten.

Saburō was enraged. "You're hung up on food, holy man, like a corpse in a river![26] Leave the feeding for later and give us the boy!"

"I hear you now!" the intendant shot back. "You want me to give you a boy? I've been concentrating on my hundred-day devotions—not looking out for a boy or a toy or whatever it is you want."

"Cursed priest!" Saburō swore. "If that's how it's going to be, then we'll have to scour the temple."

"Fine!" the intendant declared.

So where do you think the nimble Saburō searched? In the sanctum and on the crossbeams; in the kitchen, the sleeping chambers, and the sacred buddha altar; under the veranda and at the base of the outside temple walls. He even pulled down the ceiling planks, but the boy was nowhere to be found.

"This is certainly strange," Saburō mused. "There's no way out the front or back, so he ought to be here. But you, holy man—you must know where he is! Bring him out! If you won't, then swear a great oath that you're not lying. If you'll do that, we'll be on our way back to Yura Harbor."

"I know nothing about a boy," the intendant insisted, "but if you want me to swear an oath, I will. Let's see. I, this priest here before you, am not a man of this province. I come from the Uda region in the province of Yamato. At the age of seven, I ascended Mount Shosha in Harima,[27] and I took the tonsure at the age of ten. I began preaching at the age of twenty. I will swear an oath now on the sutras that I have studied since I was a child.

"Among the many sutras, there are the Kegon, Agon, Hōdō, Hannya, Hokke, Nehan, and Five Great Storehouse scriptures.[28] There are the Yakushi, Kannon, Jizō, and Amida sutras, and more than seven thousand scrolls of other ancient, sacred writs. The sutras that absolve myriad offenses are the Blood Bowl and three Pure Land scriptures. Also, there are the Kusharon treatises in thirty scrolls, the Tendai sutras in sixty scrolls, the Greater Hannya sutra in six hundred scrolls, and the Lotus sutra, which contains 69,384 characters in twenty-eight chapters in eight scrolls. May I suffer the profound punishment of these works if I lie when I say that I know nothing about a boy!"

---

26. There is an untranslatable pun here on *kui* (to eat) and *kui* (post or piling), on which a corpse might get caught in a current.

27. Mount Shosha is the site of Enkyōji Temple, founded by Shōkū Shōnin in 966.

28. Or, in the circa 1670 *Sanshō Dayū monogatari*, the "Five Mahāyāna sutras." See SSS 1:327b.

Sanshō Dayū spoke: "Listen, priest. When you swear an oath, you're supposed to waken and summon all the greater and lesser gods of Japan. That's what it means to take an oath. But all you've done is try to fool us with a list of the sutras you've learned since you were young. Just give us a proper oath."

Alas, the poor intendant! Being a monastic, he was already disturbed by the assurance he had sworn. "To demand that I pronounce another oath is just too cruel!" he thought to himself. "I wonder if I should surrender the boy or take another oath? If I give up the boy, I'll violate the precept against killing, and if I don't give him up and make another pledge, I'll violate the precept against lying. Well, I suppose I'll lie if I have to, but I won't be a party to murder!" The intendant spoke: "Sanshō Dayū and Master Saburō, if you insist on an oath, then I'll give you one. Please put your minds at ease."

The priest purified himself by gargling. Then he performed seven sets of hot water, cold water, and saltwater ablutions, for a total of twenty-one sets. He decked out a *goma* prayer altar, and he took a painting of the divine boys Kongara and Seitaka and the Mantra King Fudō in his manifestation as the Dragon King Kurikara swallowing a sword, and he hung it upside down. Next, he took a sheaf of paper from a side room and cut twelve paper prayer wands, which he set on the *goma* altar. Rather than preparing for a simple oath, he seemed to be getting ready to smite Sanshō Dayū with a terrible curse.

"Respectfully I speak," he began, clutching a single-pointed *vajra* and rattling a sacred ceremonial bell.[29] Rubbing his rosary beads with a scraping sound, he chanted, "I present these offerings and pay my reverent respects. In the regions above, Bonten and Taishaku; in the regions below, the Four Great Heavenly Kings, Dharma King Enma, and the officials of the Five Realms of Karmic Transmigration; among great deities, Lord Taizan; and in the earthly world, at Ise Shrine, Holy Amaterasu Ōmikami and the deities of the forty outer and eighty inner Ise branch shrines: I summon you now!

"At Kumano, the Shingū, Hongū, and Nachi shrines; Hiryō Gongen at Nachi;[30] Jūzō Gongen at Kannokura; the Thousand-Armed Kannon at the foot of Nachi Falls; the Eleven-Headed Kannon at Hase Temple; at Mount Yoshino, Zaō Gongen and the great deities of Komori and Katsute; Kagamizukuri Shrine in Yamato; the great deity of Fuefuki Shrine; the seven great temples of Nara; the great deities of

---

29. A *vajra* is a handheld ritual implement used in esoteric Buddhist rites.

30. *Gongen* is a term for a buddha or a bodhisattva in its Japanese manifestation as a Shinto deity.

the four Kasuga shrines; the Ox-Headed Guardian King of Tegai Gate; Great Hachiman Bodhisattva of Wakamiya; the Lower and Upper Kamo shrines; Tachiuchi; Betsutsui; Shō Hachiman of Iwashimizu Hachiman Shrine in Yawata; the deity of Mukō Shrine at Nishi-no-oka; Takara Temple in Yamazaki; Shinmei Shrine in Uji; Gokōnomiya Shrine in Fushimi; the great deity of Fujinomori Shrine; the deities of the five Inari shrines; the eight great heavenly kings of Gion; the great deities of the four Yoshida shrines; the eight shrines of Goryō; the deities of the three Imamiya shrines; Tenjin of Kitano Tenman Shrine; Umenomiya Shrine; the great deities of the seven Matsuo shrines; Jizō Gongen of Mount Atago; at the foot of Mount Atago, the Seiryōji Shakyamuni that traveled from India and China to Japan; Bishamon of Kurama Temple; the deity of Kibune Shrine; the deity of Kamo Shrine; Saichō of Mount Hiei; at the foot of Mount Hiei, the twenty-one Sannō shrines; the great deity of Shirahige Shrine in Uchioroshi; Benzaiten of Chikubushima in Lake Biwa; Great Hachiman Bodhisattva of Taga Shrine; the heavenly king of Nagae in Mino Province; Tsushima in Owari; the deity of Atsuta Shrine; in the eastern provinces, the deities of the Kashima, Katori, and Ikisu shrines; Haguro Gongen in Dewa; Mount Tateyama in Etchū; Mount Hakusan in Kaga; Tenjin of Shigiji; the great deity of Mount Isurugi in Noto Province; the deity of Togakushi Shrine in Shinano Province; the Goryō deity in Echizen; Obama in Wakasa; Monju of Kireto in Tango; Obara Hachiōji in Tanba; Furigami Tenjin in Settsu Province; the Onji, Hiraoka, and Konda Hachiman shrines in Kawachi Province; Shōtoku Taishi of Tennōji Temple; the great deities of the four Sumiyoshi shrines; Mitsunomura Shrine in Sakai; the great deities of the five Ōtori shrines; Kūkai of Mount Kōya; Kakuban Shōnin of Negoro; Izuriha Gongen of Awaji Island; the Kibitsu shrines in Bitchū, Bizen, and Bingo; and all you guardian deities of India, China, and Japan: I waken and summon you here now!

"In the land of Tsukushi, there are the Usa Hachiman Shrine, Rakanji Temple, Mount Hiko, Mount Kubote, Udo Shrine, and the Kirishima peaks. In Iyo Province, there are Ikku Shrine, Mount Godai, and the great deity of Takenomiya Shrine. There is the Great Shrine of Izumo Province, overseer of all deities of Japan. The deities' father is the god of Sada Shrine; their mother is Tanaka no Gozen. All you many gods, including the fifteen mountain-deity kings, Bonten in the boulders, Kodama in the trees, earth and kitchen deities in the houses, guardian gods of the Three Jewels, eight great guardian deities, oven gods of the thirty-six shrines, and household gods of the seventy-two shrines: I swear an oath before you now. Punish me if I lie, you 13,000-plus buddhas and awesome multitude of deities of the 98,007 shrines, but I know nothing about a boy!"

PART 3

"Well done, priest!" Sanshō Dayū exclaimed. "Beginning tomorrow, I would be honored if you would dine with me."

"Just a moment, sir," Saburō interjected. "I've noticed something strange. That leather hamper that's hanging up there is old, but the ropes around it are new. And it swings back and forth a little bit every now and then, even though there's no breeze. It's peculiar! If we go home now without taking a look, it's sure to bother me the whole year through."

The elder brother Tarō spoke: "Listen, Saburō, our father may have started to show his age, but you surely haven't. In old temples like this, the priests take their worn-out scrolls and buddha images, tattered papers and whatnot and hang them from the rafters to get them out of the way. They hang things up like that all the time. And even if the wind isn't blowing outside, the building creaks and tree spirits echo, making a breeze indoors. You may have imagined that the boy was in the hamper, but after hearing this priest's oath, you know he's not. And it's not like we don't have anyone else to serve us at our father's place. So take my word for it this time and just go home."

"Maybe I'll take your advice, Tarō," Saburō sneered. "And then again, maybe I won't! You're spouting off like some crackpot temple novice! Get out of my way!"

Saburō unsheathed his blade, cut the rope that was suspending the hamper, and lowered it toward the floor. Thrilled at the prospect of finding the boy, he pulled on the knots while the basket still dangled in the air. "It's taking too long!" he shouted, and sliced through the ropes running front to back and side to side. He lifted the lid and peered inside, whereupon the Jizō amulet around Zushiōmaru's neck threw out a brilliant golden light, blinding Saburō's eyes and causing him to fall off the temple veranda.

"Didn't I tell you?" Tarō yelled. "You're lucky it didn't strike you dead! The rest of you, hang up that hamper the way it was!" The men tied it tightly, front to back and side to side, and hung it from the rafters like it was before. Then, with Saburō leaning on his siblings for support, they all set off for Yura Harbor, a shameful sight to see.

The poor intendant had watched Saburō lower the hamper to the floor, and he had thought that the men were going to take the boy away for sure. If they did, he was going to tell them to put a rope around himself as well. But then, from inside the container, they had been saved by some Buddhist miracle or

Left, The intendant swears an oath; *right*, Saburō cuts open the hamper. From *Sanshō Dayū* (ca. 1639 woodblock-printed edition). (Courtesy of Tenri University Library)

magic of the gods! The intendant walked under the hamper and called out, "Boy, are you there?" In a weak voice, Zushiōmaru replied that he was.

"Are Sanshō Dayū and his sons gone yet?" the boy asked.

"You can relax," the priest said as he lowered the basket to the floor. Lifting the lid and looking inside, he was amazed to see the Jizō amulet shining a golden light.

Zushiōmaru leaped out of the container and embraced the intendant. "Oh, master," he cried, "I wasn't going to reveal my identity, but I should tell you now. Who do you think I am? I am Zushiōmaru, heir of Iwaki no Hangan Masauji, governor of the fifty-four districts of Michinoku. My family and I were on our way to the capital to settle a strange dispute and receive a deed from the emperor confirming our lands. But we were kidnapped and sold at Naoi Bay in Echigo Province, and my sister and I were sold from place to place until that Sanshō Dayū bought us. He made us cut brushwood and scoop saltwater, even though we didn't know how. We couldn't do the work, which is why I ran away.

But my sister is still at Sanshō Dayū's house. If she comes and asks you the way to the capital, please tell her for me, sir. I am going to escape there myself."

"You naïve little boy," the intendant warned. "Sanshō Dayū has hordes of men out looking for you, three and five leagues ahead! If you really want to get away to the capital, then I'll have to take you there myself." The priest bundled Zushiōmaru back into the leather hamper and tied it up tightly, front to back and side to side. He hoisted the container onto his back and covered it with an old robe. "At towns, inns, and provincial borders," he explained, "when people ask what I'm carrying, I'll tell them it's the Branded Jizō of the *kokubunji* temple of Tango Province. 'It's all worn out,' I'll say, 'and I'm on my way to the city to have it painted.' With that excuse, no one should give us any trouble."

Zushiōmaru and the intendant set out from Tango Province. They passed through Ibara and Hōmi, and Kamadani and Mijiri, too. They quickly came to Kunai and Kuwata and then, near the capital, to Kameyama, "Turtle Mountain," as precious as a flower or the proverbial floating log.[31] Impervious to the years, they climbed Oi-no-saka, the "Hill of Age," after which they made their way over Kuzukake Pass. They crossed the Katsura River and pressed on beyond Senjōji Village and Hatchō Nawate Road. Hastening on their way, they soon arrived at the Western Seventh Avenue Shushaka Gongen Buddha Hall.[32]

The intendant took the hamper off his back, opened the lid, and peered inside. Whether from frostbite or the constriction of the container, Zushiōmaru was unable to stand. "I'd like to visit the palace and get you that deed confirming your lands," the intendant said, staring down at the boy, "but as a monastic, there's little I can do. I'll be taking my leave now."

Alas, poor Zushiōmaru! "My savior priest," he cried, "will you return to Tango? Oh, how I envy you! It's a dreadful place, but my sister is there, so I miss it terribly. I should give you something for saving my life. How about my Jizō amulet? Or my dagger, perhaps?"

---

31. The Lotus sutra compares the likelihood of encountering a buddha in the present life with that of a one-eyed turtle chancing on a floating log in the vast, barren ocean. The word "turtle" in the name Turtle Mountain inspires this association. The "flower" is likely the *udonge*, which is said to bloom only once every three thousand years and is cited in the same Lotus sutra passage to illustrate the rarity of encountering a buddha.

32. The Gongen Buddha Hall at Gongenji Temple. According to *Oguri* and *Goō-no-hime*, both Oguri and Yoshitsune visited there as well.

The intendant spoke: "Do you really think it was I who saved you? It was the bodhisattva Jizō who hangs around your neck! Wear it with faith, boy. As for your dagger, that's something that a samurai carries from the age of seven, I hear. And since I'm a priest, the only blade I need is a razor. If you really want to give me a keepsake, then give me a tuft of your sidelocks. My present to you will be a sleeve of this robe." The holy man cut a bit of hair from Zushiōmaru's temples, after which he gave him his sleeve. Then, with tears in his eyes, he returned to Tango Province.

Poor Zushiōmaru remained at the Shushaka Gongen Buddha Hall. The beggar children from the seven Shushaka settlements gathered together and decided to take care of him, but though they looked after him for a day or two, no one did anything after that. "Let's build a cart and pull him to the city center," someone suggested, and they did. The city may be large, but the people there looked after Zushiōmaru for only five or ten days. The children therefore decided to pull him to Tennōji Temple in the south.[33] Dragging his cart from inn to inn and town to town, they eventually arrived.

Poor Zushiōmaru! Taking hold of the stone *torii* gate at Tennōji, he gave a loud cry and pulled himself to his feet. Whether it was thanks to Shōtoku Taishi or his own karmic returns,[34] he was once again able to stand. An eminent priest and Shōtoku Taishi devotee by the name of Oshari Daishi happened to be passing along at the time, and he saw Zushiōmaru there. "Young samurai," he inquired, "are you looking for employment, or perhaps wishing to take the tonsure?"

"Employment would be nice," Zushiōmaru replied.

"I have a hundred acolytes and other boys at my own residence," the holy man said. "If you were to put on a pair of their old *hakama* trousers, you could serve tea and the like." Zushiōmaru humbly accepted the priest's offer. He accompanied him to his home, where he donned a worn pair of acolyte's pants and served tea here and there with his distinctive eastern accent. He was beloved by all.

Back in the elegant capital, the emperor had thirty-six ministerial retainers. Among them was a man called the minister of Umezu, who had no heir,

---

33. South of Kyoto, that is. Tennōji (formally, "Shitennōji") is in the Tennōji district of present-day Osaka. The temple is a particularly important site in *Shintokumaru*.

34. Shōtoku Taishi was the sixth-century founder of Tennōji and an early champion of Buddhism in Japan.

neither a boy nor a girl. He visited the statue of the bodhisattva Kannon at Kiyomizu Temple and prayed that he be granted a child.[35] That night, the Kiyomizu Kannon emerged wavering from his inner sanctum and stood before the minister where he slept. "You shall adopt a son," the bodhisattva said, "and to do so, you must visit Tennōji Temple in the south." Marveling at the oracle he had received, the minister returned to his home at the Umezu estate. He was boundlessly happy. Three days later, he set out for Tennōji.

Oshari Daishi heard the news. "It seems that the minister of Umezu is coming here for a visit," he said. "Let's spruce up the reception hall, in case it's true." He had his boys decorate the ceiling with figured cloth, brocade, and gold-lace weave. In addition, the children wrapped the pillars in leopard and tiger skins, and they laid out a thousand reed mats with a Korean-pattern fringe. For a devotional image, they hung up a set of three ink paintings of Kannon, Shakyamuni, and Bodhidharma by the venerable Muxi,[36] whose works were all the rage in the capital at that time. Then they arranged flowers in the "newborn Shakyamuni" style,[37] after which they groomed themselves like a hundred little blossoms and eagerly awaited their guest.

Three days passed, whereupon the minister arrived. "What a lovely bunch of flowers!" he marveled on entering the reception hall. He examined the hundred acolytes and other boys from the highest to the lowest, three times each, but not a single child was suited to be his son. Then he saw Zushiōmaru at the back of the room. The boy was manifesting miraculous signs, including three characters for "rice" impressed on his forehead and two pupils in each of his eyes.[38] After taking a closer look, the minister declared, "I choose that tea server to be my son!"

---

35. Kiyomizu Temple lies in the eastern foothills of the Kyoto valley.

36. Muxi (Mokkei) was a Zen painter-priest of the Southern Song and early Yuan dynasties in the latter half of the thirteenth century.

37. The "newborn Shakyamuni" style is an arrangement in three vases in which the flowers in the right-hand vase are set taller than those in the left. It is named after a verse that the Buddha is said to have recited when, at his birth, he took seven steps and pointed to the heavens and the earth with his right and left hands.

38. Muroki Yatarō notes that the word *yone*, written with the character for "rice" 米, is a term for a bodhisattva. He adds that because the character's elements resemble the characters for the number 88 (八十八), *yone* 米 was thought to be auspicious. See SNKS *Sekkyō shū*, 237n.14.

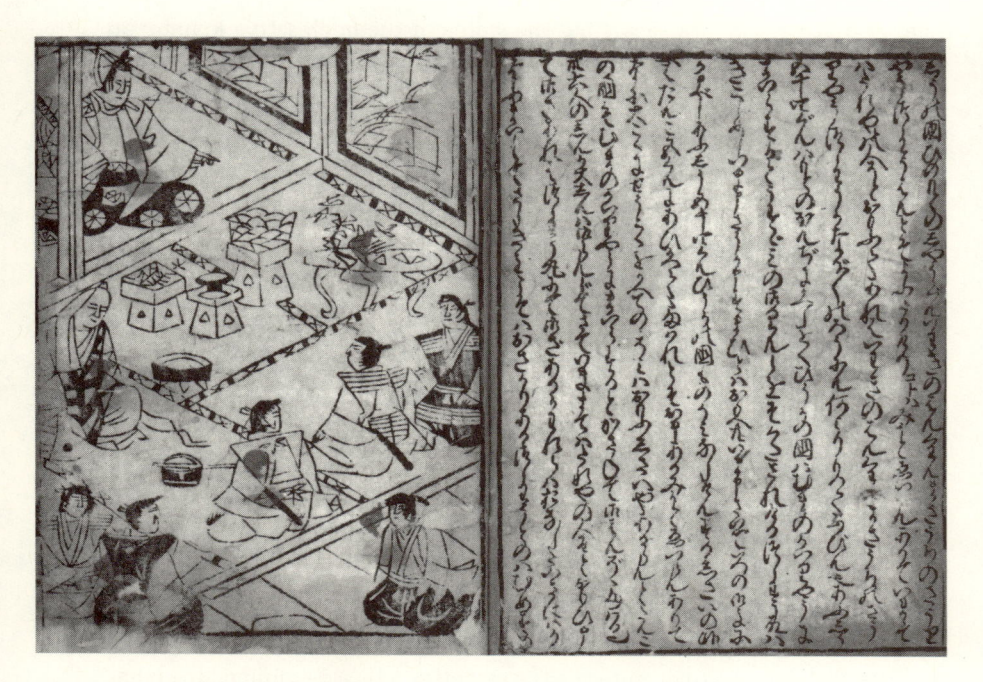

The minister of Umezu (*top left*) chooses Zushiōmaru (*bottom right*). From *Sanshō Dayū* (ca. 1639 woodblock-printed edition). (Courtesy of Tenri University Library)

The hundred acolytes and other boys stared at Zushiōmaru. "The minister talks like he's blind," they murmured. "He says he wants to adopt the lowly tea boy who was begging from a cart until just the other day!" And they all burst out laughing.

"Laugh at my son, will you?" the minister shouted. He took Zushiōmaru to the bath and had him scrubbed in a tub of steaming water. He dressed the boy in an under robe of fine brocade on a blue ground, a tie-dyed *hitatare*,[39] a flaxen *suikan* over robe, and a jeweled court cap. When he installed Zushiōmaru on an elevated seat to his left, there was not one among the hundred boys who could compare.

The minister brought Zushiōmaru to the Umezu estate, where he provided him with delicacies of the land and sea and a variety of local sweets. His joy knew no bounds. One time he sent Zushiōmaru to attend to the emperor in

---

39. *Hitatare* is a kind of matching shirt and pants typically worn under armor.

his place. Seeing the boy, the other ministerial retainers drove him from his seat, saying, "You may be the Umezu minister's adopted son, but riffraff like you can't sit in formation with us!" Poor Zushiōmaru! If he were to reveal his identity now, he thought, it would cast shame on his father, Lord Iwaki. But if he were to remain silent, the humiliation would be the minister's. Choosing to defend his adoptive father now and to leave his birth father's honor for later, he took out the lineage scroll showing his right to the Shida and Tamatsukuri districts. He placed it on a folding fan and carried it to the far front of the room. Then, leaping down to the white gravel of the courtyard, he pressed his jeweled court cap to the earth as a sign of respect for the emperor.

The Nijō major counselor picked up the scroll and read it aloud in a powerful voice: "The bearer of this document is Zushiōmaru, heir of Japanese General Iwaki no Hangan Masauji of Michinoku Province."

The emperor examined the scroll. "I had been wondering who you were," he said. "So you're Zushiōmaru, heir of Iwaki no Hangan Masauji! You've been dispossessed for a very long time, which is a sad thing indeed. I will give you back your former lands—the fifty-four districts of Michinoku. And to provide for your horses' expenses, I shall grant you the province of Hyūga."[40] The emperor commanded that an imperial edict be issued on official gray paper.

Zushiōmaru spoke: "I have something to say, sir, but I hesitate to say it. Still, if I don't speak now, then when will I ever? I have no desire for Hyūga and the fifty-four districts of Michinoku. Please allow me to exchange them all for the five districts of Tango. I have a personal reason."

The emperor peered at the boy. "What?" he said. "You have a personal reason for wanting to trade a large territory for a small one? In that case, I will also grant you the province of Tango, to provide fodder for your horses!" The emperor had another edict issued to that effect.

Having observed these events, the thirty-six ministerial retainers exclaimed, "And all this time, we were wondering who he was! So it's Zushiōmaru! Now it won't do for *us* to sit in formation with *him*." And with that, they all surrendered their seats.

Zushiōmaru returned to the Umezu estate, where everyone was exceptionally pleased. But poor Zushiōmaru! His sad complaints were moving to hear. "If only I could be a bird for a while," he moaned. "How I wish I had wings! I would fly to Tango and scoop brine for my sister. I would clutch her sleeves and tell

---

40. Hyūga Province is now Miyazaki Prefecture on the southern island of Kyūshū.

her how I've finally found my place in the world! And then I'd fly to the island of Ezo, find my mother there, and tell her about my success. I'd fly to Anrakuji Temple in Tsukushi, find my father, and tell him, too!"

The time had come to act. Zushiōmaru informed the emperor of his situation, received a deed confirming his lands, and dispatched a palanquin for his father at Anrakuji Temple. Then, declaring that he would pay his first official visit to Tango Province, he sent a notice to the *kokubunji* temple indicating his intent to lodge there, three days hence. He had it affixed to the temple's inner gate.

The intendant saw the notice. "Tango may be a small province," he thought, "but it has grand buddha halls. For the governor to put up a lodging sign at an old run-down place like this must mean that he's coming for my head!" Remembering that the word for "monastic," *shukke* 出家, is written with the characters for "leaving home," the intendant fled to parts unknown with only a single oil-paper umbrella over his shoulder.

Three days later, Zushiōmaru arrived at the Tango temple. Summoning some villagers, he said, "Hello, people! Doesn't this place have an intendant?" One of the locals replied, "Yes, sir. There was a venerable priest here until just the other day. But when he saw your lodging notice, he seems to have thought his life was in danger, and he ran away to who-knows-where."

"In that case, find him and bring him here!" Zushiōmaru declared.

"Yes, sir," his men replied. They tracked him to Anauji Temple in Tanba Province, where they twisted and tied his arms behind his back before dragging him to the *kokubunji* temple. Seeing them arrive, Zushiōmaru cried, "Why have you bound this holy man who saved my life? Release him at once!"

"I've never saved a governor's life!" the intendant protested. "You shouldn't tease a priest like that. Now hurry up and take my head!"

"Yes, your request is reasonable enough," Zushiōmaru said. "But who do you think I am? I'm the boy from inside the leather hamper! Look, here's the sleeve you traded me when you took me to the Seventh Avenue Shushaka Gongen Buddha Hall! Now give me back my sidelocks."

The priest was overjoyed. "It's been less than a hundred days!" he exclaimed. "How wonderful that you've taken your place in the world. This must be what people mean when they say that neither gold nor samurai ever lose their luster."

"But what about my sister at Yura Harbor?" Zushiōmaru asked. "Is she alive?"

"It's like this," the intendant began. "That evil Saburō tortured her to death as punishment for helping you escape. I found her body where he dumped it. I brought it here and cremated it myself. I have her bones and hair."[41] With tears in his eyes, the intendant took out Anju-no-hime's remains and offered them to her brother.

Zushiōmaru stared. "Can this really be happening?" he cried. "So it's made no difference, even if I did regain my place in the world!" And pressing his face to his sister's remains, he wept bitter, anguished tears.

The boy could not grieve forever, so, intending to punish Sanshō Dayū for his crimes, he sent a messenger to summon him from Yura Harbor. Sanshō Dayū gathered his five sons and spoke: "Hello, boys! You know, I've been living around here for a very long time, so the governor probably wants to ask me about the local sights. I'm going to see him and give him all the details. When I do, he's bound to offer me a domain. So listen, Saburō—if he grants us a province, don't settle for a small one. Tell him I've got so many children and grandchildren that I need a big one. Whatever you do, don't forget!" Thus, with his five sons leading the way, Sanshō Dayū set off for the *kokubunji* provincial temple.

Zushiōmaru watched them arrive. "Sanshō Dayū," he said, "you've done well to come so quickly! Do you recognize me at all?"

"Sir," Sanshō Dayū replied, "you are our provincial governor from the capital."

Zushiōmaru continued: "I hear that you have a lovely serving girl in your employ. Please let me take her for my bride. As your son-in-law, I can bring you wealth and rank."

Sanshō Dayū cast a glance at Saburō. "Indeed," he replied with regret, "we had two children from the Shinobu estate in the Daté district: a sister named Shinobu and her younger brother, Wasuregusa. And Shinobu was beautiful! If we had kept her and not killed her, we could have given her to you for your wife. With you as a son-in-law, we would have been rich and honored."

Zushiōmaru considered Sanshō Dayū's words. He had meant to conceal his identity, but he could do so no longer. Leaning out over his former master, he

---

41. In the 1667 *Sanshō Dayū*, the intendant explains that "that evil Sanshō Dayū and Saburō tortured her to death with fire and water as punishment for helping you escape. When I went to collect her body, I found an arm in a grassy field and a leg in a cluster of azaleas. The dogs and crows had torn her apart, but I picked up the pieces and carried them back in my sleeves." See SSS 1:67b.

said, "Listen, you! What did Shinobu ever do to deserve being tortured and killed? And who do you think I am? Wasuregusa, that's who! Now give me back my sister!

"Sanshō Dayū and Saburō—you might think it's unreasonable for me to demand you return my dead sister. But how about punishing a boy who can't cut three loads of brushwood by making him cut another seven, for a total of ten loads? And all for the crime of bringing home nicely cut wood after some woodsmen took pity on him and cut it for him! Does that sound reasonable?

"But I'm only rambling. You know, to repay hatred with hatred is like adding fuel to a raging fire. Rather, it's the way of the Buddha to meet malice with compassion. So how about it, Sanshō Dayū? Would you care for a large province or a small one? You can have whichever one you choose."

Sanshō Dayū cracked a smile. He glanced at Saburō, who spoke up, saying, "Thank you, sir. Our father has many children and grandchildren, so instead of a little province, give him a big one, please."

"Greedy Saburō," Zushiōmaru chided, "even if your father had preferred a small province, I would have given him a large one. But now he can have his wish! I grant him the great Land of the Dead!" Zushiōmaru's men seized Sanshō Dayū and dragged him to the temple courtyard, where they dug a pit some five feet deep. They buried him up to his neck and prepared a bamboo saw. "Wait, don't give the job to just anyone," Zushiōmaru instructed. "Let his own sons do the sawing! That'll give them something to cry about."

"Yes, sir," Zushiōmaru's men replied. First, they handed the saw to the eldest brother, Tarō. "I have other plans for Tarō," Zushiōmaru said, "so we'll excuse him from cutting." Next, they passed the saw to Jirō, who accepted it but immediately turned aside, whimpering pitifully. "Up until now," he sobbed, "I've never heard of a son sawing off his own father's head! Didn't I always say to treat the servants kindly, no matter what far-off places they're from? Governor, it's only right that you should do it yourself!" Choking on his tears, Jirō was unable to cut.

"Yes, I see," Zushiōmaru said. "I have other plans for Jirō, too, so we'll excuse him as well."

The saw passed to Saburō, who snatched it up and shouted, "You cowards! Playing innocent and blaming everything on Dad and me! Well, how about it, Father? If you've been wondering when you'd get to redeem your lifetime's worth of *nenbutsu* recitations, this is it! It'll be me, Saburō, who carries you over the Sanzu River and into the Land of the Dead!" Saburō began sawing through his father's neck. "The first pull," he cried, "—memorial services by a thousand priests! The second pull—services by ten thousand! Heave, ho! Heave, ho!" After 106 pulls, Sanshō Dayū's head finally fell to the ground. Later, Zushiōmaru had Saburō taken to Short Asumi Beach, where, over the course of seven days and seven nights, the local woodsmen sawed off his head on their way to and from the mountains.

Afterward, Zushiōmaru called Jirō and Tarō to see him. "Since the distant past," he said, "people have maintained that sweet and bitter vines bear sweet and bitter fruit.[42] But in your case, a bitter vine has borne something sweet! As for you, Tarō, I excused you from sawing off your father's head because of what you said when I was hiding in the leather hamper: 'It's not like we don't have anyone else to serve us at our father's place, so take my word for it and just go home.' Because of that one statement, I forgave you. And as for you, Jirō, I excused you because of how you brought food to me and my sister every night when we were suffering through the new year under that pine tub at the road along the shore. Wherever I go, I will always be grateful. I am going to divide the 808 *chō*[43] of Tango Province and give 404 of them to your brother, Tarō. I will entrust the remaining 404 *chō* to you, Jirō, as my sovereign steward." The overseer of Tango Province has been called "Lord Sovereign" ever since. Tarō later shaved his head and became a priest at the *kokubunji* temple, where he devoted his years to praying for Anju-no-hime's enlightenment and holding services for Sanshō Dayū.[44]

Zushiōmaru proclaimed that the intendant would be his godfather for having saved his life, and he formally recognized the servant-girl Ise no Kohagi from Sanshō Dayū's house as his sister. He loaded them into wickerwork palanquins and sent them off to the capital.

Next, Zushiōmaru set out to find his mother on the island of Ezo. The poor woman had passed so many days and nights weeping for her children that she had cried herself blind. Zushiōmaru found her chasing birds from a vast millet field. Clutching a bird-rattle on a rope, she heaved herself forward to the cry of, "Oh, my dear Zushiō—hey ho! My dear Anju-no-hime, and my dear Uwataki—

---

42. The aphorism applies to the similarity of parents and their children. In other words, the apple does not fall far from the tree.

43. Approximately 1,980 acres, or 802 hectares.

44. For the sake of clarity, I have changed the order of these last three sentences.

hey ho!" Zushiōmaru stared. "What an unusual bird-chasing song!" he said. "Sing it again. I'll give you a domain if you do."

"Do I look like I need a domain?" the mother spat. "I'm getting along fine like this. But if you command me to chase the birds some more, I will." Still clutching the bird-rattle, she shouted, "Oh, my dear Zushiō—hey ho! My dear Uwataki—hey ho! My dear Anju-no-hime!" heaving her body forward with every cry. Concluding that the woman must be his mother, Zushiōmaru took her in his arms and said, "Listen, Mother, it's me, Zushiōmaru! I've regained my place in the world, and I've come for you here!"

"Oh, if only it were true!" the mother moaned. "I have two children, a daughter and a son named Anju-no-hime and Zushiōmaru. They were sold far away from here, and no one knows what became of them. You shouldn't try to fool a blind person like that! You know, it's not a crime for a blind woman to hit a man with her stick!" And with that, she began flailing all around with her staff.

"You are right to be suspicious," Zushiōmaru said, "but I remember something now!" Taking the Jizō amulet from around his neck, he pressed it against his mother's eyes three times and repeated, "What joy, brightly! Be cured, brightly!" Although her eyes had been shriveled for a very long time, she suddenly opened them wide.

The mother gazed at her son. "So you really are Zushiōmaru!" she cried. "But what about Anju-no-hime?"

"It's like this, Mother," Zushiōmaru explained. "After we were sold away from you at Naoi Harbor in Echigo Province, Anju-no-hime and I were resold here and there until we were bought by Sanshō Dayū of Yura Harbor in Tango Province. He made us scoop saltwater and cut brushwood, even though we didn't know how. We had trouble doing the work, and after I ran away, he had Anju-no-hime tortured and killed. But I took my place in the world and avenged her death, and now I've come here looking for you."

"It's wonderful that you've achieved such success," the mother said, "but what sorrow for an old vine like me to have outlived my little sapling! Yet there's nothing to be done about it, I suppose."

Zushiōmaru and his mother boarded jeweled palanquins and set out on their return. Later, they visited Naoi Harbor in Echigo Province, where they had the man who first sold them into slavery, Yamaoka Dayū, rolled up in a rough reed mat and drowned. They tried to find his wife, too, but they gave up when they learned that she had died. They crossed over to Kashiwazaki, built a temple there called the Middle Practice Hall, and prayed for Lady

Uwataki's enlightenment.⁴⁵ After that, Zushiōmaru took his mother to the capital. They stayed at the Umezu estate, where the minister of Umezu met with the mother and congratulated her on her recent good fortune. Their pleasure knew no bounds.

Meanwhile, owing to Zushiōmaru's investiture, Lord Iwaki's imperial censure was lifted, and he was allowed to return to the capital. When he arrived at the Umezu estate, his wife and son rushed out to greet him. They hugged him deliriously, overwhelmed with emotion. People are quick to cry in happiness and sorrow, yet if only Anju-no-hime had remained alive in this uncertain world, their own sobs might have been for joy alone! Thinking such things, they wept torrents of tears.

The minister, the intendant, Ise no Kohagi, and others eventually reproached them, saying, "It's natural that you should lament, but please get over it." Then decorating the mythical Mount Hōrai, they held a merry drinking party for three days and three nights.⁴⁶ After the celebration, Zushiōmaru and his family built a temple in Tango Province and enshrined the Jizō amulet there for the sake of Anju-no-hime's enlightenment. Since that time, the amulet has been worshipped as the Branded Jizō Bodhisattva.

Later, Zushiōmaru declared that he would pay his first official visit to his northern domain. He provided wickerwork palanquins for his father and mother, as well as litters and palanquins for Ise no Kohagi and his godfather, the intendant. Then, riding on a horse, he set out for Michinoku with more than a hundred thousand riders in tow.

Zushiōmaru built rows of mansions on his father's former estate. He amassed wealth and honors, and his father's retainers all scrambled to return and support their lord. Whether in ancient or recent times, or even in ages to come, his fate was an extraordinary one indeed!

---

45. According to the 1656 *Sekkyō Sanshō Dayū*, they prayed for Yamaoka Dayū's wife there, too. See SSS 1:45a.

46. The eighteenth-century scholar Ise Teijō explains that it was a custom at drinking parties to erect models of Mount Hōrai, the legendary island of immortals. Quoted in SNKS *Sekkyō shū*, 151n.6.

Karukaya

PART 1

I shall speak to you now about the origins of the Parent and Child Jizō Bodhisattva that is worshipped to the left of the Main Buddha Hall at Zenkōji Temple in Shinano Province.¹ Ask me about its past, and I will tell you that it was once a man by the name of Lord Shigeuji, chieftain of the Matsura League of Chikuzen Province in Great Tsukushi.² Lord Shigeuji ruled the six provinces of Chikugo, Chikuzen, Higo, Hizen, Ōsumi, and Satsuma.³ He owned ten storehouses in the ten directions, seven springs in the south, a self-propelled carriage, and all the

---

Translated from the 1631 *Sekkyō Karukaya*.

1. Zenkōji Temple is in Nagano City on the central island of Honshū. According to the late-sixteenth-century *Karukaya* and the final paragraph of the 1631 text, the Parent and Child Jizō is enshrined in the Zenkōji Inner Buddha Hall (Oku no midō).

2. Tsukushi is an old name for the southern island of Kyūshū. The Matsura League was a warrior federation in the Matsura region of Hizen, not Chikuzen, Province.

3. These provinces are now Fukuoka, Kumamoto, Saga, Nagasaki, and Kagoshima prefectures in Kyūshū.

crystals, jewels, and precious metals that he might desire.[4] Even his manor was built with the four seasons in mind: cool in the summer, yet suited to moon viewing, snow viewing, and cherry-blossom viewing in the autumn, winter, and spring.

One time Lord Shigeuji hosted a cherry-blossom-viewing party for all his relatives and retainers. It was in the third month, at the height of spring. The blossom-viewing hall was arrayed with jeweled hairpins, golden blinds, and jugs and bamboo tubes of wine. The saké cup passed from the highest to the lowest and then back again. Shigeuji received a brimming cupful, which he was just about to drink when an unseasonal gust of wind blew down from the mountains. It rushed through the branches of the lord's beloved Jishu cherry trees,[5] and although it failed to scatter the flowering blossoms at the base of a particular branch, it dropped a cluster of unopened buds from the branch's tip right into Shigeuji's cup. The buds circled in the saké one, two, and then three times. Being a sensitive person, Shigeuji was moved by the sight. It occurred to him that even blossoms may scatter before their prime, demonstrating the truth that death may come at any time, to young and old alike.

Shigeuji addressed the room: "Listen, everyone. I would like you all to allow me to take my leave. I am going to become a priest." Hearing the master's words, the people protested, saying, "Are you upset that some blossoms fell at a blossom-viewing party? Please give up this idea of yours!"

"If the blossoms were to scatter in order," Shigeuji explained, "then the buds on the ends of the branches would linger while the open flowers fall. That would be the proper way. But see how the open flowers linger while the closed buds scatter—it's a plain demonstration of life's instability, for young and old alike."

"But you rule six provinces and command eighty thousand riders!" the people countered. "What could make you want to become a priest? Everyone knows that when a lord takes monastic vows, it's because he's lost his domain to some greater warrior and has no place left in the world. That's when a man becomes a monk!"

"If I were to become a priest after losing my domain, it would only be a way of getting on in the world. It's the man who renounces wealth and splendor to take holy vows who plants seeds for his future rebirth. You can try to stop me,

---

4. This sentence is interpolated from the late-sixteenth-century *Karukaya*, in SNKBT 90:250.

5. From Jishu Shrine at Kiyomizu Temple in the eastern hills of the capital.

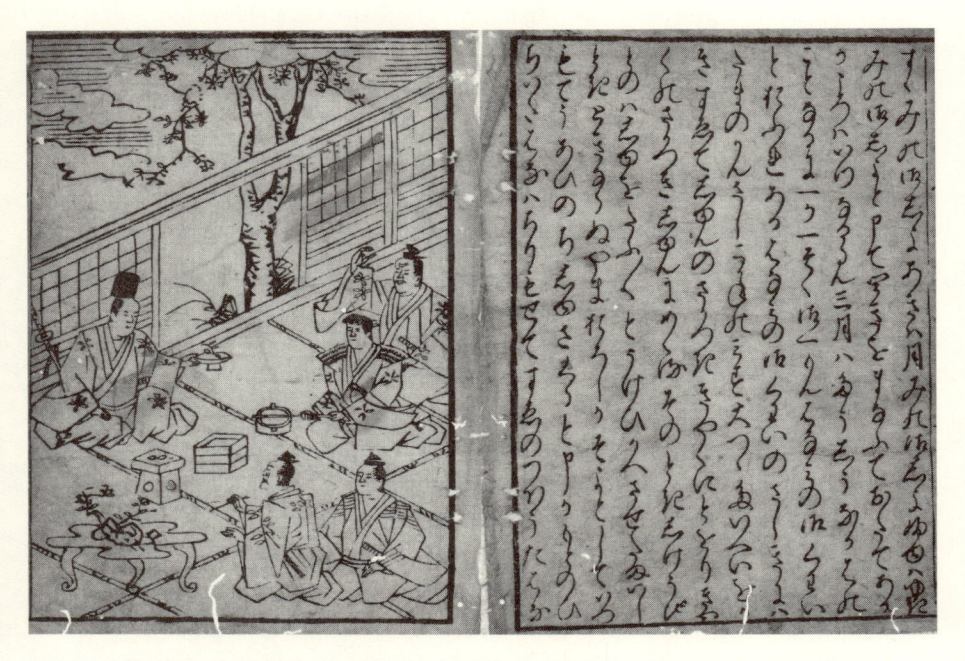

A cluster of unopened cherry blossoms falls into Shigeuji's cup. From *Sekkyō Karukaya* (1631 woodblock-printed edition). (Courtesy of Tenri University Library)

but I've made up my mind and I won't be dissuaded." Shigeuji stood up from his seat and retreated to his private buddha hall.

Word reached Shigeuji's wife. Handing her three-year-old daughter Chiyotsuru to a wet nurse, she pulled a lightweight robe over her head and hurried down a connecting corridor to the buddha hall where Shigeuji had been spending all his time. She slid open a sliding paper door and stared in at her husband. Then, without saying a thing, she burst into tears. "I need to speak with you, dear," she finally said. "I hear that at the party today, you saw some blossoms scatter and decided to become a priest. Are you upset that some blossoms fell at a blossom-viewing party? Please give up this idea of yours!"

"No one has been able to dissuade me," Shigeuji replied, "and whatever you say, you can't, either." The wife took in her husband's words. "Should I tell him now or not?" she wondered. But if she did not tell him today, then when ever would she?

"It's embarrassing to speak of," she began, "but you are twenty-one years old, I am nineteen, and our daughter Chiyotsuru is three. It's a woman's duty to receive her husband's attentions, and for this reason I am now seven-and-a-half months pregnant. Even if you won't give up your plan to spend the rest of your life as a priest, you can at least wait another three months. Once the baby is born, we'll leave it with a wet nurse. You can retreat to some mountain temple and chant the *nenbutsu*,[6] and I'll move to the foot of the mountain, put up a brushwood shack, and live there as a nun. I'll wash out your dirty robe for you once a month. What do you think, dear?"

"Women are nothing but snakes," Shigeuji thought, and concluding that it would be foolish to argue with a senseless woman, he readily agreed to his wife's request. The wife was delighted, for although everyone else had tried to dissuade him and failed, she had succeeded by telling him about the child in her womb. She decided that on the following day, she would gather all the great lords of Tsukushi and have them put an end to her husband's monastic ambitions. With this thought in mind, she was boundlessly happy.

Shigeuji was certain that despite his wife's request to wait three months, she would actually summon all the great lords of Tsukushi and ask them to put an end to his lifelong plans. And if he were to forgo his aspiration, he would lose this opportunity for enlightenment in his next rebirth. But conversely, if he were to pursue his dream, he would invite the world's disdain . . . He made up his mind. It wasn't raining, so he might as well leave today. He took out some writing paper and an inkstone and composed a letter.

"Dear wife," he wrote, "my love for you remains the same. If my feelings had changed, then you might hate me for it, but this is not the case. Although our bond in this life may be weak, we are sure to meet again in Amida's Pure Land. As for the seven-and-a-half-month-old child in your womb, if it is a boy, you should name him Ishidōmaru. Please have him become a priest when he grows up. If it is a girl, you should do with her as you like. Just remember, dear, that even if our bond in this life is weak, we will be born together on a single lotus in Amida's Pure Land."

Shigeuji cut a tuft of hair from his sidelocks. Wishing to leave the letter where his wife would find it, he set it on the floor of the buddha hall together with the sword that never left his side. He turned up the flame of an oil lamp,

---

6. The *nenbutsu* is the ritual invocation of the name of Amida Buddha, by which one may attain rebirth in Amida's Pure Land Paradise.

donned an unfamiliar pair of straw sandals, and crept out of his magnificent mansion in the dark of night.

Quickly leaving the Karukaya estate, Shigeuji passed through Ashiya, Yamazaki, and the Hakata post station. He set out in a small boat from Komatsu Bay and came to the Akama Barrier.[7] After taking in the view of the Nagato provincial capital, he sailed on to Aki Province, where he bowed and prayed in the direction of the goddess Benzaiten at Itsukushima Shrine. He sped past the provinces of Bingo and Bitchū, and when he came to Bizen, he marveled at the local Osafune swords. Hastening on through Inbe and Kōka, he entered Harima Province. He breezed by the dharma-spreading Kuromoto post station,[8] Gochaku, and Kakekawa; past the Amida post station, which, unlike its namesake, shines no light; by "Bright Stone" Akashi in the nighttime darkness; and through lonely Suma Bay.

Shigeuji soon came to Hyōgo Harbor. Continuing through the Pine Field of Sparrows and the Mikage Forest, he reached Nishinomiya Shrine; asking the way ahead, he pressed past Kanko to Unobe Village. After pausing at the Ōta post station, he crossed Yōji River, though he had no business there.[9] He exclaimed at the name of the "Difficult post station"; crossed the Akuta River, which washes away the dust; and visited "High Moon" Takatsuki in the depths of night. He asked the way at Takara Temple in Yamazaki and, with the Yawata peak towering above him, bowed and prayed to the bodhisattva Shō Hachiman. Though he had no boat, he rowed along Koganawate Road to the Rashōmon and Tōji Temple gates.[10] Rashōmon Gate had fallen into such ruin that only its foundation stones remained. Shigeuji stumbled across Fifth Avenue Bridge to Kiyomizu Temple in the eastern hills, and because he hurried on his way, he arrived after only thirty-nine days.

---

7. The Akama Barrier was at the western tip of the central island of Honshū.

8. In the late-sixteenth-century *Karukaya*, this is "Biromine post station" (the city of Himeji). See SNKBT 90:256. The first character in the name "Biromine" means "to spread" and thus allows for a pun on "dharma-spreading," which is nonsensical in the 1631 text.

9. In this and the following sentence, the author puns on the name of Yōji (Business) River, on the *aku* (grime) in the name Akuta River, and on the name Takatsuki (High Moon).

10. The author puns on the word *koga* (a form of the verb "to row") in the name Koganawate (also Koga-no-nawate). The Rashōmon and Tōji Temple gates stood at the southern entrance to the capital city of Kyoto.

Proceeding to Otowa Falls,[11] Shigeuji purified himself by rinsing his mouth and hands, after which he moved on to the central hall. Rattling the sacred summoning bell, he bowed and prayed: "Hail most merciful Kannon! If I were to ask for additional wealth or riches, I should indeed incur your wrath. Instead, please allow me to take monastic vows. My only wish is to become a priest."

Shigeuji approached a wandering preacher and called out, "Hello, holy man! Please tell me which are the most sacred temples and shrines in the capital."[12]

"Come this way," the preacher replied, and he led Shigeuji to the western gate. "Look over there—that tall, distant mountain to the west is Mount Atago. At its foot are the Saga Hōrinji and Uzumasa Kōryūji temples. Over this way are the great deities of the seven Matsuno'o, six Imaguma, and eight Goryō shrines. And over this way is the great all-powerful Tenman Tenjin of Kitano. To the north, you can see the great merciful Tamonten of Kurama Temple, the Kamo Mitarashi Shrine, and the Kibune deity. Within the city, there are the Kyōkakudō, Rokuhara, and Seiganji temples. And in the eastern mountains, there are Gion Shrine, Kiyomizu Temple, Sanjūsangendō, and Tōfukuji Temple. These are the holiest temples and shrines in the capital. Go and pray at them all, young samurai."

"But those all are shrines to local gods," Shigeuji said.[13] "Aren't there any major or cardinal temple complexes?"

"I'm just a simple priest, so please ask me in a way that I can understand."

Shigeuji rephrased his question: "Are there any temples where a layman like me can shave his head and take holy vows?"

"Yes, certainly," the preacher replied. "After the reverend Hōnen of Mount Hiei's Saitō Kitadani engaged in the hundred-day Ōhara debate at an old house in Ōhara Village, he made his way into the mountains east of here and built a new temple.[14] The area around it is called Shinkurodani, 'New

---

11. Otowa Falls is the small waterfall from which Kiyomizu-dera (Pure Water Temple) takes its name.

12. The preacher is a *kanjin hijiri*, an itinerant fund-raising priest.

13. In the late-sixteenth-century *Karukaya*, Shigeuji objects that "those are all pilgrimage temples"—temples for visiting, that is, rather than residing. See SNKBT 90:257.

14. Hōnen (1133–1212) was the founder of the Pure Land school of Buddhism. In 1186 he engaged the priest Kenshin in the Ōhara debate, which actually lasted for one day and one night and in which Hōnen expounded the doctrines of the incipient Pure Land School. In 1175, well before the famous debate, Hōnen established the Shirakawa Zenbō (Konkai Kōmyōji Temple) in what is now known as the Shinkurodani, or simply Kurodani, part of Kyoto.

Kurodani.'[15] He's busy conducting practices for the next life there, so if you visit him, you can become a priest."

"Then please tell me the way," Shigeuji said.

"Go around the Gion Forest. Then, when you get to Awataguchi, press on toward the north. You're sure to reach Kurodani if you do."

"If I manage to shave my head and become a priest there, I'll come back and thank you," Shigeuji said, and he took his leave. He walked down Kiyomizu Hill, crossed Todoroki Bridge, skirted the Gion Forest, and hurried past Awataguchi. Then he came to Kurodani.

Shigeuji met with the master.[16] "Please confer ten *nenbutsu* recitations on me," he requested. "In addition, please shave my head and make me a priest." "There's a sign outside the gate that says 'No Renunciants,'" Hōnen replied. "I'm not giving the tonsure to anyone."

Shigeuji pondered: "Why would there be a 'No Renunciants' sign at the entrance to the Pure Land? Back in my own province, I heard that the capital was such a great vast city that even passing laypeople are sometimes stopped and made to take the tonsure. But even if I can't become a priest here, I'm certainly not going home! I'll move outside the temple gate. I'll take the pillar stones for my stateroom, and the swinging doors for my folding screens. I'll refuse food and water for five or ten days and die of hunger and thirst! Then when the master hears about it, he'll surely give me rites. It's all the same whether I have my head shaved now or when I'm dead. After all, lay and monastic aren't just a matter of actually being lay and monastic." Having thus made up his mind, Shigeuji lay down to die.

Some local pilgrims watched him for a while. "Young samurai," they said, "you were lying here yesterday, and now you're lying here today. What could have gone so wrong that you won't get up?" "I come from a wild, distant province," Shigeuji replied, "and when I asked the holy man to shave my head and make me a priest, he refused. That's why I'm lying here."

The local pilgrims reported this to Hōnen, who summoned Shigeuji and spoke: "Listen, samurai. It's not that I won't give you the tonsure; it's just that young warriors like you tend to come to the temple after you've been disowned

---

15. Hōnen moved to the Kurodani district of Kitadani (Northern Valley) on Mount Hiei in 1150. For this reason, he was also known as the Kurodani master (Kurodani shōnin).

16. According to the late-sixteenth-century *Karukaya*, Shigeuji had to struggle through a crowd of supplicants in order to speak with Hōnen. See SNKBT 90:259.

by your parents or offended your lord. You all shave your heads and become priests for five or ten days, but then when your parents or wives and children come looking, you go back to being laymen. And when that happens, we're both doomed to fall into the Hell of No Respite—me for giving you the vows and you for taking them.[17] That's why I put up that 'No Renunciants' sign. But if you'll swear a great oath that even if your parents or children come looking for you here, you won't see or meet with them and you'll never return to lay life, then I'll be happy to give you the tonsure."

"What a heartless thing to say!" Shigeuji thought. "If he had told me this yesterday, I could have sworn a great oath and been tonsured by now."[18] Shigeuji proceeded to the bathhouse, where he purified himself by performing twenty-one sets of ablutions. Then he ascended the prayer altar and spoke: "Hail Usa Hachiman of Tsukushi! When I was at home, I asked for your support in battle and for prosperity throughout the land. But today my request is different. I pray that you will allow me to become a priest. I present these oblations and offer my reverent respects.

"First, I will address the heavenly realms. In the regions above, Bonten and Taishaku; in the regions below, the Four Great Heavenly Kings, Dharma King Enma, and the officials of the Five Realms of Karmic Transmigration; among great deities, Lord Taizan; and in the earthly world, at Ise Shrine, Holy Amaterasu Ōmikami and the deities of the forty outer and eighty inner Ise branch shrines: with this oath, I summon you here now!

"In Iga Province, the great deity of the first provincial shrine;[19] at the three Kumano mountains, Yakushi at Shingū, Amida at Hongū, and Hiryō Gongen at Nachi;[20] the Thousand-Armed Kannon at the foot of Nachi Falls; Ryūzō Gongen of Kannokura; Kokūzō of Yunomine; Benzaiten of Tennokawa; the eight *vajra* attendants of Mount Ōmine; Kūkai of Mount Kōya; at Mount Yoshino, Zaō Gongen and the great deities of Komori, Katsute, and the thirty-eight surrounding shrines; Taishokan of Tōnomine; the Eleven-Headed Kannon

---

17. The Hell of No Respite (Muken jigoku) is the most terrible of the eight burning hells.

18. In the late-sixteenth-century *Karukaya*, Shigeuji replies that he has no parents, children, or anyone else who would come looking for him. See SNKBT 90:260.

19. The first provincial shrine (*ichinomiya*) is the premier shrine of any given province—in this case, Aekuni Shrine in Ueno City, Mie Prefecture.

20. *Gongen* is a term for a buddha or a bodhisattva in its Japanese manifestation as a Shinto deity. Hongū, Hayatama (Shingū), and Nachi are the three Kumano shrines.

at Hase Temple; the deity of Miwa Shrine; the Ox-Headed Guardian Kings of the six Furu shrines; the great seven-hall compounds of Nara; the great deities of the four Kasuga shrines; Tenjin of Kizu; Shinmei Shrine in Uji; the Ox-Headed Guardian King of Fuji Forest; the great bodhisattva Shō Hachiman of Yawata; Jizō Bodhisattva of Mount Atago; at the foot of Mount Atago, the Seiryōji Shakyamuni that traveled from India and China to Japan; the great deities of the Umenomiya and Matsuo shrines; Tenjin of Kitano; the great merciful Tamonten of Kurama Temple; the Ox-Headed Guardian Kings of the three Gion shrines; Saichō of Mount Hiei; Yakushi of the Enryakuji central hall; at the foot of Mount Hiei, the twenty-one Sannō shrines; the great deity of Shirahige Shrine in Uchioroshi; Benzaiten of Chikubushima in Lake Biwa; the Taga deity who resides in Ōmi Province; the heavenly king of Nagae in Mino Province; in Owari Province, Gion Shrine of Tsushima and the great deity of Atsuta Shrine; the Yahagi Guardian King of Mikawa Province; the Ox-Headed Guardian King of Tōtōmi; Fuji Gongen of Suruga Province; in Shinano Province, the Suwa deity and the great deity of Togakushi Shrine; in Kai Province, the great deity of the First Provincial Shrine; Mishima Gongen of Izu Province; Hakone Gongen of Sagami Province; in the Kantō region, the great deities of the Kashima, Katori, and Ikisu shrines; Haguro Gongen of Dewa Province; the great deities of the six Shiogama Shrines in Michinoku; Zaō Gongen of Echigo Province; Tateyama Gongen of Etchū; the great deity of Mount Isurugi in Noto; Shirayama Gongen in Kaga; Goryō Shrine in Echizen; Hachiman of Obama in Wakasa; Monju of Kireto in Tango; the Akarika deity; the great deity of the First Provincial Shrine of Tajima; Obara Hachiōji in Tanba; in Settsu Province, Hirukami Tenjin, and Young Ebisu at Nishinomiya; in Kawachi Province, the great deities of Onji and Hiraoka, and the Hachiman of Konda Shrine; at Tennōji Temple, Shōtoku Taishi and the great deities of the fifteen subsidiary shrines; the great deities of the four Sumiyoshi shrines; the great deity of Mitsunomura in Sakai; the great deities of the five Ōtori shrines in Izumi Province; Awashima Gongen of Kii Province; on Awaji Island, Senkōji Temple where the world began, Eleven-Headed Kannon, and the great deity of Yuzuruha Shrine; on the island of Shikoku, the great deity of Tsurugi Peak in Awa, the great deity of Mifune in Tosa, the great deity of Tsubaki Forest in Iyo, and the Shido Practice Hall of Sanuki Province; on the distant island of Tsukushi, Usa Hachiman Shrine, Rakanji Temple, Hiko, Kubote, Mount Aso, Shiga, Saifu, Udo, Kirishima, and the Takaku hot springs. In Harima Province, the Kanbe first provincial shrine, the Arata second provincial shrine, Hōjōji Temple of the Sakami third provincial shrine, and the great deity of Murotsu; the Kibitsu shrines of Bitchū, Bizen, and Bingo; and all you guardian deities of India, China, and Japan: I summon you now! Jizō Gongen of Mount Daisen in Hōki; the Great Shrine of Izumo Province; Tanaka no Gozen, the father of deities;[21] all you tree gods in the mountains, Bonten in the boulders, eight great dragon kings in the ocean, and water gods in the rivers; in people's houses, you household gods of the seventy-two shrines, and twenty-five oven gods; you roadside deities of the highways: with this oath, I summon you here now!

"Even if my parents or wife and children come looking for me, I shall refuse to see them. If I break this vow, then in addition to me, for whom it goes without saying, may my father, mother, and everyone else in my house and family fall in the Hell of No Respite and the Three Evil Realms.[22] I am resolved, so please shave my head and make me a priest!" Shigeuji thus swore an oath to make a man's hair stand on end.

"Excellent, young samurai!" Hōnen exclaimed. "I will be pleased to shave your head." The holy man filled a small tub with warm water, and after rinsing away the filth of delusion and desire, he scattered Shigeuji's locks toward the pure lands of the four directions. "Young samurai," he said, "now that I have given you the tonsure, tell me where you're from. What province is your home?"

"I come from the Karukaya estate in Chikuzen Province," Shigeuji replied.

"In that case, I shall grant you the name Karukaya Dōshin."[23] Hōnen gave him an old robe and an old priestly stole, after which he said, "Listen, Karukaya—it's important that I confer on you the five lay precepts.[24] A priest should neither envy a man his prosperity nor grieve at his ruin." From that time forward, Shigeuji—now Karukaya—served the holy man with utmost devotion, laboring beneath the stars at night and through the mists of dawn. The master had many followers at Kurodani, but Karukaya was his leading disciple.

The days quickly passed, and it was soon thirteen years since Karukaya had come to Kurodani. After dreaming his first dream of the new year, he went to

---

21. In *Sanshō Dayū*, Tanaka no Gozen is identified as the mother of deities.

22. The Three Evil Realms are the realms of hell, animals, and hungry ghosts. The hell realm includes the Hell of No Respite.

23. *Dōshin* is a term for a low-level priest.

24. The five lay precepts are prohibitions against killing, stealing, lying, drinking alcohol, and sexual misconduct.

Top, Shigeuji performs ablutions before swearing an oath; *bottom*, Hōnen gives Shigeuji the tonsure. From *Sekkyō Karukaya* (1631 woodblock-printed edition). (Courtesy of Tenri University Library)

see the master. "Please allow me to take my leave," he requested. "I would like to move to Mount Kōya."

"Listen, Karukaya," Hōnen replied, "whether you're on Mount Kōya or at Kurodani, you'll still be reciting the *nenbutsu*, so just do it here. I'll be able to instruct you. But you're not really planning on moving to Mount Kōya, are you? I think you want to go home and become a layman again. If that's your intention, you can erase countless eons of sin with a single confession, or so people say. Confess it now and I'll give you your leave."

"What a cruel accusation!" Karukaya declared. "People say that you can judge a man's character in just three or five days, but I've served you for thirteen years, and you still don't know mine! If you think I'm lying, then I suppose I do need to confess. When I first came to this temple, I wanted to take the tonsure so much that I said I had no parents, wife, or children and that I was resolved. But I was twenty-one years old then, and my wife was nineteen. We had a three-year-old daughter named Chiyotsuru, and my wife was seven-and-a-half months pregnant with a second child. I left them all to come here. Now I've had a dream in which the child is born and grows up, and he comes with his mother to find me here. They hang on my sleeves, cry out their names, and beg me to give up the priesthood. It's disturbing and upsetting, even in my sleep. And if they really do come, think of the punishment they'll suffer from that oath I swore! That's why I want to move to Mount Kōya—because it's closed to women."

"If that's the situation," Hōnen said, "then I shall give you your leave. If Mount Kōya doesn't agree with you, please come back."

Upon receiving ten *nenbutsu* invocations, Karukaya set out from Kurodani. Asking the way ahead, he passed by the Tōji Temple gate; again asking the way, he bowed and prayed to the bodhisattva Shō Hachiman at Yawata;[25] still asking the way, he hurried onward. When he came to Tennōji Temple, he wrote "sentient beings of the dharma realm" on a wooden sutra strip and cast it into the waters of the Turtle Well.[26] He sped past the shore at Sakai, marveled to find himself in Ōno-no-shiba, and then hurried through Nakanotani Valley and over Konomi Pass. Pressing forward, he soon reached the Kinokawa River, which he crossed in a boat that was just casting off. Upon arriving at Shimizu Village on the opposite shore, he continued on his way, soon ascending Fudō Hill and coming to the Great Pagoda of Mount Kōya.

The Great Pagoda, the Golden Hall, the Mieidō Hall, and the shrines of the Four Deities stood one beside the other. Karukaya reverently bowed and prayed, after which he proceeded to the Okunoin Hall to bow and pray there, too. He later secluded himself in the Kayandō Hall in Lotus Valley, where he performed supplications for the afterlife with an ardor that was beyond compare.

But let us leave Shigeuji for a while and return to his home in Tsukushi. His wife there was the most pitiful of all. On the night that her husband

---

25. Iwashimizu Hachiman Shrine, immediately to the south of the capital.

26. Tennōji (Shitennōji) Temple is in present-day Osaka. According to the gazetteer *Setsuyō gundan* (1701), it was customary to write the name of a deceased person on a wooden sutra strip and cast it into the Turtle Well as a prayer offering. By writing "sentient beings of the dharma realm," Karukaya offers his prayer to all living beings. See SNKS *Sekkyō shū*, 29n.6.

left, she had noticed a strange silence; although she could usually hear him chanting the holy name,[27] on that night alone he had not made a sound. She pulled a lightweight robe over her head and hurried down a connecting corridor to the buddha hall, where she slid open a sliding paper door and looked inside. The oil lamp had been turned up slightly; all that remained were the telltale signs of her husband's travel preparations. "So he snuck out this very evening!" she cried. "If only I had known how quickly he would make up his mind—I would have spent this one night with him and then secretly seen him off myself!" And with that, she collapsed in a paroxysm of tears.

The wife searched the buddha hall between fits of weeping. She found her husband's letter and the sword that never left his side. Picking up the letter, she read: "Dear wife, my love for you remains the same. If my feelings had changed, then you might hate me for it, but this is not the case. Although our bond in this life may be weak, we are sure to meet again. As for the child in your womb, if it is a boy, you should name him Ishidōmaru. Please have him become a priest when he grows up. If it is a girl, you should do with her as you like. Just remember, dear, that even if our bond in this life is weak, we are sure to meet again in Amida's Pure Land."

The wife writhed in anguish. "Why am I so irresolute when my husband is so resolved? I should throw myself into some pool and drown!" Among her serving women was a person by the name of Lady Karakami, who reproached her, saying, "What a bunch of nonsense! You're pregnant! If you want to go searching for your husband after you've given birth, then I'll go with you."

The days quickly passed, and before long the wife reached full term. When she finally gave birth and looked to see whether her child was a boy or a girl, she beheld a son as lovely as lapis lazuli or a polished gem.[28] Loath to call him a fatherless child while his father was still alive, she did as her husband had instructed and named him Ishidōmaru. To speak of the boy's growth, we might say that he sprang up like a bamboo shoot that sprouts in the evening and thrives on the midnight dew.

27. The name of Amida Buddha, hence, the *nenbutsu*.

28. According to the late-sixteenth-century *Karukaya*, the boy was born clutching a Pure Land jewel in his left hand. See SNKBT 90:272.

PART 2

Time passed, and it was soon thirteen years since Ishidōmaru's birth. In the spring, the wife's serving women invited the daughter Chiyotsuru on a cherry-blossom-viewing excursion. Ishidōmaru and his mother strolled onto their own wide veranda to see the blossoms at home. A pair of swallows were raising twelve little birds on a flowering branch; they had lined their children up according to size and were twittering *chi-chi-ha-shi* in a way that was wonderful to hear. Ishidōmaru took in the sight. "Tell me, Mother," he said, "what are those birds called?"

"Didn't you know, Ishidō?" the mother replied. "They're *tsubame*. They fly here from the Eternal Land every spring and return in the autumn.[29] It sounds like they're chirping *chi-chi-ha-shi*, but actually they're twittering an important verse from the first volume of the Lotus sutra, '*shi-shi-fu-shu-setsu-ga-hō*.'[30] They are very filial birds. That's the father there, and over here is the mother. The twelve birds in the middle are their children. Ishidōmaru, you should be filial toward your mother, too."

"So all creatures have a mother and a father, just like that!" Ishidōmaru exclaimed. "Even the swallows that fly in the sky, the beasts that roam the earth, and the fish in the rivers. But Chiyotsuru and I, we have a mother but no father! Since he was a warrior, was he cut down for some argument or offense, or on a battlefield, perhaps? And when is his death anniversary? Tell me who his enemy was!"

"When you were little," the mother replied, "we never spoke of your father or me. But now that you're grown, how kind of you to ask about your dad! Your father was a man by the name of Lord Shigeuji. He was at a cherry-blossom-viewing party when he saw some flowers fall. That was the seed of his enlightenment, and it turned his heart to the Buddha. I've heard that he took the tonsure at Kurodani in the capital and that he's become a priest there. That's what people say. I've been sending him letters every year, and because they never come back and there's no reply, I know that he's still alive."

---

29. The Eternal Land (Tokiwa no Kuni) is a mythical place without change.

30. "Cease, cease! No need to speak. / My dharma is subtle and hard to imagine" (Leon Hurvitz, trans., *Scripture of the Lotus Blossom of the Fine Dharma* [New York: Columbia University Press, 1976], "Expedient Devices," 28).

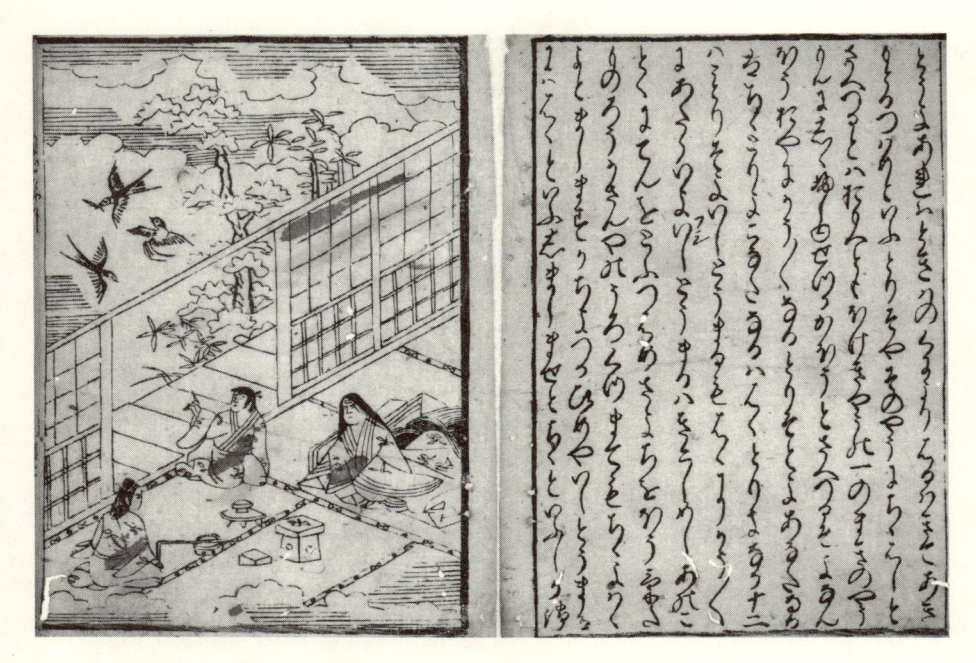

Ishidōmaru asks his mother about his father. From *Sekkyō Karukaya* (1631 woodblock-printed edition). (Courtesy of Tenri University Library)

"Listen, Mother," Ishidōmaru said, "I thought that my father was dead. But if he's alive, then please let me and Chiyotsuru go and find him." The mother was overjoyed. "If that's how you feel," she said, "then let's sneak out tonight. If we wait until tomorrow, everyone will know."[31]

After donning their travel clothes, the two poor pilgrims set out from their mansion, weeping all the while. Because of the karmic bond between parent and child, Chiyotsuru awoke to the creak of an outer door. Thinking it strange, she jumped up with a start and threw open a sliding paper screen. "Mother, are you there?" she called. "Ishidōmaru, is that you? What's happening?" But her mother was gone, and all that remained were the telltale signs of her travel preparations.[32] "Mother always said that she'd go looking for Father once Ishidō

---

31. In the late-sixteenth-century and circa 1661 *Karukaya*, the mother instructs Ishidōmaru to say nothing to his sister about their plan. See SNKBT 90:274 and SSS 2:40a.

32. In the circa 1661 *Karukaya Dōshin*, Chiyotsuru comes home from cherry-blossom viewing and discovers that her mother and brother are gone. See SSS 2:40a.

was grown," Chiyotsuru thought, "so she must have snuck out tonight. I may have been abandoned by my father, but I won't be abandoned by my mother, too!" And with that she ran out barefoot, just as she was.

Because of the deep karmic bond between parent and child, Chiyotsuru caught up with her mother at the beach some five hundred yards away. Clinging to her mother's sleeves, all she could do was cry. Then from between her sobs, she shouted, "Mother, you've shut me out like a stepdaughter! Is Ishidōmaru Father's only child? Am I not my his daughter, too? Then let me go with you to look for him!"

"Listen, Chiyotsuru," the mother said, "I haven't shut you out. It's just that Ishidō is a boy, even if he is your little brother. So he'll be a good travel companion. You may be the elder sister, but you're a girl. You wouldn't be any help on the road—you'd just be a bother.[33] If you want to know why, it's because the people near the capital have evil hearts. They kidnap and sell pretty girls like you, or so I've heard. If you were bought and sold, you'd regret it until the next life. Go back home and mind the house while we're away. If we can find your father, I'll see that you and he meet. Now go home, quickly!"

"If that's how it is," Chiyotsuru said, "then I'll look after the mansion while you're away. But I wonder if I should give you something for him. That's right, I forgot! There's the silk robe I've been sewing since I was six. I've been meaning to offer it to some priest or holy man, and I have it with me now. You can give it to Father for me! Ishidōmaru, when you present it to him, say, 'This is a silk robe made by the daughter whom you abandoned at the age of three and who will be fifteen this year. It's not very handsome, but please be so kind as to wear it for her anyway.' Since you've already decided to go looking for him, I'll wish you well on your trip. Go find him, Ishidō, and then come right back!"

With cries of farewell and good-bye, the boy and his mother took their leave. They thought that the parting would be for just a little while, but it was to be forever.

Ishidōmaru and his mother boarded a small boat at Komatsu Bay. The winds were strong, so they sailed to Daimotsu Harbor in Amagasaki. Inquiring the way ahead, they pressed past Kanko to the Unobe post station. Then, after pausing at the Ōta post station, they quickly crossed the Akuta River, which

---

33. Much of this passage is interpolated from the late-sixteenth-century *Karukaya*, which in this case is clearer than the 1631 text. See SNKBT 90:275.

washes away the dust, and hastened on through Yamazaki. They entered the capital and hurried by Tōji Temple, and because they sped on their way, they soon came to Shinkurodani.

"Well, Ishidōmaru," the mother said, "this is the place where your father is. I'd like to go inside and search for him myself, but I think I'll wait out here. I sent him letters from time to time whenever I missed him, but because they never came back and there was no reply, I've come to feel that our bond is broken. But you two are father and son, so he's sure to see you. Go on inside, Ishidō."

Ishidōmaru went to see Hōnen. "Excuse me, master," he said, "but I would like to ask you something. I come from the Karukaya estate in Chikuzen Province in Great Tsukushi. My father is a man named Katōzaemon Shigeuji. When he was twenty-one years old and my mother was nineteen—my sister Chiyotsuru was three years old then, and I was only seven-and-a-half months in the womb—he saw some blossoms scatter in the wind. All of a sudden his heart turned to the Buddha. My mother heard that he came to this temple, where he became a priest and took the name Karukaya Dōshin. So, we've traveled here to find him. Please tell me if you know where he is."

Hōnen took in the boy's words. "So the dream was true!" he thought, and he spoke: "Listen, child, your father Karukaya did come to this temple. I gave him the tonsure and made him a priest. But one night he had a vision in a dream. He saw his wife, whom he had left at home, and the child who was seven-and-a-half months in her womb. The child had been born and was grown, and he had come here with his mother to find him. Your father asked me to let him leave so that he wouldn't have to meet or see or speak with you. He has gone to Mount Kōya, which women are forbidden to climb. Oh, you poor child!" And the holy man wept into his sleeve.[34]

Alas, poor Ishidōmaru! Bidding farewell to the master, he went back outside and embraced his mother by the gate. Without saying a word, he pressed his face against her sleeve and burst into tears. "So, Ishidōmaru," the mother said, "are you crying for joy at having met your father? Tell me now, what happened?"

"Oh, Mother," Ishidōmaru began, "Father was here at the temple, but he had a dream in which he saw us coming. He ran away to Mount Kōya, which

---

34. In the late-sixteenth-century *Karukaya*, Hōnen tells Ishidōmaru to go and look for his father on Mount Kōya. See SNKBT 90:278.

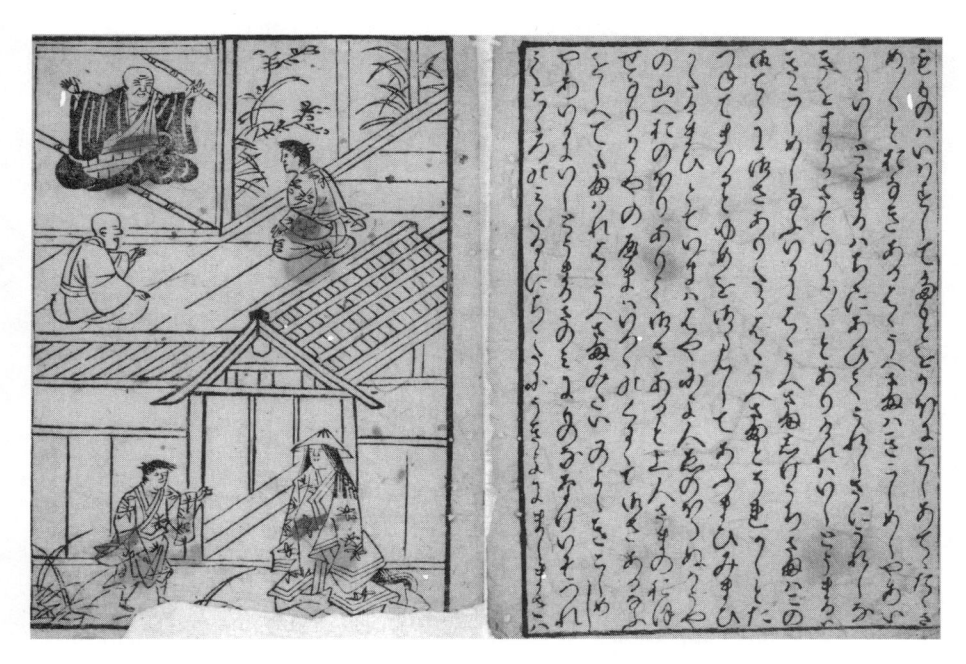

Top, Ishidōmaru meets with Hōnen at Shinkurodani; *bottom*, Ishidōmaru and his mother at the Shinkurodani gate. From *Sekkyō Karukaya* (1631 woodblock-printed edition). (Courtesy of Tenri University Library)

no women are allowed to climb, so that he wouldn't have to meet or see or talk to us. That's what the master said. Which province is Mount Kōya in? Tell me, mother, please!"

"Don't cry like that, Ishidōmaru, or you'll make me upset, too. As long as your father is alive in this uncertain world, I'll find him and see that you two meet, even if it means traveling to the farthest moors and mountains or to the ends of some tiger-infested field. Now come this way." Thereupon, with tears in their eyes, Ishidōmaru and his mother set out from Shinkurodani.

As they crossed the Fourth Avenue Bridge, the mother said, "Look, Ishidōmaru, that's the Fifth Avenue Bridge. Over to the left, you can see Gion Shrine, Kiyomizu Temple, and Inari Shrine. To the right, you can see Saga, Uzumasa, and Hōrinji Temple. That tall mountain there is Mount Atago. I'd like to have you pray at all the famous old sites in the city, but you'll have to wait and do it on the way home after we find your father."

Hand in hand, Ishidōmaru and his mother hurried on their way. They soon passed by the Toba Lover's Tomb, Autumn Mountain, and the Yodo River Waterwheel, which asks, "Do you wait for your beloved?" with every creaking turn. They climbed Mount Yawata and piously prayed, "Hail, Great Hachiman Bodhisattva, who in his original form is the buddha Amida."[35] Crossing the Katano Plain, where pheasants in imperial fields long for their young, the wife brooded and grieved to think that even birds love their children while her own husband did not. They pressed on to the Itoda post station and then bowed and prayed to the Kubotsu deity. Speeding on their way, they soon reached Master Yoji's Tamaya Inn at the Kamuro post station at the foot of Mount Kōya, three leagues from the peak.

"Well, Ishidōmaru," the mother said, "tomorrow morning we're going to climb Mount Kōya, and I'm going to find your dear father and see that you meet."

The innkeeper Yoji overheard the mother's words. "Traveling lady," he said, "there's something I should tell you. You may or may not have known this when you said that you were going to climb Mount Kōya, but the mountain is a seven-league precinct of nondiscriminatory self-practice[36] from its eight-leaved lotus peak to its eight valleys, three auxiliary cloisters, and four subsidiary halls. That means that while male trees grow on the mountain peak, female trees grow in the valley below. Male birds fly up at the ridge; female birds fly in the valley. Bucks graze on the mountainside; does graze in the valley. Trees, reeds, grasses, fowl, and beasts—all that are male may enter, and all that are female may not. Absolutely no women are allowed."

The mother turned to her son. "Listen, Ishidōmaru, it's normal for parents and children to rent a room for the night when they're traveling. But there's no point in staying at a worthless inn, and not on a night when the moon's too bright for sleeping. Let's climb the mountain right now. Your father is definitely up there somewhere. I'll bet he told the innkeeper to tell us about the mountain being closed to women if we came looking for him here. Come on, let's go."

Yoji realized that to let his guests climb would be to spurn the dictates of the mountain. Yet to prevent them from doing so would be to disrespect the

---

35. The Great Hachiman Bodhisattva at Iwashimizu Hachiman Shrine at Yawata is believed to be a native Japanese manifestation of Amida Buddha.

36. *Shichiri kekkai byōdō jiriki no miyama*, a sacred mountain on which Buddhist practitioners practice individually and nondualistically, without discriminating among phenomena.

traveling lady's wishes. He therefore spoke, saying, "Please, madam, allow me to explain. I once heard a recitation of the so-called Kōya scroll, and I would like to summarize it for you now.[37]

"The woman known as Kūkai's mother was not a lady of this land. She was the daughter of an emperor of central Tang.[38] Her father had her married to another emperor, but that man sent her back, saying that she was the ugliest woman in all of India, China, and Japan. Her father therefore placed her inside a dugout canoe and set it afloat on the western sea. She drifted toward Japan until a fisherman by the name of Tōshin Dayū of Shirakata Byōbu Bay in Sanuki Province on the island of Shikoku found her bobbing in the Chikura Offing. When he hauled up her canoe and had a look inside, he saw the ugliest woman in all of India, China, and Japan. Some say that he adopted her as his daughter, and others say that he kept her as a lowly serving woman. Her name was Akō Gozen.

"Akō thought to herself, 'Just as every mountain that's a mountain is sometimes shrouded in mist, every woman who's a woman will at some time enchant a man. Yet in all these years I have yet to attract one myself! Since that's my fate, I'll ask the sun for a child.' She stood on the roof of her house in a pair of fourteen-inch elevated clogs with a sixteen-gallon tub of water on her head and awaited the twenty-third-night moon. She then had a dream revelation in which a golden fish from the western sea swam into her womb. Although other women give birth in their tenth month, Akō delivered her own child in her thirty-third. It was a boy, as lovely as lapis lazuli or a polished jewel. When it came time to name him, she chose Kingyomaru—Goldfish Boy—in reference to her dream.

"Because the boy was not really human, he used to recite the sutras from inside his mother's womb. Later, the people of Byōbu Bay complained, saying, 'Akō's baby at Tōshin Dayū's house cries in the night. And night-crying babies bring ruin to seven harbors and seven towns.' They sent a messenger to inform Tōshin Dayū that he, too, would be unwelcome in the village if he did not have the baby abandoned. Akō was incensed. 'I won't give up my Goldfish!' she cried. 'Not after all I went through to have him!' She took her baby and left,

---

37. The Kōya scroll (*Kōya no maki*) concerns the lives of the Mount Kōya Kongōbuji Temple founder Kūkai (774–835) and his mother. Kūkai is also known as the progenitor of the Shingon school of Japanese Buddhism.

38. Tang China, that is.

wandering through eighty-eight different places, people say. That's why there are eighty-eight stops on the Shikoku pilgrimage route today.

"Akō said, 'Listen, Goldfish, people already complain about you crying at night. Are you going to start crying now for hours on end? Since the ancient past, people have said that while there's no thicket to abandon yourself in, there's always one in which to lose your child.' And with that, she discarded her baby.

"Now at that time there was a priest by the name of Karan Kashō of Makino'o in Izumi Province who was preaching a seven-day sermon at the Shido Practice Hall in Sanuki Province. Akō went to hear him speak. She listened to his sermon, and she stayed behind when all the others had left. Earlier, Karan Kashō had heard a voice chanting sutras under the sagging branches of a pine. He had dug into the ground only to discover a baby boy as lovely as a jewel. He had thought that this was peculiar indeed. Now Akō was standing here before him, sobbing and wringing her hands and feet. 'Dear lady,' he asked, 'whatever is the matter?'

"'I was fortunate enough to have a son,' Akō replied, 'but he cried at night and people complained, so I buried him under that sagging pine. I could hear him wailing until yesterday, but today he seems to be dead because I can't hear a thing. That's why I'm upset.'

"'Do you mean this child here?' the priest asked, handing the baby to his mother. Akō was overjoyed. 'I should tell you, lady, your son's bawling isn't night crying. He's reciting the sutras.' Having delivered this news, the priest set out for Makino'o.

"When her son was seven years old, Akō took him to Makino'o in Izumi Province. Because they both were buddhas, Karan Kashō met with the boy, after which the child moved to Omuro Palace.[39] Being a buddha, he learned ten characters for every one that his teacher taught. He was an exceptional scholar. The years passed, and at the age of sixteen, he shaved his head and took the priestly name of Kūkai.

"When Kūkai was twenty-seven, he wished to travel to China. He secluded himself in Usa Hachiman Shrine in Tsukushi Province where he prayed that he might gaze on the deity in its true bodily form. The deity appeared before him as a beautiful fifteen- or sixteen-year-old girl. Taking in the sight, Kūkai said,

---

39. Ninnaji Temple, also known as Omuro Palace, is at the northwestern edge of the capital.

'Do you mean to test the heart of a foolish priest? Just show me your true form.' The deity reappeared as the demon king of the Sixth Heaven. 'That's the shape of a demon king,' Kūkai objected. 'Just show me your true form.' The inside of the shrine shook with thunder and lightning and burst into flames, whereupon the six-character name emerged.⁴⁰ 'Now that is your true bodily form,' Kūkai declared. He had the characters carved into the stepping board of a boat, which is why the *nenbutsu* is also known as 'the boat-board name.' He then sailed to Tang, where he paid his respects to the Seven Emperors. He later met with Shandao,⁴¹ who gave him the title of Kōbō, 'Disseminator of the Dharma.'

"Kūkai decided to travel on to India. He had already passed the Running Sands River when Great Holy Mañjuśrī saw him approach.⁴² 'Kūkai of Japan,' Mañjuśrī inquired, 'why have you come so far?' 'To visit your Pure Land,' Kūkai replied. Mañjuśrī adopted the form of a divine boy. 'Kūkai,' he said, 'this river has no crossing, so turn back now.' 'Every river that's a river has a crossing,' Kūkai rejoined. Mañjuśrī spoke: 'You come from a small country, Kūkai. Turn back now.' 'India takes after the stars,' Kūkai persisted, 'which is why it's called Shintankoku, "Land of the Trembling Dawn." Tang takes after the moon, so it's called Gasshikoku, "Land of the Moon People."⁴³ Japan may be small, but it takes after the sun, so it is called the Realm of the Sun. It is a land of the foremost wisdom.'

"'How well can you write?' Mañjuśrī asked. 'You first,' Kūkai replied. 'All right,' Mañjuśrī said, 'watch this.' He inscribed the characters for *abirauken* 阿毘羅吽欠 on the scudding clouds.⁴⁴ The clouds were far away, but the characters were perfectly formed.

"'Finished, are you?' Kūkai said, taking in the sight. 'Then it's my turn.' Kūkai wrote the character for 'dragon' 龍 in the flowing water of the river. Mañjuśrī

---

40. The six-character *nenbutsu*, the formulaic expression of Amida Buddha's name.

41. A seventh-century priest and early formulator of Pure Land Buddhist thought, Shandao died in 681, nearly a century before Kūkai's birth.

42. Mañjuśrī (Monju) is popularly known as the bodhisattva of wisdom. "Running Sands" is actually a name for the Taklamakan Desert in Central Asia, rather than a river.

43. In fact, Shintan is an old name for China, and Gasshikoku is an old name for India. Muroki Yatarō furthermore suggests that in the reference to India, "stars" is a mistake for "thunder." See SNKS *Sekkyō shū*, 49n.12.

44. *Abirauken* is a potent Shingon incantation purported to contain in its five characters the essence of all Buddhist teachings.

inspected his writing and said, 'That character can be read "dragon" only if you add another mark. You're missing a stroke!' 'I can easily add another stroke,' Kūkai said, 'but something terrible will happen if I do.' 'Even so,' Mañjuśrī said, 'finish the character.' 'All right,' Kūkai said, and he added the final stroke, whereupon his brush touched the eye of a dragon in the water upstream, causing it to weep. The dragon's tears produced an instant flood, sweeping Kūkai five hundred or six hundred yards away. Mañjuśrī watched and cried, 'Careful, Kūkai!' With his hands, Kūkai made the sign of the stone and cast it on the river,[45] causing a five-foot boulder to appear and dispel the frothy torrent.

"Mañjuśrī cracked his whip and rode back to his Pure Land.[46] Kūkai followed close behind. Watching him come, Mañjuśrī produced a golden memorial marker thirty-three double-handbreadths long. He announced, 'Write on this, my premier disciples.'[47] Among Mañjuśrī's followers was a certain Chikei Kashō; thinking that he would write, he straddled the golden memorial marker and applied his brush. Kūkai watched. 'My country may be a small one,' he said, intending to point out the disciple's mistake, 'but the Japanese ride horses and oxen. This is the first time I've seen a man ride a memorial marker!' Chikei was enraged. 'Anyone can see that you're short and dark,' he replied, 'so who are you to judge my writing?' 'Lacquer may be dark,' Kūkai countered, employing the wisdom of Japan, 'but it is used on myriad household goods. A needle may be small, but it sews together myriad garments. And a brush may be short, but it writes myriad documents. Likewise, though I may be short and dark, I can certainly judge your writing.'

"Hearing these words, Mañjuśrī declared that Kūkai should write. 'I will,' Kūkai said, and he took up the golden memorial marker that was thirty-three double-handbreadths long. Because he commanded the power of the dharma, he immediately stood the marker on its end, dipped five brushes in ink, and threw them at its face. Although the brushes were tipped with lion's hair, they deftly wrote their way down from the top and returned to Kūkai's hand. Mañjuśrī said, 'Well written, Kūkai. But you're missing a character.' 'I'll write it for you now,' Kūkai replied, and when he had finished, the marker read, '"A"

---

45. Kūkai formed a *mudra*, a magical hand gesture employed in spells.
46. In Buddhist iconography, Mañjuśrī is typically depicted riding on a lion.
47. Or "Write on this, my premier disciple." In the circa 1661 *Karukaya Dōshin*, Mañjuśrī says, "Write on this, and I will make you my premier disciple." See SSS 2:45b.

阿 is for the buddhas of the three ages in the ten directions;[48] "mi" 弥 is for all the many bodhisattvas; and "da" 陀 is for the eighty thousand scriptures; together they are "A-mi-da Buddha."' Although the brush was tipped with lion's hair, it flew back to the inkstone from which it came. Mañjuśrī stated that he would grant Kūkai a title, and thus borrowing the 'Great' from his own name, Great Holy Mañjuśrī, he called him Kōbō Daishi, 'Great Teacher Who Spreads the Dharma.'

"Later saying that he had something to give him, Mañjuśrī took three treasures—a single-pointed *vajra*, a triple-pointed *vajra*, and a sacred ceremonial bell—and tied them in the bristles of a broom, which he then used to sweep the garden. Kūkai received the broom from Mañjuśrī's hand, and because it was given to him by his master, he placed it among his personal belongings. A golden light erupted from the three knotted places in the bristles, and when Kūkai cut through the tangles, he discovered the three treasures woven inside. Thinking that he would return home, Kūkai took the three treasures and threw them all the way from Mañjuśrī's Pure Land back to Japan. The single-pointed *vajra* landed in the capital at Tōji Temple, which is venerated as the Mount Kōya for women; the sacred ceremonial bell landed in Sanuki Province at Reisenji Temple, which is venerated as the western Mount Kōya; and the triple-pointed *vajra* landed on Mount Kōya, in what is revered as the triple-pointed *vajra* pine. Then, after more contests of wit and writing, Kūkai returned to Japan.

"Now Kūkai's mother had reached the age of eighty-three, and wishing to see her son, she began to climb Mount Kōya. Clouds suddenly filled the sky, and the mountain shook with thunder and lightning. Realizing that a woman must be approaching, Kūkai descended for a look. At a place called Standing Arrow Cedar, he saw an old nun in her eighties caught in a fissure in the ground. 'Who are you?' he asked, taking in the sight. His mother replied, 'I am Akō from Tōshin Dayū's house in Shirakata Byōbu Bay in the Tado district of Sanuki Province. I have a son who came here shortly after becoming a priest. We parted on the sixth day of the sixth month of Enryaku 8,[49] and I haven't seen him since. I've come all this way because I miss my boy.'

"Kūkai clapped his hands and exclaimed, 'It is I, Kōbō, who came here after becoming a priest so long ago! You've done well to climb this far, but the

---

48. The three ages are the past, present, and future.
49. The year is 789, when Kūkai was sixteen years old.

mountain is forbidden to women. All that are male may enter, and all that are female may not. That includes even the birds in the sky and the beasts on the earth.' Kūkai's mother was so angry at being excluded from her son's mountain that she twisted up a nearby boulder, which is now called the Twisted Rock. Fire rained from the sky, so Kūkai hid his mother in a stony hollow; the boulders there are called the Hiding Rocks.

"Kūkai's mother wept and spoke: 'However great a priest you may be, it's only because of your father's seed and your mother's womb that you're here at all to preach in this latter age.[50] And instead of inviting your one and only mother to the temple, you're ordering her back down to the village! How cruel!'

"'It's not because I'm unfilial,' Kūkai replied. He took off his seven-paneled stole and spread it on a rock. 'Step over this,' he said. Because the stole was her son's, the mother was unconcerned. She boldly stepped across, whereupon the blood of her monthly malady began to fall in tiny drops. It had ceased when she was forty-one, but now, at the age of eighty-three, it began anew. The stole burst into flames and flew up into the sky.

"Afterward, Kūkai gathered the buddhas of the three ages in the Pure Land of Constant Abiding,[51] where he created the Womb Realm and Diamond Realm Mandalas. He conducted seven weeks of memorial services for his mother, at the end of which she was released from the human world of delusion and reborn as the bodhisattva Miroku.[52] As Miroku, she is worshipped at Jison'in Temple at the foot of Mount Kōya, five leagues from the Okunoin Hall. She is also venerated as the clan deity of the twenty villages of the Kanshōbu estate; the people there make a pilgrimage to her every year on the twenty-ninth day of the ninth month. Now if Kūkai's own mother was forbidden from climbing the mountain, how could a new believer like you even think about doing so?" Yoji paused and then added: "But whether or not you choose to climb it is up to you, traveling lady."

---

50. The Latter Age of the Dharma, a spiritually degenerate period due to its distance in time from the life of Shakyamuni Buddha. In Japan, the Latter Age was generally believed to begin in 1052, so the mother's reference to it is anachronistic.

51. The Pure Land of Constant Abiding is another name for Mount Kōya, because of the belief in Dainichi Buddha's constant presence there.

52. Maitreya, the future buddha, who abides in Tosotsu (Tusita) Heaven.

PART 3

Ishidōmaru's mother was frightfully intimidated. "If that's the case, Master Yoji," she said, "then perhaps I can't climb the mountain after all. But it will be impossible for the boy on his own! He was abandoned when he was just seven-and-a-half months in the womb, so even if he does meet his father, they won't be able to recognize each other. Poor child!"

The mother doubted that she should send her son alone, but she urged him on, saying, "Well, Ishidōmaru, you go up the mountain and look for your father for two or three days. Then, whether or not you find him, come back down, even if it means going up again later. Just don't keep me waiting. And listen, Ishidō—you'll know your father by his strong Tsukushi accent. If you hear someone talking like he's from Tsukushi, grab him by the sleeve and give him a good scolding. Then bring him here. Good-bye, good luck, and come back soon!" The mother and child thus took their leave, thinking that it would be for just a little while. But it was to be their final parting in life, as they would learn only later.

Ishidōmaru started up the mountain. At Fudō Hill, he encountered five holy men on their way down toward the post station. Seeing them approach, he felt happy inside, and he wondered whether his father might not be among them. "Excuse me, reverend sirs," he inquired. "Can you please tell me where I might find a renunciant devotee?"

"What a silly question, boy!" the holy men exclaimed. "Everyone on this mountain is a renunciant devotee, including the five of us." With that, they all burst out laughing. Ishidōmaru cursed them, saying, "I asked because I didn't know. Damn you for not helping!" and continued up the hill.

A single priest approached. When Ishidōmaru asked him how many temple halls there were on the mountain, he replied, "Seven times seven, or forty-nine."

"And how many monasteries?"

"More than 7,300."

"How about priests?"

"According to the Great Teacher's golden records, some 99,000."

The boy was overwhelmed. "That's so many," he thought. "How will I ever find my father?" Ishidōmaru visited the Okunoin Hall. There were tall wooden memorial markers standing all around—monuments to people's grief throughout the land. He spent six days searching for his father at building after building, hoping all the while that today they would meet.

At dawn on the sixth day, the poor boy remembered what his mother had said at the Kamuro post station—that he should come down after two or three days, even if it meant having to go back again to search some more. He therefore decided to return early the next morning. As the sky began to lighten in the fifth hour of the night,[53] he dressed and set out for the Okunoin Hall so that he could tell his mother about it on his return.

At just that time, Ishidōmaru's father happened to be leaving the Okunoin Hall with a flower basket in his hand. He crossed paths with his son on a broad bridge, but as neither recognized the other, they simply continued on their way. Yet perhaps because of the karmic bond between parent and child, Ishidōmaru turned back around and seized his father by the sleeve. "Excuse me, reverend sir," he said, "there's something I'd like to ask. Can you please tell me where I might find a renunciant devotee?"

"What a silly question, boy!" Karukaya exclaimed. "Everyone on this mountain is a renunciant devotee. Back in their home provinces, they all were cormorant fishers, falconers, arsonists and murderers. They offended their lords, angered their parents, or simply set their hearts on the next life, abandoning their lands and shaving their heads. If you want to find a man here, you need to set up three placards with his name written on it. If it's a warrior you're after, you write his personal and family names, and if it's a farmer, you write the name of the place he's from. Then, if he wants to see you, he'll put up a sign next to yours. If he doesn't want to meet, he'll pull up your placards. That way, in three days you'll know where he is. But the way you're searching, you won't find your man in three years and three months. Poor child! Tell me who he is and where he's from. I'll help you look."[54]

"Oh, thank you!" Ishidōmaru gushed. "He's from the Karukaya estate in Chikuzen Province in Great Tsukushi, and his name is Katōzaemon Shigeuji. When he was twenty-one years old and my mother was nineteen—my sister Chiyotsuru was three years old then, and I was only seven-and-a-half months in the womb—he saw some blossoms scatter in the wind. All of a sudden his heart turned to the Buddha. My mother heard that he took the tonsure at a place called Shinkurodani in the capital and that he took the name Karukaya Dōshin. So we traveled all the way there to find him. But he saw us coming in a dream,

---

53. The fifth hour of the night is approximately 3:00 to 5:00 A.M.
54. In the circa 1661 *Karukaya Dōshin*, Karukaya takes his son to the Kayandō Hall to help him make signs. It is there that the boy explains whom he wishes to find. See SSS 2:48b.

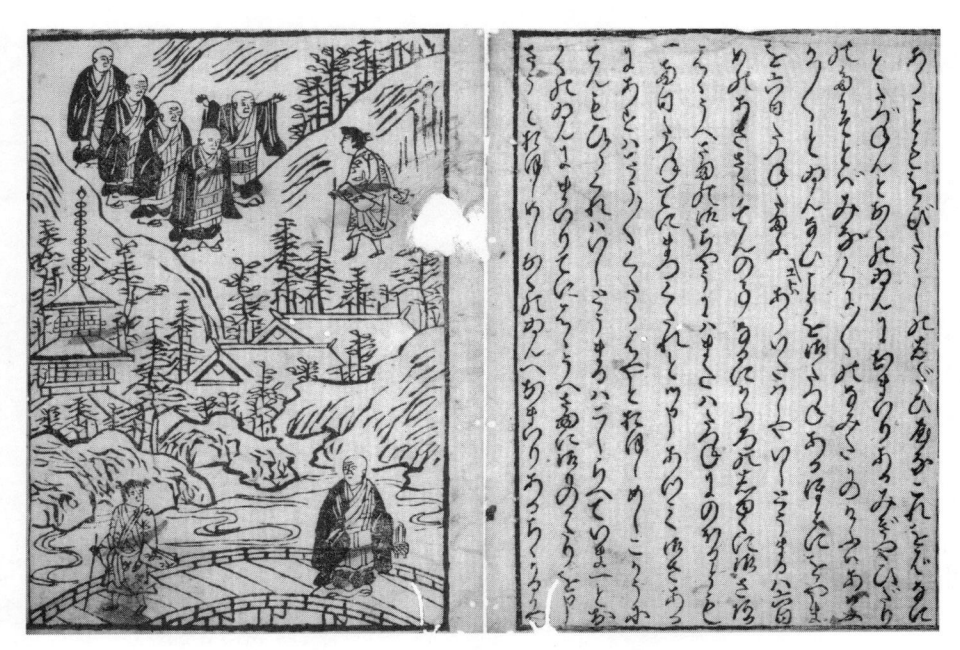

Top, Ishidōmaru questions some holy men on Mount Kōya; *bottom*, Ishidōmaru encounters his father. From *Sekkyō Karukaya* (1631 woodblock-printed edition). (Courtesy of Tenri University Library)

and since he didn't want to meet or see or speak with us, he ran away to Mount Kōya, which is forbidden to women, before we arrived. Please tell me, sir, if you know where he is."

Karukaya was overwhelmed. "And all this time," he thought, "I was wondering who the boy was! To think that he's my own son! If I had known I was his father, I never would have questioned him like that. Oh, why did I have to get involved? Just seeing him breaks my heart!" Karukaya's secret grief spilled out in tears.

Ishidōmaru stared at the priest. "Today is my seventh day on the mountain," he said, "and I've met lots of holy men so far, but you are the first one who's been kind enough to shed a tear. You look like you know where my father is. Please tell me, sir, if you do."[55]

55. In the circa 1661 *Karukaya Dōshin*, Ishidōmaru says, "It's certainly strange for you to cry when I ask about my father. And listening to you talk, I can hear your Tsukushi accent. If you're my dad, then admit it to me now!" See SSS 2:49a.

The boy was clever, Karukaya thought, and since it would be a disaster if he were to realize that he was his father, he decided to lie. "Indeed," Karukaya said, "I do know about your father. He and I shared the same master here, so we were fellow disciples. We were good friends until around this time last summer, when your father suddenly fell ill and passed away. In fact, today is his death anniversary. I was on my way to visit his grave just now, and meeting you like this has made me weep."

Ishidōmaru's senses reeled. "Can this really be happening?" he thought. "Is it some kind of dream? How sad if it's true!" He broke down and sobbed. Then between bouts of tears, he spoke: "Excuse me, sir, but I want to visit my father at his grave. Will you please show me where he's buried?" Having no plot of his own, Karukaya led Ishidōmaru to a wooden memorial marker that a traveler had put up the previous summer for his own future rebirth. "This is your father's marker," Karukaya said. "You should pray for him here." And together they prayed.

Poor Ishidōmaru collapsed beside the memorial mound. "Up until now," he cried, "I always thought that I could meet my father if only he were alive in this world! But now all I have is this marker." Again, the boy burst into tears. Pillowing his head on the ground beside the mound, he wept as if to die. "Father," he whimpered, "Karukaya, Shigeuji, are you there in the earth? I'm the son you abandoned at seven-and-a-half months in the womb. I was born and have grown up now, and I came here to find you. Answer me, please, from down in your grave! Say, 'Ishidōmaru, is that you?'" The boy shed bitter, burning tears.

Weeping all the while, Ishidōmaru took out the silk robe that his sister had given him to present to their father. He shook it open and threw it over the top of the memorial marker, letting it drape down the sides. Wrapping his arms around it at the waist, he said, "Listen, Father, I was told to tell you that this is a silk robe made by the daughter whom you abandoned at the age of three and who will be fifteen this year. It's not very handsome, but please be so kind as to wear it for her anyway. I had meant to find you someday, put the robe on you like this, and then hug you around the waist. I would have been so happy just to have seen you! But now I can hang this robe only on your marker, which isn't any comfort at all."

Ishidōmaru folded up the garment as it had been before, and then he addressed the priest: "Please, sir, this silk robe may not be a handsome one, but my sister made it. She was abandoned at the age of three, and she'll be fifteen this year. She said that if I found our father, I should tell him to be so kind as to wear it for her. But he's dead now, so I would like to give it to you instead." Despite believing that the priest was his father's fellow disciple, Ishidōmaru was in fact able to fulfill his sister's request.

Poor Ishidōmaru! Intending to have his mother offer a prayer to the wooden memorial marker, he hoisted it to his shoulder and started down the hill. "If that clever boy carries the marker down to the post station," Karukaya thought, "then as soon as she sees it, my wife will know it isn't mine. She'll recognize it as a marker for somebody's future rebirth, and all this lying will have been in vain." He therefore spoke, saying, "Wait, child! If you carry that memorial marker down to the post station, it'll be like dropping your father into the Hell of No Respite. A standing marker is like a buddha on a pedestal. If you really want one, then leave that here and let me make you a copy." Karukaya led Ishidōmaru to the Rengebō cloister, where he inscribed a proper placard and offered it to the boy. Ishidōmaru accepted it and headed down the mountain.[56]

Let us leave Ishidōmaru for a while and return to the Kamuro post station. His mother there was the most pitiful of all! The poor lady had endured a day or two of waiting, straining at the sounds of a softly blowing breeze and a creaky outer door, wondering if her son had returned or a message had arrived from her husband. Yet all her apprehension was for naught.

"Listen, Master Yoji," the poor woman said, "today's the seventh day since I sent my boy up the mountain. I keep waiting, imagining that he'll return at any moment. But how sad to think that he might not come back today! And to think that he might not come back tomorrow, either! What if he got lost on those strange mountain roads and forgot the way back here? Or what if he found his father and got so caught up in some sweet reunion that he forgot to leave, and now he's not coming back at all? Oh, Master Yoji, I'm afraid I won't last the day! I've got some gold with me, and if I die, I want you to have it. Just see that I'm cremated when I'm gone. If my son comes back from the mountain, give him my ebony rosary and the amulet that's around my neck. And please give him a lock of hair from my temples for his sister Chiyotsuru at home. He hasn't

---

56. In the late-sixteenth-century *Karukaya*, the narrator adds: "Alas, poor Ishidōmaru! Although he had met his living father, he did not recognize him as such. And even though Karukaya knew Ishidōmaru to be his son, he did not identify himself as the boy's father. The poor priest wanted to reveal himself, but fearing the vow that he had sworn at Shinkurodani, he refrained. The feelings in his heart were pitiful indeed!" See SNKBT 90:299–300.

come back yet, has he? How sad that he doesn't come! Oh, Master Yoji—even if I never hear about my husband again, I wish I could see my Ishidō one more time! How I miss my boy!"

The wife's longing must have taken its toll, or her time had simply come, for despite the sorrow of dying in her prime, she met her end that very night. Unable to await the coming dawn, she passed away at the age of thirty.

Yoji was aghast. He had meant to provide only temporary lodging, and he was dismayed to witness such a tragic turn of events. Thinking to set out early in the morning to find the woman's son on Mount Kōya, he dressed and departed as the sky began to lighten in the fifth hour of the night. Poor Ishidōmaru was coming down the mountain with the memorial marker on his shoulder when he encountered the innkeeper on Fudō Hill.

Seeing the child approach, Yoji shouted, "You there, with the marker! If you already knew about your mother dying, why didn't you come down yesterday, while she was still alive?" "This marker isn't for my mother," Ishidōmaru said. "It's my father's. And what do you mean by talking like that, calling it hers? Oh, this cursed marker!" He flung it toward the valley below.

Yoji and the boy struggled back down the mountain. Hurrying on their way, they reached the Kamuro post station in no time at all. Ishidōmaru pushed open the creaky outer door and pulled aside a folding screen, only to discover his poor mother lying on her side, her head pointing north and her face turned toward the west, just as she had been when she attained Pure Land rebirth.

Ishidōmaru immediately embraced his mother's corpse. "Can this really be happening?" he cried. "If it's a dream or a delusion, then please let it be over!" He pressed his face to his mother's cheek. "Mother, Mother," he bawled, "who'll take care of me now in these strange mountains? Where have you gone, abandoning me like this? If you had to die, then why didn't you take me with you? How could you leave me here alone like this?" Clinging to his mother, Ishidōmaru roiled and wailed, sobbing as if to die.

But the child had a duty to perform, so he fetched a cup of clear water, pried open his mother's mouth, and used his little fingers to scoop some liquid inside. "This sip of water that I'm giving you is a final offering from Father, who is with you in the afterworld," he said. "Please accept it and attain buddhahood. This next sip of water is from Chiyotsuru at home. Please accept it and attain buddhahood. This last sip is from me, Ishidōmaru, who came all this way with you for nothing. Please accept it and attain buddhahood." The boy collapsed in an anguish of tears, which was a sad sight indeed!

Alas, poor Ishidōmaru! Having no one to help him at the inn, he climbed back up the mountain to the Rengebō cloister. Finding the priest from before, he said, "Hello, sir, excuse me. My mother, who was at the foot of the mountain, has died now, too. I've come to ask you to help me with her body." Karukaya agreed, and the two set out for the valley below.

But as they approached the Kamuro post station, it occurred to Karukaya that since the boy was so clever, he probably told his mother about the priest he met on the mountain. And in that case, she would have recognized him at once. "That's no fellow disciple," she would have said. "That man must be your father!" Thus, she might have sent the boy back to deceive him in order to bring him to the inn and make him confess.

Karukaya decided to lie. "Wait!" he exclaimed, pretending to have just remembered something. "It's a custom here to take leave of your teacher before going down the mountain. As you know, I didn't ask permission when we set out this morning. So you go on ahead—I'll say good-bye to my master and be right along behind you."

"But sir," Ishidōmaru pleaded, "it all depends on the situation. It's your job as a priest to help me now." Karukaya saw the truth in this, and they continued on their way. When they reached the Kamuro post station, Yoji said, "I was wondering who you were. You're that fellow from the Rengebō cloister, aren't you? I was giving lodging to the traveling lady for a little while, and then this awful thing happened. I wanted to visit you myself, but I've got lots of guests arriving. Please take care of the body, won't you?"

Karukaya was glad to see no one else around. He slid open a sliding paper door and pulled aside a folding screen. His wife was lying on her side, her head pointing north and her face turned to the west, just as she had been when she attained Pure Land rebirth. He immediately embraced the corpse. "You must have hated me so much at the end!" he cried. "It would have been one thing if my love for you had changed, but it never did. I'll pray for you in the next life. I can only imagine the feelings in Ishidō's heart!"

Karukaya knew that if he grieved too much, the boy might recognize him as his father. Choking back his tears, he took out a razor and prepared to shave the lady's head.[57] But because this was his own wife whom he had abandoned thirteen years before, he was overwhelmed by memories of the past and unable

---

57. As a ritual bestowing-of-the-tonsure in death.

to apply the blade. Still, he eventually managed to scrape away her hair, scattering the woman's locks toward the pure lands of the four directions.

Wishing to be on their way to the cremation grounds, Karukaya carried the front shafts of the funeral bier and Ishidōmaru carried the rear. And poor Ishidōmaru! Mumbling between his sobs, he whimpered in a way that was moving to hear. "If this had happened in my homeland of Tsukushi," he wept, "then all the greater and lesser lords and their families and retainers would have gathered together, high and low alike. But here on Mount Kōya I've got no one to turn to, so it's just me and this priest and nobody else!"[58] Ishidōmaru and his father proceeded to the Thousand-Acre Plain,[59] where they piled the bier with sandalwood and set it afire. Then as they chanted *shogyō muon mujō*, "the silence and impermanence of all things," the mother's body was consumed by the three flames of worldly delusion.

After the smoke had cleared, they quietly collected her bones. Karukaya said, "Listen, boy, this is the hair that I shaved from your mother's head. If you have a sister at home, take it to her now. I'll inter these bones in an ossuary hall on the mountain." Still concealing his identity—even now—Karukaya drove away his son. The feelings in his heart were sad indeed!

Poor Ishidōmaru set out for Tsukushi with his mother's hair draped around his neck. After days of travel, he took the hair in his hands and sobbed. "When my mother and I set out to find Father, the road didn't seem so long. Not as it does today!" Weeping and moaning, he continued onward, and in no time at all he came to Great Tsukushi.

As he approached his home, Ishidōmaru heard a multitude of priests reciting sutras inside the mansion. "When people talk about bad news flying a thousand leagues," he thought, stepping inside, "this must be what they mean. What joy that word of my mother's passing has preceded me and that everyone's holding services for her now!"

The boy's nurse and nanny seized him by the arms and exclaimed, "Ishidōmaru, our fortunate child! Have you come home after meeting your father? When you left, your luckless sister Chiyotsuru started talking about

---

58. According to the circa 1661 *Karukaya Dōshin*, Ishidōmaru and his father were accompanied by Yoji and his wife. See SSS 2:52a.

59. Actually, the Thousand-*chō* Plain, which is more like 2,500 acres. Its location is unknown.

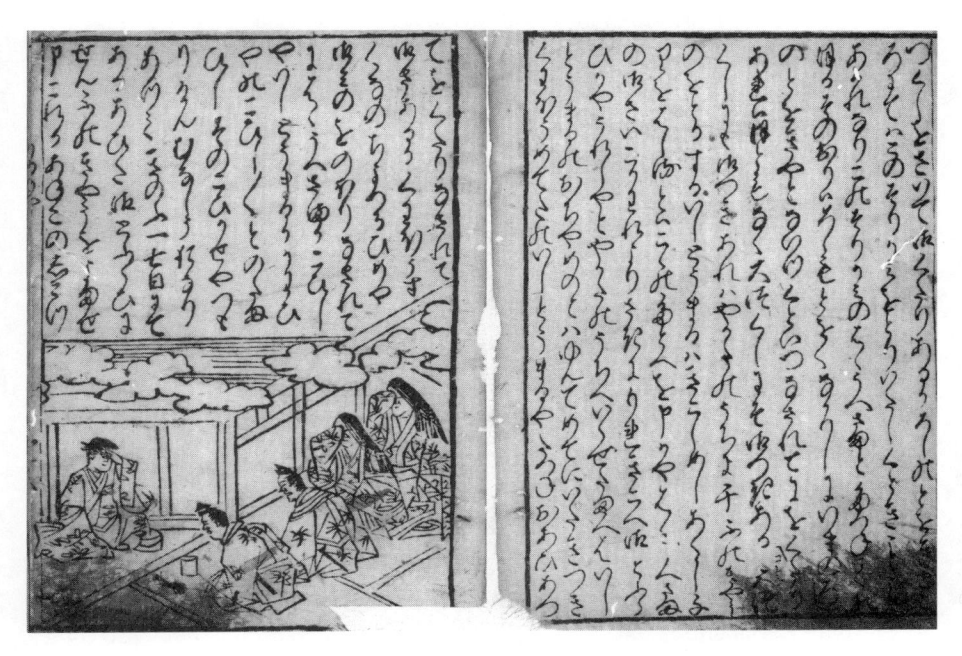

Ishidōmaru weeps at the news of his sister's demise. From *Sekkyō Karukaya* (1631 woodblock-printed edition). (Courtesy of Tenri University Library)

how much she missed you and your mother. 'I want my family!' she cried. Her longing must have taken its toll, because she died a week ago yesterday. That's why all these priests are here—to recite sutras for her in the afterworld. These are her bones and her hair." The women handed Ishidōmaru his sister's remains.

"Is this a dream?" Ishidōmaru cried. "Is this really happening? My sister Chiyotsuru, who was always there for all of us . . . is she really dead? Am I dreaming or awake? I lost my father, then my mother, and now Chiyotsuru, too—and how sad to see her bones! Yet my own worthless life goes on, for nothing!" Ishidōmaru wished to join his family, but it occurred to him that if he were to die, too, there would be nobody left to pray for their enlightenment. Having no one to rely on now, he entrusted his lands to the household, hung his sister's hair and bones around his neck, and set out again for Mount Kōya.

Back on Mount Kōya, the father Karukaya had sent his son home, but because he wondered how the child would manage the family domain, he decided to travel to Tsukushi for a surreptitious look. But when he shouldered his pack and started down the slope, he encountered Ishidōmaru on his way up Fudō Hill. "Well, hello boy!" Karukaya called out. "You've been on the mountain for a long time. Haven't you gone home yet?"

"I did go home," the boy replied, "but my sister was dead. She died waiting for my mother. These are her bones and her hair." Ishidōmaru handed them to his father.

Karukaya took in the news. "What a cruel fate!" he thought to himself. "Rather than practicing the monastic law on this mountain, I've been killing people instead! I'll tell the child that I'm his father and give him a little joy." But then he reconsidered. "Yet, if I tell him who I am, then that oath I swore at Kurodani will be in vain, and we'll all be doomed to the Hell of No Respite. Oh, how sad that I can't confess!"

Karukaya spoke: "Listen, boy, you should take the tonsure here, become a priest, and pray for your parents' and sister's enlightenment." He led his son to the Rengebō cloister, where he scattered the child's locks toward the pure lands of the four directions. For the boy's monastic name, Karukaya borrowed the *dō* in *dōshin* and named him Dōnenbō.[60] "Now pray hard for the life to come," he instructed.

Poor Dōnenbō became a woodcutter on the mountain. After a while, people began to gossip, saying that he and Karukaya were unusually close, even for a master and his disciple. Karukaya heard the rumors, and although he attributed them to spite, he also recognized the danger if it were discovered that he and Dōnenbō were father and son. He therefore took his leave, saying, "Listen, Dōnenbō, I'm going to the northern provinces to practice Buddhism. It's the way of the world that death may come at any time to young and old alike. So if you see purple clouds rising in the north, please understand that I have passed on. And if I see purple clouds rising in the west, I will know that you have died."

Karukaya shouldered his pack and set out from Mount Kōya. He performed a hundred-day *nenbutsu* recitation at Shinkurodani in the capital, but because his heart was still unsettled, he continued on to Zenkōji Temple in Shinano Province, where he secluded himself in the Inner Buddha Hall and prayed wholeheartedly for the next life.

---

60. *Dōshin* is a term for a low-level priest. It is also the second part of the name that Hōnen gave to Karukaya.

Karukaya's days were gloriously long. In the hour of the horse on the fifteenth day of the eighth month of his eighty-third year, he attained Pure Land rebirth without suffering or pain.[61] Purple clouds rose in the northern sky. In the same hour of the same day, at the age of sixty-three, Dōnenbō on Mount Kōya likewise attained Pure Land rebirth without physical discomfort. Purple clouds rose in the west to mingle with the purple clouds from the north, spreading and joining across the sky in a way that was marvelous to see. Although Karukaya never revealed himself to his son in the present world, he kept no secrets before the buddhas of the three ages in Amida's Pure Land, where father, mother, sister, and brother were joyously reunited.

A wondrous fragrance wafted through the air, and flowers rained from the sky. The buddhas of the three ages all took in the sight, and deciding to transform this magnificent father and son into buddhas like themselves, they installed them in the Inner Buddha Hall of Zenkōji Temple in Shinano Province so that they might be worshipped by sentient beings of the latter age. Karukaya and Dōnenbō are venerated there as the Parent and Child Jizō Bodhisattva. Such is their story. May prosperity reign throughout the land, and may we all strive for Pure Land rebirth.

---

61. The hour of the horse is approximately 11:00 A.M. to 1:00 P.M. According to the late-sixteenth-century *Karukaya*, Karukaya and Dōnenbō died on the twenty-first day of the third month—the same day on which Kūkai is said to have died. See SNKBT 90:312.

Shintokumaru

PART 1

Now as for the tale I tell, in the Takayasu district of Kawachi Province there was once a wealthy lord by the name of Nobuyoshi.[1] He had erected forty thousand storehouses in the four directions, eighty thousand in the eight, and there was nothing for which he lacked. Nothing, that is, except a child. He was without a son or a daughter, and for this he grieved, morning and night. He summoned his wife one day and spoke: "Listen, dear—you and I don't have a single child, and the pain of this is more than I can bear. Is there nothing we can do?"

"What a silly thing to say," the wife replied. "It's because the karma from our previous lives is so wretched. But since ancient times, childless couples have visited the gods and buddhas to pray for an heir, and when they do, they're given one, I've heard. Nobuyoshi, you should visit a god or buddha and pray

---

Translated from the 1648 *Sekkyō Shintokumaru*, supplemented by the Urokogataya *Shintokumaru*.

1. Takayasu is now a part of Osaka. Nobuyoshi is identified as a *chōja*, a man of immense material wealth.

for a child, too." The lord thought this was good advice. "Rather than just any place," he said, "let's visit Kiyomizu Temple in the eastern part of the capital. They say the Kannon there is the best in the three countries."[2]

Traveling with too many can be a burden, Nobuyoshi thought, yet with too few, the roads can be difficult to clear. Thus, to the jingling sound of hawks' bells, dogs' bells, and the horses' bit, the lord and his wife set off for Kiyomizu with one hundred attendants and a parade of palanquins on sturdy shafts. Through what places, now, do you think they passed? Through Uetsukenawate, and the Sakura district, too; over Hora Pass, and Mount Yawata beyond; trudging and plodding over Little Yodo Bridge, pressing on through Fushimi, and bowing down to pray at Sanjūsangendō, the Hall of Thirty-Three Bays: thus they sped on their way, and in no time at all they reached Kiyomizu Temple in the eastern hills.

The lord and his wife proceeded to Otowa Falls, where they purified themselves by rinsing their mouths and hands.[3] They moved on to the central hall. Standing in the Holy Presence, they rattled the sacred summoning bell and made their earnest request: "Hail most merciful Kannon! If it were wealth we sought, we should indeed incur your wrath. But all we ask is that you give us a child, either a boy or a girl." They settled in at a place near the left of the altar to pass the hours in supplication. Late in the night, the Kiyomizu Kannon—awesome to behold—emerged wavering from his inner sanctum and stood before the dozing Nobuyoshi and his wife. "Dear couple," he spoke, delivering his oracle in a dream, "that you've traveled such a distance to ask me for a child is truly very moving. However, I shall tell you now about the karma from your previous lives.

"As for you, sir, in your previous existence you were a woodsman in the Nosé district of Tanba Province. In the spring, thinking that you might like to pluck fresh ferns and bracken, you let loose a terrible fire in the mountains, burning up the bugs that live three feet down in the earth. There were many birds in that place, but none so sad as two pheasants, a husband and wife.

---

2. The three countries are India, China, and Japan. In referring to the Kiyomizu Kannon, Nobuyoshi speaks of the Kiyomizu "principal image" (*honzon*), a wooden statue of the Eleven-Headed Kannon enshrined in the main temple hall.

3. Otowa Falls is the small, spring-fed waterfall from which Kiyomizu-dera (Pure Water Temple) takes its name.

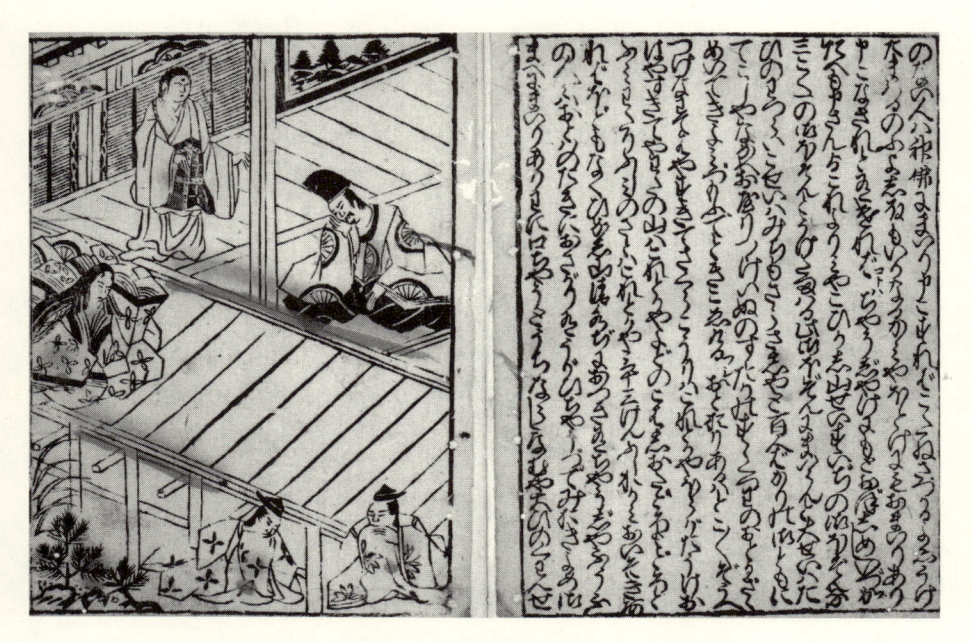

The Kiyomizu Kannon appears to Nobuyoshi and his wife in a dream. From *Sekkyō Shintokumaru* (1648 woodblock-printed edition). (Courtesy of Tenri University Library)

"Because it was spring, they had laid twelve eggs, and in this, their time of joy, the raging fire approached. In great distress, the father and mother pheasant carried water in their beaks to dampen the grass around their little ones. Still, the menacing flames crept close. The mother pheasant wrapped her wings around her twelve eggs, and the father, grasping the mother's beak in his own, tried to pull her to safety. Caught in the thorny brush, however, they had little chance to escape. The father pheasant flew to the far riverbank. 'Come! Come! Mother pheasant,' he cried. 'As long as we're alive, we'll have more children and raise them anew! Leave our babies and fly!' 'You heartless father!' the mother shouted back. 'I can't bear to leave even one of these twelve eggs behind, much less the entire lot!' and she was consumed by the fire.

"Heartbroken, the father pheasant screeched and flailed his wings, and he pronounced a curse that was most moving to hear: 'Whoever set fire to this field today, he shall surely pay a price! If he's reborn as a stone, then he shall be a paving stone on the Kamakura Highway, trampled by horses as they pass on their way. If, because of some good deed in a former life, he's reborn as a human, then he shall be a wealthy lord. Even the poor have children, but this one—he will have none! He will long for a child in the daytime and long for a child in the night, suffering on in this way until death!' With his beak, the father pheasant ripped the ends of his wings and expired. His dying vow has penetrated your heart, devouring your heirs on the inside before they can be born. This is why you have no child.

"As for you, madam, in your previous life you were a great snake beneath the Seta Bridge in Ōmi Province. Most pitiful of all were the swallows—a husband and wife—who used to fly from the Eternal Land in spring and return in the autumn![4] They had laid twelve eggs on a strut of the bridge; the mother would keep them warm while the father looked for food. All was well until one day they went out together to forage. You saw them go, and thinking it a fine opportunity, you took the nest and ate the babies inside.

"Upon their return, the swallows were desperately alarmed. They searched here and there, but they could find no sign of their young. 'That big river snake must have eaten them!' they cried. 'It didn't leave us even one. The sorrow of it all! What use is it now to return to the Eternal Land?' They took hold of each other's beak and threw themselves into the river. 'I'll eat them today, too,' you thought, and that's just what you did. That one wicked desire has permeated your heart, devouring your heirs before they can be born, and this is why you have no child. It's not my fault, so don't blame me. Please return to Kawachi in the morning." Having spoken thus, the bodhisattva vanished without a trace.

Awaking from their dream, the lord and his wife jumped up with a start. "You cruel Kannon!" Nobuyoshi shouted. "Even if our karma is bad, you should give us a child anyway, as an expedient means![5] If you don't, I won't leave. I'll cut open my stomach right here, rip out my guts, and throw them on you. I'll become a demon god and gobble up anyone who comes to see you! Maybe not in a week, but within three years I'll have weeds growing in here. This place will be a deer wallow!" The lord ranted on wildly.

One of his longtime servants interrupted: "Please listen, master. To threaten such a celebrated buddha . . . you're sure to come to some unspeakable harm!

---

4. The Eternal Land (Tokiwa no Kuni) is a mythical place without change.
5. Nobuyoshi asks to be given a child as a *hōben*, an expedient means employed by a buddha or bodhisattva to teach the dharma.

If you don't have a dream revelation in seven days, then you should make a solemn vow and pray for another seven." Nobuyoshi thought this good advice, and he had paper and an inkstone brought to him. He wrote out his petition and placed it in the inner sanctum. His wife did the same, placing her own petition beside her husband's, and they prayed for seven days.

The venerable abbot eventually took his honored seat, and rubbing his rosary beads with a scraping sound, he read aloud Nobuyoshi's vow:

> O wondrous Kannon, who soothes the broiling hearts of sentient beings of the Latter Age:[6] If you grant us a child, I shall build you a temple hall with precious wood from India. I will inlay the beam fittings with bronze and engrave upon them lifelike scenes of soaring dragons and cranes. If this is not enough, I will take your altar stage, which is old and shabby, and replace it with one decked in silver and gold, from the handrails to the bridge-post knobs.[7] If this is still not enough, I will take your summoning bell, which is also old and shabby, and replace it with a new one, the front cast in gold, the back in silver, measuring three inches thick and three feet, eight inches, wide. Your sacred shrine fence is old and shabby, too, so if this is still not enough, I will construct a new one of three thousand white-handled spears braided together with a fine crimson cord. If this is still not enough, I will scatter on your grounds three *shō*, three *gō* of gold dust, three *shō*, three *gō* of silver dust, and replenish these every month with six *shō*, six *gō* of pure gold and silver dust.[8] I have at home a fine spring steed, just turned six, so if this is still not enough, I will fit him with a gilded saddle and a silver bit and parade him before you again and again to rouse you from your sleep. My one request is for a child, either a boy or a girl.

---

6. The Latter Age of the Buddhist Law.

7. According to Muroki Yatarō, the Kiyomizu Temple altar stage (*butai*) burned down in 1629 and was rebuilt in 1633. If it indeed was worn out at the time of the story's narration, then this version of *Shintokumaru* might date to 1629 or earlier. See SNKS *Sekkyō shū*, 161n.17.

8. One *shō* is the equivalent of 1.92 quarts, and one *gō* is one-tenth *shō*. According to the nō play *Kan'yōkyū*, the Kan'yō Palace in Qin China was similarly adorned with pearl, lapis lazuli, and gold dust spread about on the ground. See Nishino Haruo, ed., *Yōkyoku hyakuban*, Shin Nihon koten bungaku taikei 57 (Tokyo: Iwanami shoten, 1998), 20.

Taking up the wife's petition, the abbot read:

> If you grant us a child, I will give you seven Chinese mirrors, seven clear mirrors, and seven copper mirrors. With these twenty-one mirrors, I will present to you an eight-foot dangling sash, five feet of hair, and a twelve-compartment handbox of heirlooms. If this is not enough, I will also present to you 108 censers, pestles, bells, and crosiers and one thousand flower trays, all decorated with gold and silver. Your sanctum curtains are old and shabby, so if this is still not enough, I will replace them with seven rills of figured cloth, seven rills of brocade, and seven rills of gold-lace weave. On these twenty-one rills, I will have accomplished artisans embroider scenes of the devas and twenty-five bodhisattvas descended from the heavens to save sentient beings of the Latter Age. I shall have them embroider the light of the sun, moon, and stars to rouse you from your sleep. My one request is for a child, either a boy or a girl.

That night, the marvelous Kannon emerged wavering from his inner sanctum, and standing between the lord and his wife, he spoke to them in a dream: "I had no heir to give you, but because you've taken such a vow, I have obtained one after all. When the child is seven, one of you—the mother or the father—will be in mortal danger. But be unstinting in your love!" "Even if we are to die tomorrow," Nobuyoshi and his wife replied, "please give us a child tonight." "I will, then, and a boy he shall be. Now be gone from this place!" and he vanished without a trace.

Nobuyoshi and his wife awoke with a start. "What a happy revelation!" they exclaimed and took leave of the Holy Presence. Immensely pleased, they set out from Kiyomizu Temple with their many retainers and soon arrived at their mansion in Takayasu in Kawachi. Kannon's promise was indeed true; the wife's monthly malady came to a halt, and after enduring her seventh-month suffering and her ninth-month misery, she loosened the birthing sash and was delivered of a child. When her women attendants lifted the baby to see whether it was a boy or a girl, they beheld a young master, beautiful like lapis lazuli or a polished gem. Nobuyoshi and his wife were joyous beyond compare.

An old and trusted retainer approached them and spoke: "You will surely give the boy a name. What will you call him?" "He's a gift of the Kiyomizu Kannon," Nobuyoshi replied, "so please think of something appropriate." "He will be wealthy like his father and long lived like me," the old retainer foretold.

Naming him after these two traits—*shin* and *toku*—they called him Shintokumaru.[9] The young master had six wet nurses and six nannies, and together these twelve ladies bathed and doted on him ceaselessly. His second and third years quickly passed, and in what seemed like a day, he was already nine.[10] Nobuyoshi and his wife were endlessly happy.

The lord approached his wife one day and spoke: "Listen, dear—let's send Shintokumaru to Shigino Temple." "That's an excellent idea," the wife replied, and they summoned their retainer, Nakamitsu. "Nakamitsu," the wife said, "we would like you to place Shintokumaru in Shigino Temple for three years. See that he gets a good education." "Yes, ma'am," Nakamitsu replied, and he set off for the temple together with the young master. Since they hurried on their way, they soon arrived and met with the abbot.

"This young master is the son of Lord Nobuyoshi in Takayasu in Kawachi Province," Nakamitsu explained. "I'll entrust him to you for a period of three years." "Fine," the abbot replied. Nakamitsu turned to Shintokumaru: "Study hard. I'll come for you in three years. Farewell," and he returned to Kawachi. Shintokumaru surpassed the other children at the temple. For every character his teachers taught, he learned two; for every ten, he learned a hundred or a thousand. In this way, he became the top student at Shigino.

There was at that time a gathering of the richest men of the three provinces of Izumi, Kawachi, and Settsu. "Let's do something splendid," someone proposed. Another person spoke: "Let's have a stone stage set up over the Lotus Pond at Tennōji Temple on the twenty-second of the second month.[11] We'll put flowers all around it and have the acolytes dance." "A perfect suggestion," everyone agreed, and it was decided that this year Lord Nobuyoshi would be in charge.

Nobuyoshi returned home and summoned Nakamitsu. "Go fetch Shintokumaru from Shigino Temple," he commanded. "Yes, sir," Nakamitsu replied, and he immediately set forth. Soon arriving at the temple, Nakamitsu met with

---

9. The explanation of Shintokumaru's name is problematic. The *toku* signifies "virtue" or "prosperity," but the meaning of *shin* is unclear. In the nō play *Yoroboshi*, the boy is called Shuntokumaru.

10. According to the Japanese count, Shintokumaru was one year old at the time of his birth.

11. Shitennōji (commonly abbreviated as Tennōji) is in the Tennōji district of Osaka. The twenty-second day of the second month is the occasion for a ceremony honoring Shōtoku Taishi, who is reported in *Nihon shoki* (720) to have founded the temple in 593.

the abbot and explained the circumstances of his visit. "Fine, fine," the abbot agreed, and he sent the boy on his way.

Shintokumaru met with his parents. "Well now, Shintokumaru," his father began, "I didn't call you back for anything so important, but there's going to be an acolyte dance at Tennōji, and this year I've been put in charge. I'm wondering whether to employ some outside boys or to have you perform instead."

"I'd rather do it myself than leave it to some other boys," Shintokumaru said. He assembled a group of acolytes, assigned them their parts, and on the twenty-second of the second month had them put on a show. The youths were exceptionally handsome; their graceful movements with their fans were exquisite beyond the powers of description. They were like bodhisattvas or fish bobbing in the waters of a river. Crowds of people gathered to watch. Rich and poor alike, everyone praised the dance.

Three of the seven days of the performance had passed. On the fourth day, from a space between the fans, Shintokumaru caught a glimpse of Otohime, the young daughter of the wealthy Kageyama lord from Izumi Province, on a northwest dais.[12] If he might have his way in this floating world, Shintokumaru thought, he would spend a night of passion with this princess, and there would be nothing left that he would wish for in his present life. He had fallen into the path of love. Abruptly stopping his dance, he returned to Takayasu with Nakamitsu. He shut himself up in his room, and pulling close a rattan pillow, he collapsed on a sickbed of love.

Nakamitsu visited him where he lay. "Young master, what are you doing here, languishing in bed? Give me your hands—I'll take your pulse and make you well." Shintokumaru gave his hands to Nakamitsu. Taking them in his own, Nakamitsu spoke: "Your upper pulse is calm, but the lower one is disturbed. You've got none of the 404 ailments . . . you're sick with love!" He released his grip. "Tell me all about it, and don't hold anything back. I'll see to it that everything works out."

The young master lifted his heavy head. "So it's true that a person's inner feelings show through—and how ashamed I feel! There's nothing now for me to hide. When I was dancing, there were three palanquins on a northwest stand. The girl in the middle—do you know who she was, Nakamitsu?" Nakamitsu took in his words. "So she's the one," he said. "She's the daughter of Lord Kageyama

---

12. Like Nobuyoshi, Kageyama is described simply as a *chōja*, a man of affluence.

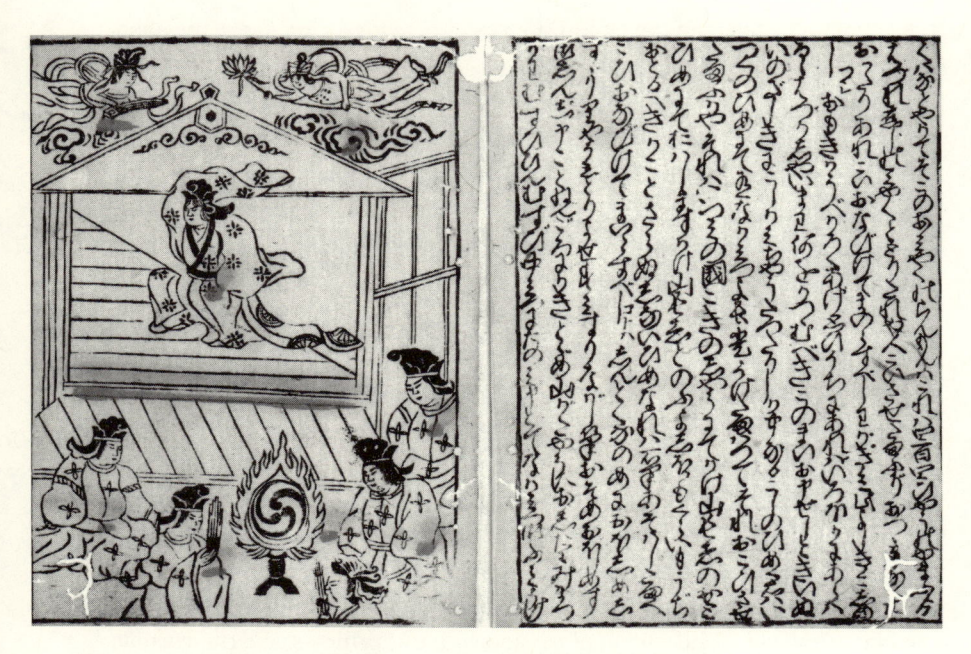

Shintokumaru performs an acolyte dance. From *Sekkyō Shintokumaru* (1648 woodblock-printed edition). (Courtesy of Tenri University Library)

of the Kogi estate in Izumi Province. He and your father are of the same rank and pedigree. She's not married, you know, so why don't you send her a note? I'll take care of everything."

Shintokumaru was exceptionally glad. He sent for an inkstone and paper, ground some ink, wet his brush, and fervently wrote out the wishes and feelings in his heart. He folded his missive in the *yamagata* style, bound it with a *matsugawa* knot, and entrusted it to Nakamitsu. Accepting the letter, Nakamitsu bid his master farewell and immediately set out from Takayasu. When he arrived at the coast at Sakai, he bought various medicines and a twelve-compartment handbox, and after changing his appearance to that of a peddler, he again hastened on his way.

Soon arriving at the Kogi estate in Izumi Province, Nakamitsu crossed the pontoon bridge over Lord Kageyama's moat and strode right in through the inner gate. Standing tall in the great garden, he began hawking his wares—

most amusing indeed! "Lipstick, face power, folding paper—anything you like! Aloeswood and musk! Come and get it!" he shouted, pacing this way and that. Various ladies heard his cries. "What an unusual peddler! What do you have?" they asked. Nakamitsu placed his wooden pack on the veranda and sat down on the ground below. Chinese medicines, Japanese medicines, the contents of his twelve-compartment handbox . . . these he sorted into a number of small containers from inside his wicker trunk. The women appraised them with delight.

Thinking that the time was right, Nakamitsu produced Shintokumaru's love letter. "Listen, ladies," he said. "Three days ago, when I was vending at Lord Nobuyoshi's place in Takayasu in Kawachi Province, I found this lovely letter at the crossroads behind the house. I kept it because of where it was. You can use it for writing practice if you like or, if not, for just a bit of fun." The women took the letter. Unaware of Nakamitsu's deception, they opened it for a look. "What?" they cried. "The characters for 'moon' and 'stars' are written at the top, 'spring blossoms' in the middle, and 'rain' and 'hail' at the bottom. Some crazy person must have written this nonsense and thrown it away on the road!" Having failed to grasp a single word, the women burst into boisterous laughter.

PART 2

Ah, dear Otohime! From behind her seven-, eight-, and nine-layered curtains she gracefully emerged, less like a person, it seemed, than a gently swaying breeze. She approached her women and spoke: "Ladies, what have you been laughing about? If it's something unusual, do tell me. My heart is in need of distraction."

"This salesman here gave us a letter," the women replied, "but it doesn't make any sense! That's why we were laughing." They refolded the paper and offered it to their mistress. Otohime took it and spread it out for a look. "The brushwork is dignified," she observed, "and the characters, refined. I don't know who wrote it, but when people talk about 'doing someone in with a letter,' they surely mean messages like this. You know, ladies, it doesn't do a bit of good to know a hundred things if the one thing you need to know, you don't. Well, then, there must be an easy way to read this note. I'll break it down now. I wonder, though . . . should I read it literally or as poetry?

Top, Otohime (*left*) motions for Shintokumaru's letter; *bottom*, Nakamitsu pretends to be a peddler. From *Sekkyō Shintokumaru* (1648 woodblock-printed edition). (Courtesy of Tenri University Library)

"The first words are 'the lofty peak of Mount Fuji.' We should read this 'I gaze, pining, at the hovering moon.'[13] This allusion to the three mountains—it means 'if I say it aloud, then let it come true.' 'The deer on the ridge': 'though I am not the autumn stag, this love is hard to bear.' 'The faintly tinted leaves': 'my true colors show through.' The figure of the 'pure waters of the open field' means 'speak of this to no one—keep it in your own heart alone.' 'The boat in the offing' is 'bring it to port, this drifting heart of mine,' and the image of the coastal reeds and salt shacks at Ise—these are 'sway with me a night in the gusting wind.' We should read 'the rushes of the lake' as 'bend to me when I pull,' and 'hailstones of the ground bamboo' as 'fall to my touch.' Where it's written

---

13. Otohime's interpretation of the letter is based on a series of word associations, many of them obscure. For a similar letter, see *Oguri*.

'ferns on the eaves'—this means 'nightfall on the road to see you; I cannot wait a moment more.' 'A short sash' is 'someday we shall meet, this love to be fulfilled' and the 'featherless bird beside an unstrung bow'—this is 'I try to stand and yet cannot; I burn and burn with flames of love.' There is a poem at the end: 'The one who loves is Shintokumaru, only child of Lord Nobuyoshi of Takayasu in Kawachi. The one he loves is Otohime.'[14]

"Oh, how embarrassing! And all the while I was wondering whom it was for. What will happen to me if my father and brother find out?" Otohime ripped the letter into two and three parts with her teeth, tossed them in the gutter, and fled inside. Her women were in an uproar. "We thought he was a peddler who comes around all the time," they said, "but he's here to abduct our lady! Is anyone out front? Somebody do something!" Nakamitsu was taken aback. "I've really done it now," he thought, "—and all at the bidding of my confounded master! But they say a man's spirit is like a temple pillar—large and stout—while a woman's wits are in her bosom, not her mind. I'll try to intimidate them." He spoke: "Listen, ladies—the letter's all torn up now, so just give it back." "Absolutely not!" the women replied.

Word reached Lord Kageyama. "I understand there was a letter for you from Shintokumaru, the only child of Lord Nobuyoshi in Takayasu in Kawachi," he said to his daughter. "Hurry up and write your reply." "Yes, sir," Otohime answered, and she called for an inkstone and paper. She wrote at length of all that was in her heart, and folding her correspondence in the *yamagata* style, she bound it with a *matsugawa* knot. She sent it out to her ladies, and they, in turn, handed it over to Nakamitsu. Nakamitsu placed it in a box inside his wicker basket, and after arranging and shouldering his wooden pack, he skipped out the inner gate. Breathing a sigh of relief, feeling as though he had stepped on a tiger's tail or avoided the bite of a deadly snake, he hastened on his way. He soon reached Takayasu in Kawachi and visited Shintokumaru in his room.

The young master was delighted to receive a reply. When he spread it out and read what was inside, his happiness knew no bounds. Nakamitsu explained everything to Nobuyoshi and his wife, and she, in turn, began to speak out around the house: "Our Shintokumaru, you know—when the Kiyomizu Kannon gave him to us, he said that when he turned three, Nobuyoshi or I would be in

---

14. Although identified as a poem, these sentences are neither metered nor set off in the text in the manner of a verse.

mortal danger.[15] But he's turned three, five, and now even thirteen, and still nothing's happened! Even the great Kiyomizu Kannon is a liar. In this day and age, it's no wonder that people lie to get by!" As lessers take after their superiors, the entire household was consumed with riotous laughter.

It is a long way from Takayasu in Kawachi to Kiyomizu in the capital, but by expedient means the bodhisattva heard everything she said. "That odious wife with her impudent talk," he fumed. "It was because I had feelings for the child—my special charge—that I stood on top of Nobuyoshi's roof, beckoning good and driving evil off a thousand leagues. And now she calls me, her guardian, a liar! People won't revere the gods as gods and the buddhas as buddhas if I let this one stand. I'll take her life tonight." He unloosed his pestilence demons.

"Well, demons," the Kiyomizu Kannon spoke. "There are many who live in the house of Lord Nobuyoshi in Takayasu in Kawachi. This evening, take from among them the master's wife." Having received their command, the demons flew off in a whirlwind and blew into Nobuyoshi's home. Ignoring the many people there, they took hold of the mistress and began to tear away her spirit. Because she was in the midst of entertaining, she begged leave of the household, withdrew to an inner room, and fell prone, dying, on a rattan pillow.

Shintokumaru and the Nobuyoshi lord knelt at her right and left. "Darling Nobuyoshi," the wife spoke, "I've never minded the breeze before, but now it cuts me to the quick. My bones and joints feel as though they're coming apart. I don't think I can last the night. If I should die, take good care of our one and only Shintoku. And you, Shintokumaru—listen to me now. Your father's still in his prime, and if I die, he'll need a wife. Treat your new mother as you would me, and remember—if you get along with her, it'll make me happy in my grave. If you don't, then even if you read a thousand or ten thousand sutras for me, it won't do a bit of good. And oh, Nakamitsu! If I should die, serve Shintokumaru well. I'm entrusting everything to you. My dear family, my dear husband, and, most of all, my dear Shintokumaru, keeping me in this world! We were so fortunate to have you . . . and yet the woe of a mother who has to go first . . ."

These were her final words. Earth is as earth, the grass is as grass, and in the quieting of a human voice, all is still. The wife vanished like the morning dew. Having watched her slip away, Nobuyoshi clung to her lifeless corpse. "Am

---

15. According to part 1, their lives would be in peril when Shintokumaru turned seven, not three.

I dreaming or awake?" he cried. "Can this parting be real? Come back and stay with us for a while in this wretched world!" Shintokumaru, too, embraced his dead mother. "Is this a dream?" he moaned. "Is it real, this good-bye? I'm still so young . . . who'll take care of me now that you're gone? If you have to go, then take me with you, please!" Roiling and clutching, pressing his face to hers, Shintokumaru shed bitter, anguished tears.

The time soon came for the funeral rites when it would no longer do to weep and wail. To the chanting of a chorus of priests, the wife was placed in a six-strutted casket and carried to the cremation grounds. Alas, poor Shintokumaru! He followed his mother the entire way, his wretched complaints so moving to hear. "Torn from my mother as a child," he sobbed, "—what'll become of me now?" The bier was piled high with sandalwood and set afire. All things are fleeting in this world, and thus amid the three flames of worldly delusion, the body was consumed. After the smoke had cleared, the bones were collected and the ashes swept together. A tomb was built and a wooden memorial marker raised, and everyone returned home. Poor Shintokumaru! Reading sutras in the buddha hall, he felt such sorrow in his heart, such immeasurable pain!

The extended family gathered to discuss various matters. Lord Nobuyoshi was still in his prime, they said, and he would have to have a wife. Among the thirty-six nobles in the capital, Lord Rokujō had a younger daughter who was then eighteen years old. It was decided that she should be his bride. An auspicious day was chosen, and the wedding held without delay. Nobuyoshi received his wife amid much singing and dancing, with infinite joy.

Back in the buddha hall, Shintokumaru heard the news. "My coldhearted father," he brooded. "It's hardly been a hundred days since my mother died—what does he mean by getting married? He's so unfeeling. Oh, for my dear, dead mother!" There was nothing he could do but cry. He looked through a great many sutras, but there were none that spoke highly of women. He erected a placard declaring the buddha hall off-limits to women, and for seven days he read sutras for the benefit of his mother. The sorrow in his heart was beyond compare.

As a sign of her good karma, perhaps, the new wife gave birth to a son. Nobuyoshi named him Little Jirō, and when the wife found out, she was upset.[16] It galled her that he had not been made heir, seeing how fortunate she was to

---

16. The boy is called Oto no Jirō, literally, "younger-brother second son."

have had a child. She concocted a plan to place a curse on Shintokumaru and have Little Jirō designated the heir. She approached her husband and spoke: "Darling Nobuyoshi—I'm from the capital, you know, and since I made a request of the Kiyomizu Kannon, I need to visit his temple." "If that's the case," Nobuyoshi replied, "will you go by palanquin or horse?" "Either way, I'm sure to stir up gossip. I'll leave Little Jirō with his nursemaids and go quietly instead." She prepared for her journey and set out from Takayasu with a Buddhist pilgrim.

Through what places now do you think they passed? Through Uetsukenawate and Sakuragauri; over Hora Pass to Fushimi and beyond. Hastening on their way, they soon arrived at Kiyomizu Hill. The wife took lodging, found a blacksmith, and had him make six-inch nails for her during the night. At the break of dawn, she visited Kiyomizu Temple. After rattling the sacred summoning bell, she made an earnest request: "Hail most merciful Kannon! Though my visit here is of no great importance, it has come to my attention that Shintokumaru is your special charge. From today, please make Little Jirō your special charge, too. Also, please take Shintokumaru's life. If you won't, then please cripple him with a repulsive disease." Taking out her nails, she said, "These I strike into Shintoku's four limbs," and she pounded eighteen of them—the number of the festival day of Kannon—into a living tree in the Holy Presence.[17]

Proceeding to Yasaka Shrine, whose festival day is on the seventh, she struck seven nails into a lattice in the sacred grounds. She then hammered eight, seven, and fourteen at the Goryō, Nanano, and Imamiya Shrines, twenty-five at Kitano Tenman Shrine, and twenty-one at Yasha Shrine at Tōji. Visiting the Inaba Buddha Hall, she said, "These are for Shintokumaru's eyes," and she pounded in an additional twelve. She struck in the remaining nails to incite the water gods of the Kamo and Katsura Rivers. In all, she hammered in 136 nails at various shrines and sanctuaries in the capital. Returning to Kiyomizu, she bowed three times in the Holy Presence and ardently prayed: "Before I leave this place, please smite Shintokumaru with a repulsive disease." She then returned to Takayasu.

Alas, poor Shintokumaru! Even though he read sutras for his mother, his stepmother's prayer took a terrible toll. It was a powerful curse, and throughout his body, 136 nail holes burst into festering sores. His two eyes ruptured as well, leaving him utterly incapacitated. The woebegone young master had

---

17. The festival day (*ennichi*) of Kannon is the eighteenth day of every month.

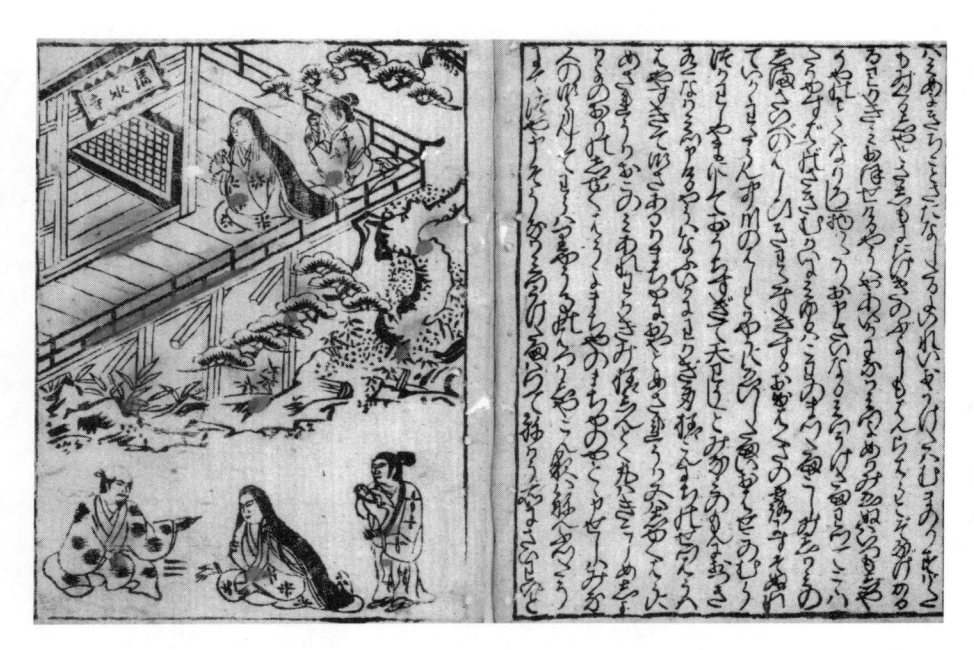

Top, The stepmother curses Shintokumaru at Kiyomizu Temple; *bottom*, the stepmother purchases nails. From *Sekkyō Shintokumaru* (1648 woodblock-printed edition). (Courtesy of Tenri University Library)

come to a pitiful pass, and taking to his room, he fell prostrate on a rattan cushion. The sorrow in his heart was beyond compare.

The stepmother arrived in Takayasu. Peeking through a gap in a sliding paper screen, she was exceptionally pleased to see Shintokumaru's sores. In her boundless joy, she bowed down in the direction of the capital to pray. Later, she approached her husband and spoke: "Listen here, Nobuyoshi—when I was in the capital, I heard people saying at all the crossroads that when there's an invalid in a warrior's house, the family loses the protection of the gods for seven generations. I hear that Shintoku's got some putrid disease. It's sad, I know, but I want you to abandon him someplace, like Hitomatsumoto, perhaps. If you won't, then please be so kind as to give me my leave."

"I'm a wealthy man," Nobuyoshi replied, "and I could easily take care of five or ten such invalids. If you don't want to be under the same roof, I'll build a separate house and look after him there." "That's fine," the wife said, "but as for me and Little Jirō, we'll be on our way."

Nobuyoshi was perturbed. "If I were to send this wife away and marry someone else," he thought, "the face would change, but the merciless heart would be the same." He made up his mind to abandon the boy, and calling Nakamitsu, he spoke: "Hello there, Nakamitsu. It seems that Shintoku has contracted a horrible disease. I know it's sad, but I want you to go off and abandon him somewhere." Nakamitsu listened to Nobuyoshi's words. "Even though it's your command," he said, "his mother asked me with her dying breath to look after him. Please excuse me this time and send someone else instead." "So my dead wife's your master now, and not me? If you won't abandon him when I tell you to, I'll have nothing more to do with you, either!"

Nakamitsu humbly withdrew. Loitering in an inner room, he fretted in a manner that was most affecting to behold. "Tripped up by the salt seaweed," he muttered, "I can't go forward and I can't go back. Truly, I don't know what to do. If Shintokumaru's own father—his own flesh and blood—can have a change of heart and turn his back on the boy, then it should be easy for me, a stranger, to forsake him." He called to Shintokumaru through a sliding paper screen: "How are you, young master? Has your sickness improved? This is Nakamitsu here." "Oh, Nakamitsu," Shintokumaru said, "what a rare treat! Some terrible karma has come my way, and it's struck me with this dreadful disease. My eyes are blind, so it's like night all the time. And no one visits me because of my loathsome sores. How wonderful that you should come!"

"Master, I don't know what to say . . . ," Nakamitsu replied, fighting back his tears. He continued: "I hear that a famous priest from the capital is visiting Tennōji Temple—the place where you performed that acolyte dance. He'll preach for seven days, they say. Shall we go?" Shintokumaru spoke: "As chance would have it, tomorrow's the third anniversary of my mother's death. Let's go, then." "Yes, together," Nakamitsu agreed, and he saddled up a packhorse. Now what do you think he packed? A metal pail, a little bowl, a narrow staff, a spiral mat, and a straw hat and raincoat. He placed Shintokumaru on the horse's back, and avoiding the front gate with its many prying eyes, he led his young master out the rear.

Lord Nobuyoshi, too, was much to be pitied. As this was a final farewell, he came out as far as the gate. "So, Shintokumaru," he said, "I hear you're off to Tennōji. Hurry home soon." "Is that you, father? Forgive me for answering from up on this horse. I'll try to come right back." Seeing his son in such a miserable state, the usually sturdy Nobuyoshi was wracked with sorrow. "When he was an acolyte," he mused, "he was known in the three provinces of Izumi,

Kawachi, and Settsu for his good looks. But now, with this disgusting disease, it hurts to look at him, even on a horse."

"Listen here, Nakamitsu," Shintokumaru said, "it's been like one long night since I went blind. Tell me about the road as we travel." "This here's Takayasu Babanosaki," Nakamitsu explained, "and over there, that's Kowanomatsu." They passed through Tamakoshi, Mishi, and Kaminoshima and crossed over Saibe Bridge. Shintokumaru composed a poem:

Kizuru wo ide	Departing Kizuru,
Hagusa no tsuyu ni	our hems are soaked
suso nurete	with the Hagusa dew.
ikaga wataran	How now shall we cross
Nakagawa no hashi	the Nakagawa bridge?[18]

Continuing on through Obase, Konomura, Mount Tsukawashi, and Nishite, they soon arrived at the southern gate of Tennōji.

Nakamitsu spoke: "Well now, young master, we're too late for today's sermon, so shall we rent a room at an inn or take lodging at the temple? What's your choice?" Shintokumaru gave it some thought. "Temple rooms are for good times," he said, "and at an inn, I'd be ashamed to have everyone stare at me and laugh. Let's just spend the night praying in the *nenbutsu* hall."

Nakamitsu thought this was just as well. He led the horse to the veranda of the *nenbutsu* hall and set the boy down heavily. This was Shintokumaru's first such journey. Dazed from the rocking of the horse, he lay down to rest. And poor Nakamitsu! In the evening he talked to the boy about various things, but knowing that he would abandon him in the night, he was unable to sleep a wink. Later, kneeling beside his young master's head, he brushed back the boy's stray locks and wondered whether he should wake him to say good-bye. But that would be wrong, he decided, and feeling as though he would die from grief, he said farewell from inside his heart. "So long," he muttered and turned to leave. Yet he was again overcome with sorrow, and he returned once more. Though strong of heart, he clung to his young master and wept at the misery of this, their final separation.

---

18. *Hagusa* is both a place-name and a homonym of *hagusa* (*kusa no ha*), or "leaves of grass." The second and third lines could be read as "our hems are soaked from the dewy grass."

Eventually wresting loose the sleeves of bitter parting, Nakamitsu took up the horse's lead and prepared to go. But the horse had feelings, too, and although Nakamitsu pulled, it refused to budge. Choking back tears like the early-summer rain, Nakamitsu found himself unable to move. His woeful lament was stirring to hear! "Up until now," he cried, "I never expected to lead a horse without my master on its back." He gazed wistfully at Shintokumaru and then set out on his return. Although he hastened on his way, the journey was slow. Upon arriving in Takayasu, he met with Lord Nobuyoshi and explained how he had abandoned the boy. The pain in Nakamitsu's heart was beyond compare.

PART 3

Alas, poor Shintokumaru! Upon awaking, he called out for his attendant: "Hello there, Nakamitsu. By the cawing of the crows, it seems to be dawn. Would you bring me some water to wash with, Nakamitsu?" But as Nakamitsu had left him in the night, there was no one to answer his call. Thinking this strange, he felt about for his pillow and discovered something odd. He found a metal pail, a little bowl, a narrow staff, a spiral mat, and a straw hat and raincoat. Giving the matter some thought, he realized that he had been abandoned.

"Of all the places to leave me," he stewed, "how awful that they should have picked Tennōji! The straw hat and raincoat are for warding off the rain and dew—my father must have thought of that. The staff is for finding my way on the road, and the spiral mat, for begging alms at the stables—this must be what Nakamitsu meant. With the little bowl, my stepmother must be telling me to go out and beg in the seven settlements around Tennōji. But I won't—I'll starve before I do!" Stoic as a holy man, he stood firm in his resolve.

Feeling sorry for his special ward, the Kiyomizu Kannon appeared to Shintokumaru in a dream. "Dear Shintoku," he said, "your disease doesn't spring from within—it comes from someone's curse. Now go out and beg in the streets to sustain your life," and he vanished without a trace.

Shintokumaru awoke. "What a wondrous revelation!" he thought. "If I had spoken badly of my father and taken up begging without falling ill first, then I would certainly have had reason to feel ashamed. But if I beg now, the dishonor would be my father's, for it was he who abandoned me when I was ailing. I'll do as I'm told and beg." Donning his straw hat and raincoat, Shintokumaru

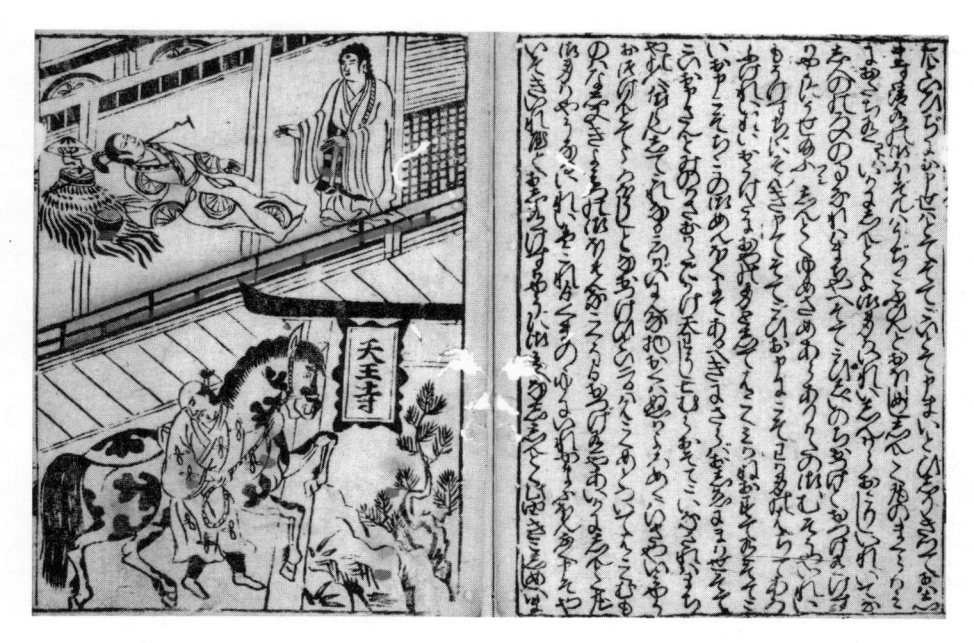

Top, The Kiyomizu Kannon appears to Shintokumaru in a dream; *bottom,* Nakamitsu sets out from Tennōji Temple. From *Sekkyō Shintokumaru* (1648 woodblock-printed edition). (Courtesy of Tenri University Library)

begged in the seven settlements around Tennōji. The city people stared. "Do you think that beggar wants something to eat?" they asked. "Look at how he staggers! Let's give him a name!" and they called him Yoroboshi, "the staggering priest." The people took care of him for a day or two, but after that, no one did anything.

The Kiyomizu Kannon spoke to Shintokumaru from the sky: "Hello there, Shintokumaru. Your kind of disease can be cured in the Kumano hot springs. Hurry to Kumano and bathe." Having delivered this instruction, he disappeared into the air.

"That must have been my guardian deity, the Kiyomizu Kannon," Shintokumaru thought, and he bowed down three times and prayed to the sky. He then set out from Tennōji, just as he had been told, inquiring the way to Kumano for a hot-spring cure. And through what places do you think he made his way? Hastening past the hundred acres of Abeno, he asked the road ahead;

bowing down to pray at the four shrines of Sumiyoshi—again asking the way—he soon reached the beach at Sakai. He gazed far into the west at Ishizunawate, his heart filled with sadness at the splashing sounds of the fishermen's nets. Pressing on through Ōtori, Shinoda, and the flourishing Yunokuchi, he stopped to rest at a Jizō hall at the Kogi estate.

The Kiyomizu Kannon disguised himself as a pilgrim, approached Shintokumaru, and spoke: "Hello there, invalid! The rich man who lives here gives alms to beggars like you. Go receive some charity and prolong your life," and he casually walked on. "I think I will," Shintokumaru thought, and he hurried forward, not realizing that this was the home of Otohime, with whom he had exchanged letter vows of love. He crossed the pontoon bridge and slipped into the great garden. "Something to eat, please, for an invalid on his way to Kumano," he begged. There was someone there who recognized him from before. "Hey everyone," the person said, "that's Shintokumaru, the son of Lord Nobuyoshi in Takayasu in Kawachi Province—the one who sent the letter to our Otohime! Look at his sores . . . what kind of karma could've done that?"

Even though Shintokumaru's eyes were blind, his ears were sharp. Humiliated, he headed out the front gate. His bitter complaints were moving to hear! "Of all afflictions," he cried to himself, "blindness is the worst. It's because I'm blind that I'm so needlessly shamed. Now even if I do get a cure at the Kumano springs, I'll never wash away this humiliation. I'll go back to Tennōji, and even if people give me food, I'll turn it down. I'll starve!" Shintokumaru struggled back to Tennōji from the Kogi estate and crawled under the veranda of the recitation hall to die. The pain in his heart was beyond description.

Three days later, Otohime's attendants told her about everything that had happened. "Shintokumaru," they said, "the son of Lord Nobuyoshi in Takayasu in Kawachi Province—the one who sent you that letter—he's become a disgusting invalid, and he came here begging for alms." "Oh, you ladies," Otohime said, "so it's true what I heard about him losing his mother, being cursed by his stepmother with a horrible disease, and being abandoned at Tennōji. He must have been looking for me the other day, and he must think I was laughing at him with you! Ah, the resentment he must feel."

Utterly beside herself, Otohime approached her father and mother. "Dear Father," she cried, "I've heard that Lord Shintoku is wandering the provinces as a repulsive leper. Please give me leave to find him. Please, Father and Mother, please!" "Here now, Otohime," the father said, "what do you mean, going to look for him after a promise in a single letter? I won't allow it for a minute."

Otohime whimpered: "Father, what a foolish thing to say! Even couples who've been together till they're eighty, ninety, or a hundred years old—they grieve when death pulls them apart. So think how much worse it is for me and Shintoku, who've had less time together than the dew on a flower! I didn't make a promise to stick by him in the good times and run away in the bad. It's staying together in the bad times that makes a couple what they are. Please, Father and Mother, please let me go for a little while!"

Otohime's mother spoke: "If that's the way you feel, then let's just send someone to look instead." "Oh, Mother," Otohime said, "if it doesn't affect them personally, they won't look their hardest. Please let me go . . . I have to find my husband!" And she collapsed on a sickbed of love. Otohime's older brother, Tarō, approached his parents and spoke: "Listen, Father. Otohime looks like she'll die from longing. They say that when people part in life, they can still meet again, but when they part in death, they never can. So please, Father and Mother, please let her go."

The mother spoke to Otohime: "If this is how it is," she said, "then whether you find him or not, be sure to send us news." She took out some gold coins she had stored away and handed them to her daughter. Otohime hung them around her neck, next to her skin. She prepared to set out on her search but then stopped: she had heard that she was beautiful, so thinking to alter her appearance, she put a simple sleeveless frock on her back and took up a sheaf of temple bills.[19] Having adopted a pilgrim's garb, she ventured out from the Kogi estate.

She passed through Shimoizumi and Ōtori in Shitachi, and even though she looked for her beloved in the three hamlets of Yamanaka, there was no sign of him at all. She searched at Kawanabe and Ichiba in Kii Province but again not a trace. She begged passage in a boat across the Ki River. "Have you come across a crippled acolyte on this sea road?" she asked a passing traveler. The person replied, "I don't care if he's your friend or your brother—I'm not keeping an eye out for him." These were cruel, disheartening words. She asked because she had to, and the insensitivity of those who would not help her was hard to bear.

Hastening on in tears, she soon arrived at Fujishiro Pass. She sat down to rest. Someone on his way to Kumano had tried to paint the surrounding scenes,

---

19. Temple bills (*fuda*) are small, personal labels that pilgrims pasted on the gates and pillars of temples and shrines.

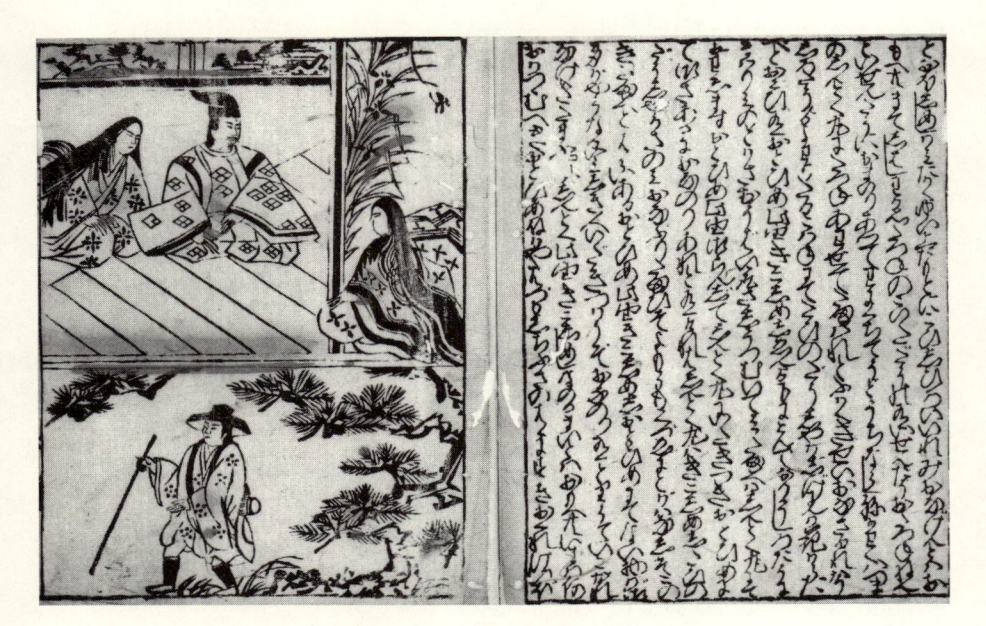

Top, Otohime pleads with her parents; *bottom*, Otohime sets out in disguise. From *Sekkyō Shintokumaru* (1648 woodblock-printed edition). (Courtesy of Tenri University Library)

and unable to depict the feelings in his heart, he had cast away his brush, which is why the tree there is called the "discarded-brush pine."[20] But for Otohime, without Shintokumaru, not even this was of interest. "Oh, how I miss my husband!" she cried. "And after all this searching, not a single trace! He must have taken it hard when he heard the ladies laughing, and gone and drowned himself somewhere. He probably thinks I was laughing with them. He must hate me for it!" Overwrought, she decided against visiting Kumano. "I'll return to the Kogi estate," she thought, "and find him from there, even if it kills me." Thinking to hold memorial services or to join him herself, she plodded back from Fujishiro. But though she searched here and there, she found no sign of her beloved.

20. The painter is said to have been Kose no Kanaoka, founder of the Kose school of painting in the latter half of the ninth century.

If she were to return to her father, Otohime thought, he was unlikely to give her leave again, so passing by her home, she continued on to the Kamigata region. As she gazed far into the west, her heart was filled with sadness at the splashing sounds of the fishermen's nets. She searched on and on, longing for her husband, yet she could not find a clue. She visited Sumiyoshi Shrine, and where, there, do you think she looked? In the recessed hall of the four deities and under the arched bridge as well—but there was no sign of her husband. Continuing past the hundred acres of Abeno, she soon arrived at Tennōji Temple, where she looked in the Golden Hall, the Lecture Hall, the Six Hours Hall, and even the waters of the Turtle Well—but all to no avail.

She climbed on top of the stone stage where Shintokumaru had performed the acolyte dance and longed for him anew. Never again would she return to Izumi Province, she thought. Rather, she would cast herself into the lotus pond below. After tying up her hair, she filled her sleeves with gravel and prepared to jump. She paused, however, when she remembered that there was still one more place left to search. Proceeding to the Recitation Hall, she rattled the sacred summoning bell. "Please let me find my husband, Shintokumaru," she earnestly prayed.

A weak voice called out from behind the hall: "Pilgrim, farmer, please give me alms." Otohime leaped from the veranda, circled to the back of the hall, and snatched away the beggar's straw hat and raincoat. It was Shintokumaru. Taking him in her arms, she said, "It's me, Otohime! Tell me your name!" "Pilgrim," Shintokumaru said, "don't tease me like that! It's no crime for a blind man to hit someone with his stick, so just back off." He drove her away with his staff. "But I'm Otohime! Who else would hug a wretch like you? Tell me your name," she cried, weeping bitter, copious tears.

Although at first he had thought to deny his identity, Shintokumaru knew now that he had nothing to conceal. "Oh, Otohime," he confessed, "I'm so ashamed! My mother died and my stepmother cursed me with this awful disease. Parents are supposed to be kind, but my cold-blooded father dumped me at Tennōji. I heard that the Kumano hot springs would do me good, so I was on my way there when I accidentally begged at your house. But this miserable blindness! The women there were laughing at me, and I was so ashamed, I made up my mind to starve. Yet my life won't end, and now on top of it all, I've met you, too! Ah, the humiliation! Please go away."

"If I didn't intend to be with you," Otohime replied, "then why do you think I came all this way?" She lifted Shintokumaru up on her back and carried him into town. All the people stared, touched by the sight. She took out the coins her mother had given her and exchanged them for rice. "Listen, Shintokumaru," she said, nursing him all the while, "I hear you're the special ward of the Kiyomizu Kannon. Let's go visit him together," and as husband and wife, they set out for the capital. Through what places did they pass? Crossing Nagara Bridge, they inquired the way ahead; past Ōta station and the dusty course of the Akuta River, again they asked the way. Still deep in the night at high-moon Takatsuki—"and where does that high moon set?"—"at Takara Temple in Yamazaki!" Bowing down to pray at Sekido Hall, pressing on past Autumn Mountain and the Toba Lovers' Tomb,[21] they hurried on their way. In no time at all, they arrived at Kiyomizu Temple in the eastern hills.

They proceeded to Otowa Falls and purified themselves thirty-three times.[22] Later, approaching the Holy Presence, they rattled the sacred summoning bell and made a reverent supplication: "Hail most merciful Kannon! We hear that Shintokumaru is your special ward. Please cure him of this disease!" They passed the evening in prayer. In the dead of night, the Kiyomizu Kannon emerged wavering from his inner sanctum. He stood before Otohime and spoke:

"Dear Otohime—since the distant past, people have called on me to do various things. Shintokumaru's stepmother came and hammered eighteen nails in my Holy Presence—135 nails at shrines and sanctuaries throughout the capital—so don't blame me.[23] When you leave here tomorrow, you'll find a feather duster on the outer temple steps. If you pull Shintokumaru upright and stroke him with it from top to bottom and bottom to top, chanting 'What joy, a cure!' his illness is sure to be overcome." The bodhisattva vanished without a trace.

Otohime jumped up with a start. "What a marvelous dream revelation!" she cried, and she bowed down before the altar three times to pray. Upon taking their leave, they found the feather duster on the outer temple steps. They carried it with them to a simple shack, where Otohime lifted Shintokumaru to his feet. Chanting the invocation, she brushed him with it three times, from top to bottom and bottom to top. One hundred thirty-five nails sprang from

---

21. The Lovers' Tomb, or *koizuka*, is the grave of Lady Kesa (Kesa *gozen*) in Kyoto's Toba district, now Fushimi-ku.

22. Thirty-three times for the thirty-three manifestations of Kannon.

23. According to part 2, the stepmother hammered 136 nails.

Shintokumaru's sores, and he was restored to his former self. Overjoyed, Otohime took him in her arms; their delight was truly without measure. Husband and wife, they returned to the Holy Presence and paid obeisance thirty-three times. Finally bidding farewell to the Kiyomizu Kannon, they left to take up temple lodgings.

Back in Kawachi Province, Lord Nobuyoshi had come to a grievous pass. "Abhor another and you yourself shall be abhorred," people say, as half our malice springs back on ourselves. The stepmother's looks remained unaffected, but not those of the Nobuyoshi lord. To everyone's dismay, his eyes were completely crushed, and even his servants fled as they would. Destitute and forsaken, he found himself unable to stay in Takayasu, and he left to wander in Tanba Province.

Word of these events spread to Izumi Province. Hearing all that had happened, Lord Kageyama approached his son, Tarō, and spoke: "Listen, Tarō. I hear that Shintokumaru's been healed and that he's in the capital. Why don't you get together a group from our province and escort him here." "Yes, sir," Tarō replied. After preparing his retinue, he set off for the capital. As he hurried on his way, he soon met Shintokumaru at Sakai Bay. Exceptionally pleased, he provided him with a horse, and Otohime with a wickerwork palanquin. Accompanied by a train of attendants, he sped them to Izumi Province amid great clamor and excitement.

They soon arrived at the Kogi estate, where Lord Kageyama was pleased to meet with Shintokumaru. Weeping for joy, Otohime's mother approached her daughter and spoke: "I was so worried for you on your woeful journey! People always say that tears are for the good times as well as the bad. Mine are for my happiness at seeing you again." Her appearance at that moment was beyond compare.

"When I was blind," Shintokumaru said, "some people treated me kindly. If I knew who they were, I would certainly pay them back, but I can't recognize them now." Unsure who had helped him, Shintokumaru handed out many treasures, and for seven days he distributed alms at Abeno Plain. News of this spread to Tanba Province.[24] Not realizing that the almsgiver was his son, Lord

---

24. The final portion of the 1648 *Shintokumaru* has been lost. The following sentences are thus translated from the last two pages of the Urokogataya *Shintokumaru*, published in Edo around the Tenna and Jōkyō eras (1681–1688).

Nobuyoshi set out from Nosenosato with his wife and Little Jirō to receive a handout. Upon reaching the distribution place, he began to shout: "We're exhausted and nearly starved! Please give us alms."

The attendants from the Kageyama mansion spotted him at once. "Look what's become of the wealthy Lord Nobuyoshi from Takayasu in Kawachi!" they cried, and burst into laughter. Nobuyoshi heard their jeers. "I shouldn't have come," he thought, "—not for this misery," and he turned to flee. Shintokumaru jumped down from his dais and ran to his father's side. "It's me, Father . . . Shintoku," he said, taking Nobuyoshi in his arms. Weeping all the while, he took out the feather duster and pressed it to his father's eyes. Chanting, "What joy, a cure!" he brushed him with it three times. Nobuyoshi's eyes, which had been completely crushed, were immediately restored, to his immense delight.

At this most joyous time, Shintokumaru beckoned to his men. "Take the wife and Little Jirō and give them their leave," he said. "Yes, sir," the men replied, and they led them off to the tribunal, where they cut off their heads and threw them away. The young master returned with his father to Kawachi, and there they built a great many mansions, all in a row. For Shintokumaru's mother, they built pagodas on mountain peaks and temple halls in valleys, floated ships on great rivers and laid bridges over streams, and commissioned countless monks to perform services for her speedy enlightenment. Theirs was a most unusual fate, touching to all!

Oguri

PART 1

Now the tale that I tell concerns Lord Oguri Hōgan, son of a Second Avenue chamberlain.¹ This Oguri Hōgan was a child of the Shō Hachiman Shrine in Sunomata Village in the Anpachi district of Mino Province.² He was born in the tenth month of his mother's pregnancy and raised by six nannies and six nurses, for a total of twelve doting attendants.

The years quickly passed, and Oguri was soon seventeen. With the strength of seventy-five men, he was unlike any human being. He took a bride, but complaining that her fair skin made her look like a daughter of the Snow

---

Translated from the seventeenth-century Tenri University Library *Oguri nara ehon*.

1. Second Avenue in the Kyoto capital. The title *hōgan* (also *hangan*) designates a lieutenant in the Imperial Police.

2. Sunomata Village in contemporary Gifu Prefecture, on the outskirts of Nagoya. According to the *Oguri emaki*, Oguri was born as a result of his parents' prayers to the statue of Bishamonten at Kurama Temple, near Kyoto. He then became a godson of the bodhisattva Shō Hachiman at the age of eighteen. See SNKBT 90:161, 164.

Woman,³ he sent her back. Then saying that a dark-skinned girl looked like Benkei's baby,⁴ he sent her away, too. He married a tall girl, but claiming that she was the child of a deep-mountain tree, he also turned her out. Next he said that a short girl was like a daughter of "Little One-Inch" Issun Bōshi,⁵ and he returned her as well. He had soon rejected seventy-five brides, yet he still lacked a wife. Hearing tell of his son's behavior, Oguri's father, Lord Kaneie, declared that Oguri could no longer stay in his stately home, and he banished him to Hitachi Province.⁶ It was thus that poor Oguri came to live in Hitachi.

One time a peddler visited him and spoke: "Hello, Master Oguri! I hear that you have no wife with you in your mansion. But over in the mountains in Sagami Province, there's a man named Lord Yokoyama with five children, both boys and a girl. He has a single daughter, and because she was born in response to his prayers to the shining sun and moon, a diviner named her Terute-no-hime, 'Shining Sky Girl,' when he came and divined. Lord Yokoyama has been raising her with the utmost care. Her looks have all the thirty-two signs of feminine beauty. You should wed a young lady like that."

Oguri listened. "Then whoever's daughter she is," he announced, "I'll make her my wife!" And without having seen her, he fell sick with love, instantly engulfed in a darkness of desire. The peddler was overjoyed. "Well, Master Oguri," he said, "if that's the way you feel, then I can help ease your longing. Please compose a letter, and I'll see that it's delivered." Oguri was exceptionally pleased. "In that case," he replied, "I suppose I should. Deliver it well, Gotōzaemon."

Upon accepting Oguri's letter, the peddler placed it securely inside a compartment of his wicker trunk and prepared to take his leave. Oguri watched. "Wait a moment, Gotōzaemon," he said, and he presented him with ten rolls of cloth and a thousand *ryō* of gold.⁷ "This is for coming to see me." The peddler was delighted, and shouldering his wooden pack, he set out from Hitachi.

---

3. The Snow Woman is a famous ghost with a snow-white face, white robes, and icy skin who haunts the falling snow.

4. Benkei was Minamoto no Yoshitsune's legendary warrior-monk companion, known for his dark complexion.

5. "Little One-Inch" is a famous character in medieval fiction known for his brave heart and miniature size.

6. Hitachi Province is now Ibaraki Prefecture in the east.

7. An exceptionally generous gift, considering that the four travelers in *Sanshō Dayū* were sold for a total of only five *kan*, the equivalent of two-and-a-half *ryō* of gold. According to the *Oguri emaki*, Oguri gave the peddler ten *ryō* rather than a thousand. See SNKBT 90:172.

Hastening on his way, the peddler quickly came to Lord Yokoyama's province. He strode in through the outer gate, whereupon a guard stopped him, saying, "No travelers allowed inside. I can't let you through." Gotōzaemon immediately dropped his wooden pack. He produced a hundred folding fans from inside his wicker trunk, and calling them a "seasonal gift," he offered them to the men on duty. "It says on the placard that it's strictly forbidden," the men all said, "but since you're a peddler, you can go in."

Gotōzaemon was immensely pleased. Making his way to the northwest women's quarters, he stepped into the kitchen and announced, "I'm a salesman from the capital! I've got makeup and medicine, rolls of cloth and woven silk! Aloeswood, musk, brick tea, and *tōchinkō*, *sai*, and *taishi* incense! Lipstick, face powder, eyebrow pencils, tooth-blackening trays and dyes, combs, hairpins, and various other items!"

Hearing his cries, the women said, "Come here, peddler." Gotōzaemon set down his wicker trunk and produced Oguri's letter. "Listen, ladies," he began. "I picked up this bit of writing outside your gate. You can use it for calligraphy practice if it's good, or if not, you can tear it up and throw it away with the garden waste."

"Your being a peddler and not trying to sell us stuff—what a funny thing to say!" the women exclaimed. They unfolded the letter and took a look. "It doesn't appear to be poetry," they said, "or any kind of ancient verse. Why, it's not written in any of the six poetic styles!" And with that, they all burst out laughing.

Now from behind her single-layered curtain, Terute-no-hime could hear the other women carrying on. "Hello, you all," she called out. "What are you laughing about? If it's something amusing, then please tell me, too."

"It's nothing very interesting," the women replied. "This peddler has brought us a letter that was left out on the road. He said to use it for writing practice if it's good, and then he just gave it to us. We opened it for a look, and since we couldn't make any sense of it, we all started laughing."

"If it's a funny sort of riddle, then I'll enjoy it, too."

"Yes, my lady," the women replied, and they presented it to their mistress. Terute-no-hime quickly opened it and stared. "Well, everyone, how about that!" she exclaimed. "It's just as they say—you can know a thousand things, but you can't know everything. Let me read it aloud for you." Terute-no-hime pored over the writing. "It may not be murder with a knife or a sword," she thought, "but this is how you do someone in with a letter!"

She began by praising the brushwork on the wrapping. "Whoever could have written this? He must have studied the style of the bodhisattva Mañjuśrī or maybe the hand of Kūkai on Mount Kōya.[8] The touch is exquisite, and the calligraphy outstanding." She continued to scrutinize the letter. "The first words are 'a short sash.' I wonder how we should read this? Maybe as 'someday we shall be tied together, this love to be fulfilled.' 'The boat in the offing'—this may mean 'when will I reach the shore?'[9] The third thing written here is 'the eulalia grass in the fields'; this seems to be 'someday it will go to seed, and we'll bend together when we meet.' The fourth phrase is 'the pure waters of the open field.' Perhaps we should read this as 'tell no one of this love—just keep it to yourself.' I won't bother reading it all. But there's something written here at the end: 'The one who loves is Lord Oguri of Hitachi Province. And the one who's loved is . . . I.'"

Suddenly anxious, Terute-no-hime beckoned Jiju-no-mae and spoke: "Oh, Jiju, listen. Don't have anything more to do with that man who delivered this note. If my father finds out, he'll punish us all." "How could I have shown you that letter without knowing what it was?" Jiju replied. "Next time I'll be more careful."

Later, Gotōzaemon called for Jiju-no-mae. "So, ladies," he said, addressing the group of women, "won't you give me a reply?" "Who ever heard of answering a letter left out on the road?" Jiju retorted. Gotōzaemon glared at her menacingly. "Use that as an excuse and you'll be reborn as a duck or a broiled clam, or maybe an animal or a paving stone on the Kamakura highway."

Being a woman, Jiju took him at his word. She went to her mistress and said, "Excuse me, my lady. The peddler asked me for a reply, and when I said that we didn't answer messages left out on the road, he threatened me, saying that people who don't send responses are reborn as beasts and birds, demons, trees, and stones. So won't you please compose a reply?"

Terute-no-hime considered. "In that case," she said, "it wouldn't be so hard to send a message." She took out paper and an inkstone. After folding a double sheet of light *torinoko* paper in the *yamagata* style, she ground some ink, wet her brush, and composed a letter in the vernacular. "You and I have never even

---

8. Both Mañjuśrī and Kūkai are famous for their writing. For a story of their legendary calligraphy competition in India, see *Karukaya*.

9. In the *Oguri emaki*, Terute-no-hime explains this as "I'm burning with love, so bring me to shore." The riddle depends on the similarity of the verbs *kogu* (to row) and *kogaru* (to burn with love).

met," she wrote. "But your 'short sash' must mean that 'someday we shall be tied together, this love to be fulfilled.' By the 'boat in the offing,' you mean 'when will I reach the shore?' By the 'eulalia grass in the fields,' you must be saying that 'someday it will go to seed, and we'll bend together when we meet.' With the 'pure waters of the open field,' you mean 'tell no one of this love—just keep it in your own pure heart alone.' I understand all the rest of your allusions, too. If word of this were to get out and reach my father, Lord Yokoyama, he'd have you exiled or killed, and there would be nothing I could do." Having thus set down her thoughts at length, Terute-no-hime bound her missive in the *yamagata* style and entrusted it to Jiju-no-mae, who passed it on to the peddler.

Gotōzaemon was overjoyed. He placed the letter inside a compartment of his wicker trunk and hurried back to Hitachi Province, arriving there in no time at all. Visiting Oguri at his mansion, he said, "Hello, Master Oguri, I've brought an answer to your epistle," and handed him the message. Oguri opened it and read. He was exceptionally pleased. "If that's how she feels," he declared, "then I'll visit her as her groom!"[10]

Oguri selected the hundred best warriors from among his thousand men, high and low alike. Then from among those hundred, he chose the very best ten to accompany him on his journey. Dressed more splendidly than ever, he wore a brilliant yellow *suikan* jacket over a colorful small-sleeved robe, a jeweled crown, and, at his waist, an heirloom sword by the name of First Demon. Even his ten retainers were dressed as handsomely as flowers. Eager to be on his way, he swiftly set out from his mansion, and because he hurried, he soon arrived at Lord Yokoyama's province.

As soon as they saw Oguri, the men on duty outside Lord Yokoyama's gate confronted him, saying, "Whoever you are, you can't come inside." Oguri glowered at them, daggers in his eyes. "He's not like any ordinary man," the guards whispered among themselves, frightened by his fury. "How terrifying!" One of the men found his voice. Speaking with an indifferent air, he said, "Whether or not you come in, it's no business of ours."

Being the fiercest man in the land, Oguri smashed the "no entry" placard and pushed his way inside. He made his way to the northwest women's

---

10. Oguri is encouraged by Terute-no-hime's interpretations of his riddles. In the *Oguri emaki*, he concludes that if she herself is amenable to marriage, her family's approval is not important. See SNKBT 90:178.

Oguri celebrates his marriage to Terute-no-hime. From *Oguri* (seventeenth-century *nara ehon*). (Courtesy of Tenri University Library)

quarters, where he and his bride exchanged nuptial cups. Afterward, the saké circulated among the guests, who sang and danced with a boisterous clamor.

Lord Yokoyama's heir was named Saburō,[11] and when Saburō heard the sounds of singing and carousing, he thought it awfully strange. Approaching his father, he said, "Excuse me, sir, but what's happening in the northwest women's quarters? There's a rowdy party going on over there. It's suspicious." "Well, Saburō, go and find out," Yokoyama said.

Saburō strode into the women's quarters. Peering into the reception room through a gap between some doors, he saw ten warriors dressed as handsomely as flowers. He beckoned to Jiju-no-mae and said, "Tell me, Jiju, who is that in there?"

"Why, that's Lord Oguri of Hitachi," the serving woman replied. "He introduced himself with a letter, and now he's pushed his way into our mansion and taken my lady as his wife."

---

11. According to the *Oguri emaki*, Saburō was the third son and Ietsugu was the heir. The narrator of the 1675 *Oguri Hangan* identifies Shinzaemon as the heir. See SNKBT 90:182 and SSS 2:60b.

Saburō returned to his father. "Excuse me, sir," he reported, "but the person throwing the party in the northwest women's quarters seems to be a man named Oguri from Hitachi Province. He's forced his way in and married our Terute."

"What a hateful situation!" Yokoyama exclaimed. "However fierce that man may be, how dare he burst in here and marry my daughter without even asking me first! If that's how it is, I'll send him a message at the women's quarters." And as his envoy, he sent Saburō.

Receiving Yokoyama's message, Oguri said, "I was planning on paying my formal respects to my father-in-law, but to think that he's sent you, Lord Saburō, to greet me instead! What a wonderful honor! I'll go and see him right away."

Saburō returned to his father and spoke: "Listen, sir, you can't cut down a great savage scoundrel like him with a knife or a sword. You'll have to trick him and kill him." "Good thinking, Saburō!" Yokoyama cried. "In that case, hurry up and call him here to meet me."

Saburō returned to the northwest women's quarters. "Come along quickly," he instructed. "My father will see you now."

Oguri changed his clothes and went to see the master. "Hello, Lord Yokoyama!" he began. "I had been planning to come and see you before your messenger arrived. But I was so happy when you sent your man to *me*!"

Since Yokoyama intended to deceive his guest, he regaled him with a lavish banquet of delicacies from the land and sea and a variety of local sweets. He served him an assortment of saké, both pouring for Oguri and receiving cups poured in return. Once when the saké had passed back to Yokoyama, Oguri got up to dance a piece called "The Crane's Waving Wings." Saburō seized the chance to speak: "Listen, Master Oguri, my father doesn't care for that sort of thing. If you want to entertain us, then we've got a warhorse here at the house and you can show us how you ride." Oguri wanted to say that it would be no fun by himself, but because this was his first meeting with his father-in-law, it would disgrace Oguri as a samurai not to oblige.

Oguri summoned the stable master and examined the horses. Being an accomplished warrior, Yokoyama had forty-eight famous steeds tethered in a row. Oguri looked them over and announced that not a single one was right for him to ride. "In that case," the stable master said, "we've got a horse called Onikage, 'Demon Bay,' over in the fields about a half mile from here. You can ride him." "Fine," Oguri replied, "I'll ride your horse," and he set out for the fields.

Oguri watched as they walked. Rather than letting him ride the horse, his hosts looked as if they were going to trick and kill him. The stable master spoke:

"Our Demon Bay feasts on men. Just look inside his pen!" Oguri saw new and old human bones scattered around like divination sticks. "Well, even if he eats people," Oguri said, "he won't eat me."

Oguri's ten retainers addressed their master: "If you ride this horse, sir, you're sure to be killed. If that were to happen, then the ten of us would take turns cutting off its head. We'd see that you were avenged, but we'd rather not if it means that you would be dead." The men spoke with powerful determination.

Thinking that such a ferocious beast must also be clever, Oguri decided to reason with it before riding. "Hello there, Demon Bay," he said. "If you're a living being, too, then listen up to what I say. Other horses are sometimes tethered outside temple gates, where they can hear sermons and preaching. But because you eat people, you're tied up in a horrible pen like this. So what do you think is going to become of you in the next life? If you'll let me ride you this one time, I'll build a golden buddha hall at the foot of Mount Fuji for you when you're dead. I'll have your body encased in pure lacquer, and everyone will worship you as the Horse-Headed Kannon.[12] You know, oxen are worshipped as manifestations of Dainichi Buddha." Because the horse, too, was a living being, it knelt down before him, all but saying, "Climb on." By convincing it with reason, persuading it to bow, Oguri had achieved an impressive feat.

"Now I'll show that animal what I can do!" Oguri thought to himself. He placed his hand on the grating of the horse's pen and surveyed his surroundings. The stable was a fright. Camphor pillars ten arm spans in circumference were planted on all four sides. The ridgepoles were zelkova, eight arm spans around, and Demon Bay was tethered by five sets of chains, each of which was three feet in circumference. Examining the grating, Oguri saw that it was made of iron beams six inches thick.[13]

Being the fiercest man in the land and saying that he would show that horse what he could do, Oguri seized the grating, ripped it into pieces and stood them in a corner. He threw a horse blanket and a bridle onto Demon Bay and then, with a single yank, tore loose the fastening chains and tied them into a set of reins.

Oguri was ready to ride, but thinking that a horse like that ought to be praised, he decided to tell it its virtues first. "Your eyes are like the setting moon," he cooed, "and your bangs are like rich rice ears waving in the wind in

---

12. Batō Kannon, one of the six principal forms of the bodhisattva Kannon.

13. According to the circa 1711 to 1736 *Oguri no Hangan*, there was also an opening in the ceiling for dropping people inside, in order to feed the horse. See SSS 2:87b.

the eighth month in autumn.¹⁴ Your ears are shaped like the eight scrolls of the Lotus sutra, and your four feet are like the faces of *go* boards. Your tail is like a leafy weeping willow that's turned to the wind in the third month in spring. What a lovely horse!"

Striking the beast with a secret riding crop, Oguri raced this way and that through the half mile of fields, after which he galloped into Yokoyama's courtyard. From among all the family and retainers who had gathered there to watch, Oguri summoned Saburō. "Since I'm already riding around," he said, "I'll do whatever tricks you like."

Saburō took out a twelve-rung ladder and leaned it against the side of the northwest women's quarters. "Well, Lord Oguri," he said, "try riding up this." "I've done that kind of thing before," Oguri thought, and striking his secret crop, he gingerly rode up the ladder with a clippity-clop, clippity-clop. He galloped this way and that on the roof of the women's quarters, and then rode back down, head first.

"What's next?" he asked. Saburō took out two or three sliding paper doors studded with needles and aligned them on the ground. "Try riding over these," he said. "That's easy, too," Oguri thought, and without even tearing the paper, he rode over the sliding doors, clippity-clop, clippity-clop, showing his steed where to step.

"Anything else, Lord Saburō?" Oguri asked. Saburō took out a single *go* board. "Up here, up here," he snapped. "All right," Oguri thought, and he stepped onto the *go* board, clippity-clop, clippity-clop, so that all four of his horse's hooves were balanced on the square.

"Anything else, Lord Saburō?" Oguri asked. Yokoyama and his family and retainers all curled their tongues in awe. Taking in the sight, Oguri repeated his question: "So, Lord Saburō, any more requests?" But no one made the least reply.

Boasting all the while,¹⁵ Oguri rode Demon Bay into the inner garden and tethered him to an old cherry tree, eight arm spans around. Then he sat back

---

14. This is the eighth month according to the lunar calendar.

15. In the 1675 text, Oguri asks Yokoyama, "Why did you name such a gentle horse 'Demon Bay'? You should give me five or ten such steeds as a wedding present. I'll take them back to Hitachi and have my men ride them around the garden." See SSS 2:64a. In the *Oguri emaki*, Oguri offers to break in Yokoyama's other horses for him, too. See SNKBT 90:192.

Oguri rides Demon Bay on a *go* board. From *Oguri* (seventeenth-century *nara ehon*). (Courtesy of Tenri University Library)

down in the reception room and let out a thunderous laugh. Demon Bay took affront at the sound. He wrenched the old cherry tree up by its roots and bolted this way and that. Seeing what had happened, the people all scattered like a bunch of baby spiders, shouting, "Demon Bay broke free! We're all doomed if he runs loose! I don't want to die!" Soon there was no one to be seen for three leagues in all four directions.

Yokoyama surveyed the situation. "Indeed," he said, "if Demon Bay escapes from here, I won't have anyone living in my domain anymore. We'll have to calm him down somehow and tie him up again." But no one would go near the beast.

Deciding to entreat his son-in-law, Yokoyama said, "Listen, Lord Oguri. Won't you please tie up that horse for us?" After answering that he would, Oguri approached Demon Bay and chanted the brush-tethering invocation.[16]

---

16. A magical incantation for tethering horses on treeless plains.

The animal stopped in its tracks, whereupon Oguri climbed on its back and rode it into its usual pen. He tied it up as it had been before and reattached the grating and the gate bar. Then he said, "Well, Demon Bay, I'll be taking my leave now. So long." And with that, he returned to Yokoyama's mansion.

Back inside the house, Oguri made his way to the northwest women's quarters. But alas, poor Oguri's luck had reached its end, because Saburō had hatched a frightening plan. He had tried and failed to kill Oguri with the horse, and now he approached his father and spoke: "Excuse me, sir, but I have an idea. The day after tomorrow, let's pretend to throw a party for Lord Oguri. We'll put up a model Mount Hōrai.[17] You should send a messenger to invite our guest." "Good thinking, Saburō!" Yokoyama cried.

Having received his father's consent, Saburō went to see Oguri. "Hello, Lord Oguri," he said. "Tomorrow, we'd like to have you come and see our model Mount Hōrai." "Since you'll be there, Lord Saburō, I'd be pleased to attend," Oguri replied. Saburō was overjoyed, and he reported the news to his father. Yokoyama, too, was immensely pleased, and he began making preparations. But let us leave him for a while.

Oguri was truly the most pitiful of all. Terute-no-hime heard word of her father and brother's plan, and she warned him, saying, "My dear husband Oguri, I'm going to speak, and I want you to listen. Please think about how my father and brother had you ride that horse yesterday." She paused. "Look, Oguri—please don't go to see their model Mount Hōrai tomorrow. I have a Chinese mirror that's been passed down to me in my family for fifty generations, and it shows that things look bad. If you don't listen to me when I tell you not to go, you'll be like the foolish summer moth that flies into a flame. There's a saying that the oil lamp shines brighter when it's about to go out and that a man loses his wits when he's about to meet his end. I think your luck's run out this time, so please, please don't attend that party tomorrow!

---

17. Meaning, "We'll hold a drinking celebration." The eighteenth-century scholar Ise Teijō explains that it was a custom at drinking parties to erect models of Mount Hōrai, the legendary island of immortals. Quoted in SNKS *Sekkyō shū*, 151n.6. In the circa 1673 and 1675 texts, Saburō proposes erecting a model of Mount Hōrai in the courtyard and then, during the ensuing festivities, poisoning Oguri and all his men. See SSS 2:384a, 64b.

"In case you're still not convinced, let me tell you about my dreams. In the first one, an eagle swept down from the sky and smashed your precious rattan bow into three pieces. It carried one of the pieces up into the heavens and another one down into the depths of hell. It set up the last piece as a memorial marker on a burial mound that was built for you on Uwano Plain. Now isn't that a bad dream to have before going to their Hōrai party? What's more, there's my Chinese mirror! When good things are going to happen, Shō Hachiman appears on the front; a crane and a turtle dance on the back; and a plover pours drinks in the middle. But Hachiman is gone now, and the crane doesn't dance. All I can see is the long dark night.[18]

"In my third dream, you were riding backward on a dappled gray horse with the saddle and stirrups set facing toward the rear. You were dressed in gray robes, and the characters for *namu* were stamped on your forehead.[19] People carried banners and baldachins to mark your passage, and a hundred monks walked ahead, leading you to your grave. I was terribly grieved and tried to follow you from behind, but I lost sight of you on Uwano Plain. If it was so disturbing in a dream, then what'll become of me if it all comes true? Please don't go to see their model Mount Hōrai!"

"Well, even if you did have such an unsettling dream," Oguri said, "just keep it to yourself. If I don't go to see their Mount Hōrai, I'll be disgraced as a samurai." And with that, he tied up the hem of his small-sleeved robe and chanted a dream-disrupting spell.

Dawn soon broke in the fifth hour of the night.[20] Oguri's ten retainers were dressed as handsomely as flowers. Not knowing that he was going to die, poor Oguri dressed more splendidly than ever, after which he and his men went to see Yokoyama. Gazing at the model Mount Hōrai, Oguri praised it, saying, "Well, how interesting!" Yokoyama, Saburō, and all their family and retainers stood shoulder to shoulder, admiring the diorama.

Soon the saké cup emerged and passed to the guests. Yokoyama offered Oguri a drink. "You'll have to excuse me," Oguri said, "but I'm abstaining for a while because of a certain tree-shrine ritual." Yokoyama protested, saying,

---

18. The long dark night of delusion, a metaphor for the darkness in which unenlightened beings transmigrate according to their karma.

19. *Namu* is a word meaning "hail," as in the *nenbutsu* invocation *Namu Amida Butsu*, "Hail Amida Buddha."

20. The fifth hour of the night is approximately 3:00 to 5:00 A.M.

"But we set up this elaborate display just for you! If you won't have a drink, then it'll all have been for naught. So do have a drink."

Saburō had stood up to pour the saké, and now saying that he remembered something, he retreated deep inside the mansion and returned with a pair of empty conch shells. He placed one in front of Oguri and the other in front of his father. Then he prepared to pour the drinks, but with a decanter that was divided on the inside. "For today's entertainment," he cried, "you two can drink together!" He filled Oguri's shell with one kind of saké, and his father's with another.

"With these conchs that we drink," Yokoyama declared, "I offer you the lands of Musashi and Sagami! Bottoms up, Oguri! We'll drink these together."

Poor Oguri! Upon swallowing the saké, he felt it penetrate his body to the core, dislocating his forty-four bones and flooding his 99,000 pores. Weakening by the moment, he realized that the saké had been poisoned. His ten retainers were likewise affected from the instant that they drank. Some fell on one another dead, while some died seizing the screen paintings behind them for support. Their bodies were soon scattered around like divination sticks.

Oguri took in the sight. "How mortifying!" he exclaimed. "It's just like you two to kill a famous samurai with poisoned wine. What a cowardly thing to do! Come out here, Yokoyama! And you, too, Saburō! We'll die together by the sword!" He untied the cord on the sheath of his dagger and quickly loosened the clasp, but his dying breath seemed to come faster than the flight of a three-feathered arrow. And thus despite his youth, he expired at the age of thirty-seven, disappearing like the morning dew.[21]

PART 2

Yokoyama was elated to have killed Oguri and his men. "Let's hurry up and see them to their graves," he said, and he did. Because Oguri had been killed according to his karma, Yokoyama had him buried in the ground. But since his ten retainers had died unjustly, he had them cremated instead.

---

21. According to the *Oguri emaki*, Oguri died at the age of twenty-one. Alternatively, the circa 1673 and 1675 texts report that he died at twenty-three. See SNKBT 90:201 and SSS 2:386b–87a, 66b.

"It's dishonorable for a samurai to kill another man's child and not kill his own," Yokoyama later said. He therefore summoned the brothers Oniō and Onitsugu and spoke: "Hello, men, listen. Oguri's dead now, so I want you to take Terute-no-hime away to Musashi Province and drown her in the Sagami River, at the Orikara Abyss."[22]

"Yes, sir," the brothers replied. After proceeding to the northwest women's quarters, they beckoned to Jiju-no-mae and spoke: "Hello, Jiju. There was an argument at yesterday's party, and Lord Oguri was killed. Terute-no-hime should prepare for the worst. She's been ordered to be drowned in the Sagami River, and we've been told to do it."

Jiju hurried to Terute-no-hime with tears in her eyes. "My lady," she said, weeping all the while, "the brothers Oniō and Onitsugu came here to report that there was an argument at yesterday's party and that Master Oguri was killed! They also came to tell you to prepare for the worst. They said that out of all the people here, they've been ordered to drown you in the Sagami River. It's sad, they say, but there's nothing they can do."

Terute-no-hime took in her attendant's words. Then she addressed the brothers, saying, "There's a time and a place for formality, but this isn't it. Come inside and explain what's going on."[23]

The brothers did as they were told. "What have we got to hide?" they began. "At yesterday's Hōrai-viewing party, Lord Yokoyama murdered your husband with poisoned saké. He killed his ten retainers in the same way, too. Then he said that it's dishonorable for a samurai to kill another man's child while saving his own, and he gave us our orders. We don't bear you any ill will, but you'll need to get ready now, quickly."

As if in a dream, Terute-no-hime retreated deep inside her rooms. Taking out a single set of small-sleeved robes with a light and dark drum-crest design, she presented it to the brothers, saying, "Please keep this as a memento." The brothers wept and accepted the gift. With tears streaming down their cheeks, they cried, "To have to drown the lady of the house that our family has served for generations! And with our own hands! Orders are orders, so there's nothing we can do. But oh, poor Terute-no-hime! Can we really take the life of such a beautiful girl?" The brothers broke down and cried all the more.

22. The Orikara Abyss is near the mouth of the river at Sagami Bay.
23. Because Terute-no-hime was the daughter of their master, Oniō and Onitsugu would normally speak to her through an intermediary.

Poor Terute-no-hime set about disposing of her possessions. "Send my twelve-compartment handbox to a mountain temple," she said, "and tell the monks to conduct services for me in the next world. I'll give my Chinese mirror to you, Jiju-no-mae. You should pray for me in the afterlife, too. Please give my crystal rosary to my mother. Be sure to tell her that although the world may be turned upside down, when she gazes out her window and sees the bamboo bent under the weight of snow, she should look on these crystal beads as a reminder of her daughter." With that, she handed the rosary to Jiju-no-mae.

Terute-no-hime later addressed the brothers, saying, "Oniō and Onitsugu, hurry up and see me to my death." "Yes, ma'am," they replied. They fashioned a barred palanquin and, bringing it to her, said, "Please get inside." Terute-no-hime did, and they set out on their way.

Because this was the end, all of Terute-no-hime's female attendants, including even the most humble, came out to say good-bye. Sixty ladies-in-waiting and eighty scullery maids mobbed the barred palanquin. Insisting on accompanying their mistress on her way, 140 of them escorted her to the river, walking to the right and left of her stern conveyance.

"My ladies and maids," Terute-no-hime said, staring out at her women, "it makes me so glad that you've come all this way! But please go back now. I'll never forget your kindness, not even in my grave."

"But we can't live on without you," the women replied. "We'd rather serve you on a lotus pedestal in the Pure Land."

"I appreciate your devotion," Terute-no-hime said. "Still, more than giving me your lives a thousand times over, I'd prefer it if you'd recite the *nenbutsu* for me one time instead."[24] Crying, "Like them or not, a master's orders can never be ignored," the women fell facedown on the beach and wept.

"We'll be rowing out into the offing now," Terute-no-hime explained. "When the men wave their torch, you'll know that I'm dead. You should recite the *nenbutsu* for me then."[25] After taking their leave, Terute-no-hime and the brothers set out on the waves.

---

24. The *nenbutsu* is the ritual invocation of the name of Amida Buddha.
25. According to the circa 1673, 1675, and circa 1711 to 1736 texts, the brothers delivered these instructions. See SSS 2:388b, 68a, 95a. According to the *Oguri emaki*, the brothers then placed the barred palanquin on a boat with Terute-no-hime still sealed inside. See SNKBT 90:203.

"Should we drown her here or there?" Oniō and Onitsugu fretted, unable to decide. The younger brother spoke: "Listen, Oniō. Poor Terute-no-hime looks so pitiful! Even if it's our lord's command, we can't just take the lady of the house that our family has served for generations and drown her in the abyss! Word might get out if we let her go, and then we'd be drowned instead, but let's save her anyway. She's like the bud of a spring blossom, ready to bloom, but we're like old flowers ready to fall. So what could be so bad about trading places? Let's just save her."

"Well put," Oniō replied. "In that case, let's do it." The brothers cut away the sinking stones and waved their torch in the air. The women watching from the shore all thought that this was the end. The sound of them chanting the *nenbutsu* was like the wailing of the fifty-two species at the death of Shakyamuni Buddha.[26]

The brothers spoke: "Excuse us, ma'am, but we feel so sorry for you that we've decided to give our lives for yours. You can drift in this boat. Then wherever you wash ashore, please live to see another day. As people say, as long as there's life, even a jellyfish can grow bones." Saying good-bye, the men pushed the craft out to sea,[27] after which they returned to Yokoyama's mansion. Such is the story of their compassion.

Alas, poor Terute-no-hime, set adrift on the waves! Bobbing and swaying in a raging ocean storm, she was eventually blown to the shore of Mutsura Bay.[28] Spying her barred palanquin, some local fisherman said, "So that's why there haven't been any fish lately! People have been floating these repulsive things in their festivals. Whack it with your oar!"

---

26. The Nirvana sutra explains that fifty-two kinds of beings gathered to mourn at the death of Shakyamuni Buddha. They included humans, animals, and a variety of mythological creatures.

27. Terute-no-hime later explains that the brothers placed her barred palanquin on a boat. According to the *Oguri emaki*, they simply set her adrift in the palanquin. See SNKBT 90:205.

28. Mutsura Bay is an inlet in the Kanazawa district of contemporary Yokohama. According to the circa 1673 and 1675 texts, Terute-no-hime washed up on the shore of Naoi Bay, the same place where Yamaoka Dayū kidnapped and sold the four travelers in *Sanshō Dayū*. See SSS 2:389b, 68b.

Terute-no-hime is set adrift on the ocean. From *Oguri* (seventeenth-century *nara ehon*). (Courtesy of Tenri University Library)

The fishermen split open the palanquin and peered inside. They saw a strikingly beautiful young lady, mired in tears. "No human woman's as lovely as that," they declared. "What are you . . . some kind of ghost or shape-shifting demon?" The girl made no reply; she only hung her head. "Then she's a shape shifter!" one of the men shouted, enraged. "Kill her!"

Terute-no-hime spoke: "No, I'm not a ghost, and I'm not a shape-shifting demon. I didn't do anything wrong, either. I was unjustly set adrift, and now I've washed up here. Whatever you do, save me, please!"

"Wicked women aren't cast out on the ocean like that for doing nothing," the fishermen agreed. "Let's just beat her to death." Among them was a man named Uragimi no Tayū, who was particularly concerned about his next-life rebirth. Upon seeing the young lady, he said, "I don't have a child, so let me adopt her, please."

"We don't mean any disrespect," the younger fishermen said, "but we can't let you have her. Let's kill her instead!" Uragimi repeated his request, saying, "Look, boys, I'll give you saké if you let me have her." The fishermen all dropped their oars and stepped out of the way. Uragimi was elated, and he quickly led Terute-no-hime to his home.

Approaching his old wife, Uragimi spoke: "I got us a child at the beach! Fix her some hot tea, quick! You've got a child, now, dear!" But the old woman was not the least bit pleased. "She'll probably have his baby," she thought, and her heart was filled with jealous hatred. After a while, she spoke: "It's crazy to take in a girl who's been blown here on the wind like that. When you adopt a child, it's supposed to be a boy you can raise to stand in for you when you need it—that's what it means to adopt. So why would you say such a thing? Not unless your feelings for me have changed . . . You know, we could sell a child like that to some slave boat for one or two *kan*. That would keep us in tea, which would be a fine thing for a daughter to do!"

"I won't fall into hell with an evil old hag like you," Uragimi rejoined. "The girl and I'll get by on people's charity instead." He hung a flat metal bell around his neck.[29] "You can have all our possessions in return for your kindness until now. Good-bye, wife." And with that, Uragimi stepped outside.

Seeing her husband leave, the old woman wondered how she might ever get along without him. "Wait, dear," she cried. "I didn't mean it! I was just saying that for fun. Please come back!" Being such a spiritual person, Uragimi took her at her word. "In that case," he said, "I will," and he foolishly returned.

"Listen, dear," the old woman said, "from now on, let's think of the girl as our adopted daughter. How does that sound?" Uragimi was exceptionally pleased, and saying that he had to make a living, he hurried back to the beach.

Later, the old woman came up with a sinister plan. "If I let that girl stay," she thought, "she's sure to take my place in the end. Men always hate dark-skinned women, so I'll see that she gets covered in soot." She chased Terute-no-hime into the loft of a salt-making shack and burned seven bundles of green pine branches below. Alas, poor Terute-no-hime! Enveloped in the piney smoke and caring nothing for her complexion, she felt her life begin to wane. But then her patron deity Shō Kannon appeared, saving her from the fumes.

As soon as the old woman saw Terute-no-hime come down from the loft, she thought to herself, "Not even brushwood smoke affects a stuck-up girl like that!" Having wasted so much effort, she devised another scheme. "Men always get tired of weepy women," she thought, "so I'll make her cry!" She found an

---

29. Such a bell is a ritual implement used by itinerant Buddhist mendicants for beating time to the *nenbutsu*.

iron needle and began pricking the girl around her hips. Poor Terute-no-hime! Stabbed here and there, she sank into a slough of tears.[30]

Feeling pity for the girl, Kannon stood in for her again, whereupon she was relieved of her pain. Taking in the sight, the old woman thought, "Whatever I do to torment her, it has no effect! It must be true that low-down women who come to steal your husband are born bold from head to toe." And with that, she took her back home.

Uragimi later returned from the beach. He purified himself by rinsing his mouth and hands, after which he entered the family buddha hall and began reciting the *nenbutsu*. "Hey, young lady," he called, "come and recite the *nenbutsu* for your next-life rebirth." Having been tortured by the old woman, Terute-no-hime could only lie in a heap, her eyes blinded by secret tears.

The old woman addressed her husband: "Instead of telling her to pray for old folks like us," she said, pretending to laugh, "you tell a young girl like that to pray for her own next-life rebirth! That's your mistake, dear."

When dawn broke in the fifth hour of the night, Uragimi set out again for the ocean. A little while later, the old woman noticed that a slave boat had come, and she immediately thought to sell the girl. "This one's for sale," she signaled to the boat, raising both hands to show a price of ten *kan*. The slave boat captain understood at once, and he raised two fingers in reply. "Even if it's for only two *kan*," the old woman thought, "I'd still like to sell her," and she did. She was pleased with the deal, but she worried what to tell her husband when he came home.

"Where's our little lady?" Uragimi called when he returned. "Come out and make me some tea!" As soon as she heard him, the old woman replied, "Hello, dear, listen. The young lady missed you when you left, so she followed you out. Do you think someone bought her and took her away?" The old woman pretended to cry.

Uragimi watched his wife as she wept. "Your tears look like tears of joy," he said. "When people cry, their tears spring from their 99,000 pores. But yours look like happy tears at having sold our girl for one or two *kan*. I won't fall into hell with an evil old hag like you! As I said before, you can have all our possessions. I'm going out to look for our girl. Wherever I end up, I intend to become a buddha there!" Having made up his mind, Uragimi left the house.

---

30. In the circa 1673 and circa 1711 to 1736 texts, the old woman tries to beat Terute-no-hime to death with a pine branch. See SSS 2:391a, 97a.

Uragimi inquired at all the inns from bay to bay. "If that's the person you're looking for," someone said, "she got sold farther on for more money." "How awful!" Uragimi exclaimed. He continued searching here and there, but he never found her. Lamenting his age, the poor man recited the *nenbutsu* for his last few times. "This first invocation I'll recite for myself," he moaned. "And this next invocation I'll recite for the young lady I'm trying to find. If she's still alive in this wretched world, then let it be a prayer for the expiation of her sins and for her peace and tranquillity. If she's dead, then let it allow her to be received into the Pure Land and reborn with me there on a single lotus blossom." With these sad words on his lips, Uragimi passed away at the age of ninety-three, vanishing like the morning dew. Such is his story.

But there was no one as pitiful as Terute-no-hime. Repeatedly sold for higher prices, she was acquired by someone in Naoi Bay in Echigo Province. It was not to be for long, though; deciding to sell her for a profit, her owner passed her on to someone in Tsuruga Bay. As her cost increased, she was sold to someone at Soto-no-hama Beach and from there to a person as far east as Hinomoto in Michinoku Province. Her price climbed from two to seventeen *kan*. Sold on and on from place to place, she was eventually bought for seventeen *kan* by the mistress of the Yorozuya Inn at the Ōhaka post station in Mino Province.[31]

The mistress was overjoyed. "I've bought the best courtesan in Japan!" she cried. "How wonderful! She'll earn a fortune for me now whether I'm sleeping or awake! Hooray!" She and her husband were boundlessly pleased.

One evening the mistress took out a set of twelve-layered robes and presented them to Terute-no-hime. "From now on," she instructed, "you're to make a living entertaining men. Please support us well!" Poor Terute-no-hime! Taking in the mistress's words, she replied, "I have a strange sickness, ma'am, and it will kill me if I touch the skin of a man. So you'll have to excuse me, but I can't possibly entertain. Please sell me someplace else before I lose my value. There's just no way that I can entertain men."

"If that's the kind of girl you are," the mistress declared, "then I'll sell you off in Awa Province! The people there'll slash the tendons in your wrists and ankles and let you live on a single cup of grain a day! You'll chase birds from the millet fields during the daytime, and at night you'll be food for sharks!

---

31. In the northwest part of contemporary Ōgaki City in Gifu Prefecture. The name Yorozuya Inn is interpolated from the *Oguri emaki* and the circa 1673, 1675, and circa 1711 to 1736 texts.

Wouldn't you rather make a living entertaining men here than be sold and suffer in a place like that? Just take your pick!"

"Even if it comes to that," Terute-no-hime replied, "—having the tendons in my wrists and ankles slashed, and becoming food for sharks—I don't mind dying, ma'am, but I won't work as a whore!"

"Well, in any case," she said, "all the girls here go by the name of their province. Where do you come from? Speak up! I paid a precious price for you, so don't think that you can go having your own way. Tell me where you're from!"

Terute-no-hime wondered: "Should I tell her I'm from Hitachi? Or should I tell her the name of my father's province? But wait—" she thought, feeling a surge of loyalty toward her husband, "if I take Oguri's province name as a part of my own, it'll be a comfort when people call for me in the mornings and evenings." She therefore replied that she came from Hitachi.

"Then from today," the mistress said, "we'll call you Hitachi Kohagi. How about that, Kohagi?" Running back and forth to cries of "Come here, Hitachi Kohagi," and "Go there, Hitachi Kohagi," Terute-no-hime was a pitiful sight to see.

Later, the mistress took out seven *mon*. She said, "Look, Hitachi Kohagi. I want you to use these seven *mon* to buy me some seven-colored tangy greens.[32] How about it?" "I can't buy seven-colored tangy greens with seven *mon*," Terute-no-hime countered. "We don't even speak of seven-colored greens. So how am I supposed to buy them, ma'am?" "Believe me," the mistress growled, "if you get a single color wrong, you'll be entertaining men for a living."

Unaware of any seven-colored greens, Terute-no-hime stopped at a crossroads and wept. But then she remembered something. "Back in my better days," she thought, "we had seven servants to whom we gave Chinese names. We called them Tōnan, Seinan, Ichiji, Kairō, Kagomori, Ugomori, and Dark Night Companion Boy. *Tōnan* is a word for field horsetails from the first days of spring. *Seinan* is a name for parsley. *Ichiji* means *hitomoji*, or 'single character,' which is another word for leeks. *Kairō*, or 'old man of the ocean,' is shrimp. *Kagomori* and *ugomori* are kinds of yams, and 'dark night companion boy' is another way of saying 'little lord,' which is a name for small dried sardines!"

---

32. The mistress asks for *shichi iro no karana no mono*. *Shichi iro*, or "seven-colored," can also mean "seven types." *Karana no mono* can mean either "tangy vegetables" or "Chinese-named things," depending on the characters used to write it. Her instructions are meant as a riddle.

Terute-no-hime bought the seven kinds of "greens" and brought them to her mistress. Although the woman was actually impressed, she said, "These are all wrong," and returned them at once. As there was nothing she could do, Terute-no-hime took them back again. "The mistress is so difficult!" she thought. "She must not know the answers." The mistress took out her list, and Terute-no-hime read it in her presence. "The first thing written here is *tōnan*," she said. "Isn't that a name for field horsetails from the first days of spring? The second thing is *seinan*. That's a word for parsley, isn't it? The third is *ichiji*. Doesn't that mean *hitomoji*, or 'single character,' which is another name for leeks? The fourth is *kairō*, 'old man of the ocean.' That's a word for shrimp, right? Five and six are *kagomori* and *ugomori*, which are kinds of yams, aren't they? And the seventh thing written here is 'dark night companion boy.' Isn't that another way of saying 'little lord,' which is a name for small dried sardines? I don't think my 'seven-colored greens' are wrong at all, ma'am."

The mistress secretly praised her to the others. "What a wonderful, knowledgeable young lady!" she said. "I doubt that there's anyone as clever." But she refrained from showing her the least bit of favor. Hoping to make her a courtesan, she inflicted her with further trials instead.

"Hitachi Kohagi," she said one day, "I've got twelve scullery maids working at my inn. I'm going to give them all a promotion and let you do their work by yourself. If you don't like it, you can start entertaining men. Just take your pick!"

"Even if I have to do the work of twelve such maids, ma'am," Terute-no-hime replied, "I won't be a whore!"

"If that's your choice . . ." the mistress retorted, and she immediately made her a scullery maid. Alas, poor Terute-no-hime! Reduced to the rank of a lowly kitchen drudge, she did her work in an orange unlined robe with a piece of rope to tie up her sleeves. Taking in the sight, the mistress said, "Hey, Kohagi, finish up your job and go fix our hundred ladies' hair!" Poor Terute-no-hime knew that the task was beneath her. "But even so," she thought, "I'll work for as long as I'm alive." And after finishing her chores, she went to arrange the hundred ladies' hair.

"After you've finished that," the mistress said, "we'll have a hundred horses arriving with a hundred grooms. You should feed and water the horses and serve the grooms a meal. When you've finished that, go and fetch us some pure spring water from eight *chō* away from here so that we can make the tea."[33] Poor Terute-no-hime did the work, despite its being so far beneath her.

Because she was a special charge of the Thousand-Armed Kannon,[34] the bodhisattva felt pity for the girl. Thus with the aid of Kannon's thousand hands, Terute-no-hime was able to accomplish her chores as easily as if she were scratching an itch. During her free moments, she would retreat to a quiet corner to recite the *nenbutsu* for the sake of Oguri and his ten retainers. As soon as the others saw what she was doing, they dubbed her Nenbutsu Kohagi and began calling her that as a matter of course. This is Terute-no-hime's tale.

Now there was no one as pitiful as Oguri. Having been murdered with poisoned saké, the poor man and his ten retainers made their way over Mount Shide and the Great Sanzu River to the court of King Enma, lord and judge of the dead. "Here come some sinners," the great king said as he watched them approach. Hearing the news, his demon retainers were endlessly pleased.

King Enma asked the men where they were from. "Your Majesty," Oguri replied, "don't you know me? I am the ruler of Hitachi Province. As punishment for forcing my way into a marriage, and because my foes were too weak to fight, I was served poisoned saké, which brought me here."

"So you're without sin, then—is that correct?" the King inquired.

"Yes, Your Majesty," Oguri replied. "I can't recall any transgressions. But if I'm mistaken, then please drop me down into whatever place you see fit. How about it, King?" Oguri's ten retainers chimed in: "And if any of us are guilty of any crimes, Your Highness, then please dispose of us, too, however you wish. But we have one request: we've accompanied our lord all this way, so please send us with him wherever he goes."

"Oguri was killed according to his karma," King Enma declared, "so there's nothing I can do. But because you ten retainers died unjustly, you should return right away to the human realm."

---

33. Eight *chō* is slightly more than half a mile. According to the *Oguri emaki*, the spring was eighteen *chō* away. See SNKBT 90:214.

34. Senju Kannon, one of the six principal forms of the bodhisattva Kannon. Earlier, Terute-no-hime was saved from the brushwood smoke by Shō Kannon, another one of the six principal incarnations.

Oguri in the court of King Enma. From *Oguri* (seventeenth-century *nara ehon*). (Courtesy of Tenri University Library)

    The retainers protested, saying, "Even if you were to send the ten of us back, we wouldn't be able to achieve our deepest desire.[35] But if you send Oguri back by himself alone, we could see it easily fulfilled. So please return him instead, Your Majesty."

    "What a trusty bunch of fellows!" the king exclaimed, and he called for Mitabōshi and Mirume, his spying eyes.[36] "Go and check on the bodies of those eleven men," he instructed.

    "Yes, sir," the two replied. Mitabōshi and Mirume climbed to the top of Mount Sumeru. They raised a *vajra* staff and struck Japan with a single blow, whereupon they saw in a glance all the sins and crimes throughout the land. They returned to King Enma and spoke: "Excuse us, Your Majesty. When we looked for the bodies of those eleven men, we found that all ten retainers had been cremated because they were killed without cause. The body of the one called Oguri is buried at a place known as Uwano Plain at the foot of Mount

---

35. Their desire to seek vengeance on Yokoyama.

36. Mitabōshi and Mirume are supernatural spies in the service of King Enma. Mirume also appears in *Aigo-no-waka*.

Fuji. A memorial marker has been erected for him there. But all the bodies of his ten retainers are gone."

"About these sinners," the king began, "Oguri isn't guilty of the slightest crime. And because his ten retainers have shown such loyalty to their lord, I would like to return them all to the human realm together with their master. But if their bodies have been destroyed, there's nothing I can do. I'll have to send Oguri back by himself to achieve his deepest desire."

The king stamped Oguri's chest with his personal seal. He wrote, "I am entrusting this man Oguri to my premier disciple at the base of Mount Fuji. Please build him a cart. If someone sets him in the Totsukawa River hot springs at Kumano Hongū Shrine,[37] it will be like offering him medicine from the afterworld, curing him of all his ills."

"Now as for you ten retainers," King Enma declared, "your loyalty to your lord has been outstanding. I shall therefore install you beside me as my assistants." The men were thereafter celebrated as the Ten Kings of Enma's Court. Since time immemorial, loyal retainers have always become buddhas. And since that particular day in the past, people have spoken of the Ten Kings of Enma's Court.

PART 3

But enough about his retainers—let us return now to Lord Oguri, who was truly the most pitiful of all. The disciple of Mount Fuji thought to himself, "How strange! The kites and the crows at Uwano Plain are making a ruckus. I wonder if an ox or a horse has collapsed there or if some strange ghost has appeared. I think I'll go and have a look."

The disciple set out for Uwano Plain. Surveying the fields, he saw Oguri's burial mound split wide open, with the memorial marker fallen over at the front. There was also a person sitting there in silence, his belly distended in the shape of a large ball. The disciple stared, wondering who it might be, when he realized that it was Oguri. Utterly amazed, he approached for a closer look.

There was a message in King Enma's own hand on a wooden placard around Oguri's neck. Being the king's premier disciple, he was all the more surprised.

---

37. One of the three Kumano shrines in contemporary Wakayama Prefecture.

Following Enma's instructions, he quickly built a cart and added the name Gaki Amida Butsu to the placard.³⁸ "Well, Gakiami," he said, "even if you ride, you're going to need a lead." He attached two strands of rope. Then, he appended a few more words to the wooden sign. "For those who draw this cart: pulling a single pull equals memorial services by a thousand priests; pulling a second pull equals memorial services by ten thousand." "Come on, then," he said, "I'll get you started." And with that, he began to pull.

Asking the way ahead, the disciple hauled Oguri past Mount Fuji and on through Suruga Province. With cries of "Heave, ho! Heave, ho!" he pulled him by the "overflowing branches" of Fuji no Morieda,³⁹ where blossoms bloom on the boughs of pines. Further inquiring the way ahead, he dragged him to the Shimada "Island" post station, not an island despite its name.⁴⁰ Crying "Heave, ho! Heave, ho!" he arrived at the Kakegawa River in Tōtōmi Province. Again asking the way ahead, he pushed past Nissaka and quickly came to Mount Utsu. He soon passed the Shōno post station, arriving at Yoshida in Mikawa Province. Hastening forward to the cry of "Heave, ho! Heave, ho!" he rapidly proceeded to "Hot" Atsuta Shrine in Owari Province.⁴¹ Wondering who called it hot when it was really so cold, he hurried on his way again and soon came to the front gate of the Yorozuya Inn at the Ōhaka post station in Mino Province.

Alas, poor Oguri! Although he had had someone to pull his cart until now, there was no one here who would take up the task,⁴² and so for three days he remained abandoned by the gate of the mistress's inn. Such is his story.

---

38. Hungry Ghost Amida Buddha. The disciple calls him a hungry ghost because of his swollen abdomen, and he adds the name Amida Buddha in accordance with medieval Pure Land Buddhist practice.

39. Actually Fujieda in contemporary Shizuoka Prefecture. The name Morieda can be written with characters meaning "overflowing branches."

40. The name Shimada contains the word *shima* (island), which allows for a play on words. The Shimada post station is now Shimada City in contemporary Shizuoka Prefecture.

41. Atsuta Shrine is in Nagoya in contemporary Aichi Prefecture. The author puns on the word *atsu* (hot) in the name Atsuta Shrine.

42. Due to a lacuna in the Tenri University Library manuscript, I have translated the first part of this sentence from the circa 1625 *Oguri* (SSS 2:406a). According to the *Oguri emaki*, the disciple pulled Oguri only as far as Mount Fuji, after which Oguri depended on strangers to be towed (SNKBT 90:221). The narrators of the circa 1673 and 1675 texts explain that "various people saw the cart, high and low alike. Some pulled it for the sake of a parent, and some for the sake of a spouse." See SSS 2:396a, 73a.

Now there was no one as pitiful as Terute-no-hime, the scullery maid Nenbutsu Kohagi at the Yorozuya Inn. "How sad!" she thought to herself upon seeing the cart. "I'd like to pull it for the sake of my husband Oguri and his ten retainers. I'll ask the mistress for some time away." She waited for an appropriate occasion and then presented the woman with her request.

"Excuse me, ma'am," she began, "but will you please allow me to take three days off? The reason is because when I saw that alms cart outside the front gate, I noticed that the placard around the beggar's neck says that pulling a single pull equals memorial services by a thousand priests and that pulling a second pull equals memorial services by ten thousand. I've lost both my parents, and I'd like to pull the cart for them. If I drag it for two days, I can walk back in one. So won't you please allow me three days? You know, ma'am, there's a saying that we should be kind to travelers and caring in life."

"You want three days?" the mistress snapped. "You antagonize me by refusing even to entertain men, and then you ask for three days? I don't care if a crow's head turns white or a horse sprouts horns! Nenbutsu Kohagi, I won't give you the least time away!"

"But wait, ma'am," Terute-no-hime said. "Please listen to what I have to say. In the past, people used to used talk about these things in verse. They said that villages raise foundlings and that where there are large trees, birds are sure to dwell. Boats will enter a harbor, and when they're cold, geese will take to the water while chickens roost in trees. It's precisely because of you, ma'am, that for the last three days that beggar Gakiami has been parked outside your gate. If you'll allow me three days, I promise to take your place if something bad ever happens to you or your husband."

"What a responsible thing to say!" the mistress declared. "So you'll agree to take my place if something bad ever happens? In that case, I'll add kindness to your compassion by giving you five days away. Go ahead and pull that cart, Nenbutsu Kohagi!"[43]

Terute-no-hime was overjoyed. She set out for the front gate and took a wheel rut for her pillow the whole night through. As dawn broke in the fifth hour, she returned to her mistress to borrow an old court cap. Although

---

43. In the *Oguri emaki*, the mistress warns Terute-no-hime that "if five days should turn to six, then both you and your parents are sure to fall into the Hell of No Respite." See SNKBT 90:224.

Terute-no-hime prepares to pull Gakiami (Oguri) on his cart. From *Oguri* (seventeenth-century *nara ehon*). (Courtesy of Tenri University Library)

perfectly sane, she made herself up to look as if she had lost her mind, thinking that it would help her to persuade others to pull the cart. "If I get a reputation at the towns and inns along the way," she thought, "it'll cause my husband Oguri some consternation in his grave. But it can't be helped."

Terute-no-hime tied some sacred streamers to a length of bamboo grass.[44] She mussed her hair and, pretending to be mad, shouted, "Hello, children! Come and pull the cart! I'll beat time for you, crazy lady that I am!" The children were thrilled. With cries of "Heave, ho! Heave, ho!" they pulled the cart to the Kagami post station at the border of Mino and Ōmi Provinces. Then they passed by it, hardly even noticing it was there.

Hurrying ever onward and wishing she had more time, Terute-no-hime led the way past the "ribbed" Abara post station—not enough roof planks? No wonder the moon shines through![45]—and beyond famous Nakahara in Ōmi

---

44. Bamboo grass is a conventional symbol of insanity, particularly in nō.
45. The name Abara (ribs) allows for the playful reference to gaps in the roof.

Province. She quickly pulled past the Yasu Market and over the easy Yasukawa River, wondering who named it that when it ran so swift and wide.[46] She sped past "overflowing" Moriyama Village, though the rain did not fall there, and to shouts of "Heave, ho! Heave, ho!" she raced through the grassy Kusatsu post station, though the dew failed to light on Gakiami's cart. To further cries of "Heave, ho! Heave, ho!" she pulled past Noji no Shinohara, the magnificent clang of the Ishiyama Temple bell ringing in her ears. Upon traversing the Seta Bridge, she hauled her cart right to the gate of the Tamaya Inn at Seki Temple in Upper Ōtsu.[47]

Alas, poor Terute-no-hime! Although she wished to pull the cart for one more day, three days had already passed. "How sad to leave you here in front of this place!" she said. "If your ears could hear, Gakiami, I'd tell you all that I know, and if your eyes could see, I'd write it out for you to read. But you're deaf and blind, so I won't. Leaving you feels just the way it did when I parted from my husband, Oguri."

Terute-no-hime visited the Tamaya Inn, where she borrowed an inkstone and a brush. Then she added a message to the wooden placard around Oguri's neck. "If you make it to the Yunomine hot springs at Kumano Hongū Shrine and recover from your ills,"[48] she wrote, "come look for the scullery maid Nenbutsu Kohagi at the Yorozuya Inn at Ōhaka in Mino Province. She'll be sure to give you lodging for a night." "Well, Gakiami," she said, "I'll be going now. Goodbye." And with that, she set out on her return. This is Terute-no-hime's tale.

Now there was no one as pitiful as Oguri. With cries of "Heave, ho! Heave, ho!" various volunteers pulled him past Upper Ōtsu and Seki Temple; past famous Jūzenji Temple in the Shinomiya Fields at "pursuing" Oiwake Yamashina, though no one pursued them there;[49] and over "Sunny Hill" Hi-no-oka Pass, though the morning sun did not appear. To further cries of "Heave, ho! Heave, ho!" the people quickly pulled Oguri's cart to "meeting mouth"

---

46. Yasukawa can be written with characters meaning "easy river."

47. A different Tamaya Inn from the one in *Karukaya*. Ōtsu lies on the southwest shore of Lake Biwa.

48. Yunomine is another name for the Totsukawa River hot springs near Kumano Hongū Shrine.

49. The place-name Oiwake allows for a pun on the verb *ou* (to chase or pursue). Oiwake lies at the northeastern edge of the Yamashina valley immediately to the east of Kyoto.

Awataguchi, despite no one to meet them there, and on into the flowering capital, home of the Imperial Palace.

Hurrying on their way and wishing they had more time, the people pulled Oguri to the Seventh Avenue Shushaka Gongen Buddha Hall, where they bowed down and prayed. They skirted the Four Tombs of Tōji Temple, and to cries of "Heave, ho! Heave, ho!" they pulled past Autumn Mountain and the Toba Lovers' Tomb,[50] moved by the thought of ancient love. Crying "Heave, ho! Heave, ho!" they pulled across the Koida River, arriving at what seemed to be Kogano-nawate. Pressing ever forward, hurrying on their way and wishing they had more time, the people pulled Oguri over the Yodo Bridge; over Kitsune Crossing, yipping like foxes;[51] over Katsura River—does the moon lodge in your current?—and past the thousand homes of Yamazaki.

With cries of "Heave, ho! Heave, ho!" they crossed the Akuta River, which washes away the dust, and came to the Hirose River. Wondering who named the rapids of such a small stream "broad,"[52] they quickly passed through Settsu Province and arrived at Tennōji Temple in Osaka.[53] Hearing that Tennōji was a Sumitomo votive temple,[54] the people bowed down and prayed with peaceful hearts. Then hurrying on their way and wishing they had more time, they pulled Oguri to the four shrines of Sumiyoshi at Sakai Bay, where they entreated the great deity to "please deliver this Gakiami safely to the Yunomine hot springs!"

With cries of "Heave, ho! Heave, ho!" the volunteers pulled Oguri to famous Sakai Beach, and because they hastened ever onward, they quickly approached the Kumano region. At a place called the Kamuro post station, there happened to be three holy men on a pilgrimage to Kumano.[55] Upon reading the

---

50. The Lovers' Tomb is the grave of Lady Kesa (Kesa *gozen*) in Kyoto's Toba district—now Fushimi-ku.

51. In the medieval period, Kitsunegawa (literally, "Fox River") was a Yodo River crossing to the southwest of the Kyoto capital.

52. The name Hirose is written with characters meaning "broad rapids."

53. Shitennōji (Tennōji) Temple in the Tennōji district of contemporary Osaka. In *Sanshō Dayū* and *Shintokumaru*, both Zushiōmaru and Shintokumaru spend time there.

54. The meaning of this is unclear. There is a similar passage in the sixteenth-century *kōwakamai* entitled *Atsumori*. See Asahara Yoshiko and Kitahara Yasuo, eds., *Mai no hon*, Shin Nihon koten bungaku taikei 59 (Tokyo: Iwanami shoten, 1994), 228.

55. Presumably the same Kamuro post station as in *Karukaya*, located midway between Osaka and Kumano Hongū Shrine.

placard around Oguri's neck, they said to themselves, "We're also on our way to Kumano. Let's pull the cart and receive memorial services by a thousand and ten thousand priests!" Realizing that a treacherous mountain road lay ahead—a path impassable by cart—they built a palanquin, placed Oguri on top, and took turns carrying the load. Hurrying on their way and wishing they had more time, they eventually came to the Yunomine hot springs at Kumano Hongū Shrine.

Since the medicinal waters were a gift from the afterworld, after seven days in the pool Oguri's vision was miraculously restored. After two weeks he could stand erect, and at the end of three weeks, he was restored to his former self.[56] Now fully healed and eager to be on his way, Oguri set out from the Kumano mountains.

Seeing him leave, the Kumano deity took the form of a woodcutter and cut two cedar staves. Intending to sell them to the great, powerful Oguri, he spoke to him in his disguise: "Hello, you man of the hot springs! Won't you buy these staves?"

"Up until now I've been pulled in a cart and called Gakiami," Oguri replied, "which is bad enough. So I don't think I'll buy your *vajra* staves."

"Then you don't have the money to pay for them?" the deity inquired. "In that case, I'll let you take them for free." Handing Oguri the two cedar staves, he said, "If you throw one of these into the Hinan River,[57] it will become a boat. The other one will become a mast. Together, they're called the Pure Land Skiff. Step on board and it will take you anywhere you want to go." With that, the deity vanished without a trace.

"And I thought he was just a woodcutter," Oguri mused, taking in the sight. "But what a joy to worship the Kumano deity!" He bowed down and prayed toward the three Kumano shrines. Then accepting the two staves, he set out in the direction of the foothills. Following the deity's instructions, he threw one

---

56. The *Oguri emaki* explains that in seven, fourteen, and twenty-one days, Oguri regained his ability to see, hear, and speak and that in forty-nine days (in Buddhism, the time that it takes for a being to be reincarnated), he was completely restored. The *emaki* also states that his journey to Yunomine took a total of 444 days, the significance of which is unclear. See SNKBT 90:230.

57. According to the circa 1673, 1675, and circa 1711 to 1736 texts, Oguri should throw it into the Otonashi River near Kumano Hongū Shrine. See SSS 2:400a, 76a, 104a. The Hinan River is unknown.

into the Hinan River, whereupon it floated to the surface as the Pure Land Skiff. He raised the second one as a mast and stepped on board. Indeed, although there was no one to row and no one to pole, Oguri sailed to his home province in no time at all—thanks to the deity's divine intervention, it seems.

Approaching his father Lord Kaneie's gate, Oguri begged for a boon, crying, "Alms, please, for a mendicant monk!" But poor Oguri! The guards shouted, "There's no place here for a beggar priest!" and chased him away with a broomstick.

One of Oguri's former nurses happened to hear the commotion. "Excuse me, guards," she called, "but today is Master Oguri's death anniversary. If there's a mendicant monk outside, please call him in so that I can give him an offering." "Yes, ma'am," the men replied. "Hey, you monk," they shouted, "get inside!"

Oguri refused, saying, "Once I've been chased out of a place, I'm not one to visit there again." Oguri's nurse heard him speak. "You poor wandering priest," she cried, "please come back!" Stepping outside, she seized him by the sleeve and beckoned him inside. "I'm offering you alms," she said, "because today is my lord Oguri's death anniversary." She stared intently at his face. "Reverend sir," she continued, "there's something strange about you, so I'd like to ask: my lord Oguri had the character for 'rice' impressed on his forehead, and you do, too.[58] What province do you come from, sir? Tell me, please."

"There's no point in explaining it all here," Oguri replied. "I'm just a mendicant monk."

"Reverend sir," the nurse rejoined, "who do you think I am? I was a nurse to Lord Oguri. I've been here since he went away, my useless life lingering on and on." She pressed her sleeve to her face and sobbed.

"I had meant to conceal my identity," Oguri said, watching her weep, "but I can't any longer. I myself am Oguri, the son of my father Lord Kaneie. Yokoyama murdered me with poisoned saké, but thanks to the intercession of Great King Enma, I've come back from the dead. People call me a mendicant monk, which is how I've made my way here."

---

58. A miraculous sign suggestive of a bodhisattva. Muroki Yatarō notes that the word *yone*, written with the character for "rice" 米, is a term for a bodhisattva. He adds that because the character's elements resemble the characters for the number 88 (八十八), *yone* 米 was thought to be auspicious. See SNKS *Sekkyō shū*, 237n.14. According to the *Oguri emaki*, Demon Bay also saw the mark on Oguri's brow. See SNKBT 90:187.

The nurse wondered whether she was dreaming. Marveling at her own jubilation, she retreated deep inside the mansion, where she addressed Kaneie and his wife. "My lord and my lady," she began, "listen, please! A beggar priest was passing by, and since it's Master Oguri's death anniversary today, I invited him inside. When I gave him alms, he turned out to be your son! Go take a look!"

"What a strange thing to say!" the wife exclaimed. "Yokoyama murdered him with poisoned saké. He's gone from this world. Unless there are two of him, that is . . . What a funny thing for you to claim!" And with that, she burst out laughing, which was certainly reasonable.

"But that's just it," the nurse persisted. "Yokoyama murdered him with poisoned saké, and when Oguri got to Enma's palace, the great king sent him back here because Yokoyama had killed him unjustly. I thought it was strange, too, but the character for 'rice' is impressed on his forehead, so there isn't any doubt. Go take a look!"

The wife made her way into a small side room and gazed at her son through a gap. Kaneie saw that she was ready to rush in and embrace him. "She's being rash," he thought to himself. "After all, there are many things in this world that look alike. If he's really Oguri, then he should have the martial skills I taught him. I'd like to see if he does."

Kaneie took out a thirteen-span arrow and fit it to a ten-man bow.[59] He called out to Oguri from behind a sliding paper door and let his arrow fly. Having learned such tricks from before, Oguri caught it in his left hand. Kaneie loosed a second speeding shaft, which Oguri caught in his teeth. "Then there's no doubt!" Kaneie cried, taking in the sight. "Come to me!"

People say that a man may weep for happiness or sorrow; upon meeting face-to-face with his father, Oguri shed tears of joy. Kaneie erected placards that read, "Our former Oguri has returned from the dead! High and low alike, everyone who served him before is hereby summoned to serve him again." Within a day or two, more than a hundred thousand riders had appeared. Day after day, they reported for duty in a constant stream.

---

59. An arrow that was thirteen handbreadths long and a bow that required ten men to string. Shinoda Jun'ichi explains that a regular arrow was only twelve handbreadths long. See SNKBT 90:233n.18.

Kaneie scrutinized the situation, and just as before, he granted his son the two provinces of Musashi and Sagami.[60] Hearing the news, Oguri spoke: "I have no desire for Musashi and Sagami. There's something that I have in mind, so please give me Mino Province instead." Kaneie therefore added it to the other two, "to provide fodder for your horses," he explained.

Oguri was exceptionally pleased, and he let it be known that he would pay his first official visit to Mino Province with an entourage of more than a hundred thousand riders.[61] In Mino, he had a notice posted at the Yorozuya Inn at the Ōhaka post station declaring his intent to lodge there.

Observing the notice, the mistress wondered what it could mean. "There must be some establishments that are larger than my own," she thought to herself. But concluding that she could not disobey the new governor's decree, she immediately set about cleaning her inn. She had the ceilings adorned with leopard and tiger skins, and she had the pillars wrapped in gold-lace weave. Then, after preparing an assortment of delicacies from the land and sea, she began to wait.

Because Oguri hurried on his way, he soon came to the inn. The mistress welcomed him with the utmost care, saying, "Although I can only offer you these shabby, most inappropriate accommodations, I could never refuse your lordship's command."

"Shabby lodgings don't bother me at all," Oguri replied.

The mistress bustled about. Thinking that first she would serve some saké, she selected the best twelve of her hundred courtesans, dressed them up in twelve-layered robes, and sent them out to pour drinks. But Oguri was unimpressed. "Ma'am," he complained, "don't you have a woman here by the name of Nenbutsu Kohagi? Send her out instead."

The mistress withdrew. She summoned Terute-no-hime and spoke: "I want you to go pour drinks for that lord who's visiting us now." She took out a set of twelve-layered robes and handed them to her.

"It's not the first time you've asked," Terute-no-hime shot back, "and ma'am, I don't think I will."

---

60. Actually, it was Yokoyama who had offered Oguri the provinces of Musashi and Sagami. In the *Oguri emaki*, Kaneie takes Oguri to see the emperor, who grants him the five Kinai provinces of Yamashiro, Yamato, Kawachi, Izumi, and Settsu. See SNKBT 90:234. In the circa 1673 and 1675 texts, the emperor offers him Musashi and Sagami in addition to Hitachi. See SSS 2:402a, 77b.

61. According to the *Oguri emaki*, Oguri arranged to visit Mino with a more reasonable contingent of more than three thousand horsemen. See SNKBT 90:235.

"So you've forgotten your joy now, just like that? Don't you remember when you were going to pull that cart, how you said that you'd take our place if something bad ever happened to me or my husband? Well, if you don't go and serve him drinks, we're sure to suffer his wrath.[62] So just do it, Kohagi."

Poor Terute-no-hime! Cornered by her mistress's logic, she thought to herself, "If I agree to serve the saké, my husband Oguri will surely resent it in his grave. But if that's how it is, then so be it! I'll go and pour the drinks." Casting aside the rope that was holding up her sleeves, she picked up a decanter and set out to see the guest.

Oguri watched her approach. "Well, so you're the one called Hitachi Kohagi, are you?" he said. "Who are you descended from in Hitachi? The name brings back such memories! Tell me now, please."

"I was made to come and pour you a drink," Terute-no-hime replied, "not to tell you my life story. So go ahead and have some saké." She dropped the decanter and turned to leave.

Oguri seized her by the hem. "Wait a moment, Nenbutsu Kohagi," he said. "When I was called Gakiami and being pulled along the Eastern Sea Road in a cart, you dragged me from the front of this inn to the gate of the Tamaya Inn at Seki Temple. I was Gakiami, and this is your writing on the placard that was around my neck." He showed her the sign.

"How peculiar!" Terute-no-hime exclaimed. "Now what could I have to hide? I was once wed to a man named Oguri from Hitachi Province. We were as close as the dew on a morning glory. But he died unexpectedly, and strangely I was left to mourn. Then I learned that if I pulled your cart, I could receive memorial services by a thousand priests. Thus, for my husband Oguri's sake, I asked the mistress for five days off. So you see, it really was I who pulled your cart!"

"I've heard that when you ask people about their ancestors, you should first tell them of your own. I myself am Oguri of Hitachi Province. Yokoyama murdered me with poisoned saké, but thanks to the compassion of King Enma, I've come back from the dead. I was pulled through the seven provinces of the Eastern Sea Road to the Yunomine hot springs at Kumano Hongū Shrine, where Enma blessed me with medicinal waters. And now he's sending me back to Hitachi."

Taking in Oguri's words, Terute-no-hime wondered whether she was dreaming. She embraced him, crying, "If this is a dream, then let me awake! And if I'm

---

62. In the circa 1673, 1675, and circa 1711 to 1736 texts, Oguri threatens to kill the mistress and her husband if they fail to send Hitachi Kohagi to serve him. See SSS 2:402b, 77b, 105b.

awake, then let this vision disappear! To meet someone who has died . . . it's like finding an *udonge* flower,[63] precious and rare! What could I keep from you now, either? I am Yokoyama's daughter Terute-no-hime. But please don't hate him! He thought that since he shouldn't kill someone else's child without killing his own, he ordered two brothers to drown me in the Orikara Abyss. The younger one, Onitsugu, saved my life! I was in a barred palanquin, and he put it on a boat and pushed me out to sea. The wind and the waves were ferocious! I drifted into Mutsura Bay, where the fisherfolk were going to beat me to death for being a shape-shifting demon, but a merciful man named Uragimi no Tayū saved me by taking me in as his child. But his old wife was evil, and when her husband was away, she sold me for two *kan*. I was sold and resold as far east as Tsuruga and Soto-no-hama Beach, changing hands seventy-five times before the mistress here bought me for her inn. But when I wouldn't entertain men, she was so annoyed that she gave her twelve scullery maids a promotion and made me do all their work by myself. 'After you finish that job,' she would say, 'go fix our hundred ladies' hair! After that, go fetch the tea water eight *chō* downhill from here and boil it for tea! Then serve a meal to the hundred grooms and feed and water their hundred horses! Then clean the house and the reception rooms!' I've suffered so much!" Having told her story to her husband, Terute-no-hime could only weep.

Oguri summoned the mistress and spoke: "Well, you're an evil, immoral woman! Even if that girl had a thousand arms, it would be outrageous to order her around like that! I wonder what I should do with a villainous witch like you . . ." His expression had changed, and now angry beyond measure, he began striking the floor mats with a fan. The mistress hung her head in silence.

"Listen, Oguri," Terute-no-hime said, "stop being so upset. It's only because the mistress bought me for the inn that we were able to be reunited. It's all thanks to her. For my sake, forgive her, please." "I was speaking like that for you," Oguri replied. "But if that's what you wish, then I'll forgive her." And with that, he appointed her deputy governor of Mino Province.

The mistress was grateful merely to have been saved, but now to have been appointed deputy governor! Recognizing that this was entirely because of Nenbutsu Kohagi, she bowed down in reverent appreciation, which was natural indeed.

---

63. The *udonge* flower is said to bloom only once every three thousand years, as seldom as a buddha appears in the world.

Until that morning, Terute-no-hime had served at the mistress's beck and call. That she had prevailed over her owner and was now herself the mistress of three provinces was solely due to her insight and understanding. People also say that it was because as a child bestowed by Kannon, she enjoyed the bodhisattva's protection day and night.

Oguri later placed Terute-no-hime in a jeweled palanquin and announced that he would take his leave. Upon hearing the news, the mistress presented Terute-no-hime with her hundred courtesans to see her on her way. The hundred women were happy simply to have escaped prostitution; now accompanying their new mistress to Hitachi Province to serve her there, their joy knew no bounds.

Oguri suggested that they attack Yokoyama on the way. Word reached Yokoyama, and because there was nothing else that he could do, he immediately filled his dry moat with water, threw up some rough gates and barricades, and grimly awaited the assault.

Hearing of her father's situation, Terute-no-hime wept and spoke: "It's natural for you to be angry, Oguri, but there's a saying that we ought to repay enmity with kindness. I don't feel any sympathy for my parents either, but a child's debt isn't for the child to decide. So please pardon him this time for my sake." "I'll do whatever you ask," Oguri replied. "If you want me to forgive him for your sake, then I will."

Yokoyama heard the news. Declaring that he finally understood the expression that "of all the myriad treasures, none is greater than a child," he sent Oguri a thousand *ryō* of gold along with the horse Demon Bay.[64] Oguri took in the sight. He never expected a dowry, but in deference to Demon Bay, he went along with the gesture.

Demon Bay died soon thereafter, and true to his word, Oguri built him a golden buddha hall at the foot of Mount Fuji. He encased the horse's body in pure lacquer, and after designating him the Horse-Headed Kannon, he enshrined him in the new temple. It was from this time, too, that oxen came to be known as manifestations of Dainichi Buddha.

---

64. One *ryō* equals four or five *monme*, or a little more than half an ounce. In the *Oguri emaki*, Yokoyama also sends Oguri his son Saburō, who, he says, bears all the blame. Oguri has him rolled up in a rough reed mat and drowned. In the circa 1673 and 1675 texts, Terute-no-hime orders Saburō to disembowel himself, and he does. See SNKBT 90:245–46 and SSS 2:404b, 79a–b.

Oguri accepts presents from Yokoyama. From *Oguri* (seventeenth-century *nara ehon*). (Courtesy of Tenri University Library)

Now Oguri and Terute-no-hime shared a deep marital bond, and as the months and years slipped by, their only regret was for the passing time. At the age of eighty-one, Oguri disappeared like the morning dew. Terute-no-hime likewise expired, dewlike, at the age of sixty-one.

To be reunited with a lover who has already died—in all the past until now, such events have seldom occurred. For this reason Oguri came to be venerated as the Mantra King Aizen.[65] Terute-no-hime was worshipped as a god of love and marriage.[66] People built her a shrine in the Kitano district of the capital, where even today they cherish and pray to her for prosperity in generations to come.

---

65. Aizen Myōō (Rāgarāja), one of the Five Great Mantra Kings. Aizen is known as a deity of love and desire; in the Edo period, he was venerated for protecting prostitutes and for aiding in matters of love. According to the *Oguri emaki*, Oguri was worshipped as the Shō Hachiman of Sunomata Village in the Anpachi district of Mino Province. See SNKBT 90:246.

66. A *musubi no kami*, known for joining men and women in amorous relations.

Sayohime

PART 1

Ask me about the origins of the Benzaiten of Chikubushima Shrine in Ōmi Province,[1] and I will tell you about an especially fortunate man known as Matsura Chōja, "the Millionaire of Matsura." He went by the name of Lord Kyōgoku, and he lived a long time ago in a place called Tsubosaka in Matsura Valley in Yamato Province. He was known throughout China and Korea, where people spoke of his fabulous wealth. Indeed, how could even the great, ancient Sudatta have compared?[2] Lord Kyōgoku built rows of storehouses in the four directions, as well as scores of gates with splendidly gabled roofs. He owned myriad treasures and all the seven kinds of jewels, such that he wanted for nothing. In spring he passed his days beneath flowering trees, while in autumn he spent his nights in the light of the moon, forever reveling in his splendor.

Translated from the seventeenth-century Kyoto University *Sayohime nara ehon*.
    1. A statue of the goddess Benzaiten on Chikubushima Island in Lake Biwa.
    2. Sudatta was a man of legendary wealth and charity in the age of Shakyamuni Buddha in India.

Yet despite Lord Kyōgoku's marvelously fine fortunes, there was in fact one thing that he lacked, and that was a child, whether a boy or a girl. Because this alone weighed on his heart, he turned to his wife and spoke: "Why don't we visit the statue of Kannon at Hase Temple,[3] give him a large offering, and tell him about our grief?" "That's just what I was thinking!" the wife replied, and they set off together.

Lord Kyōgoku and his wife bowed thirty-three times in reverent supplication,[4] after which they pronounced a great prayer-vow: "Hail most merciful Kannon, whose blessings allow even flowers to bloom on withered trees! Please give us a child, either a boy or a girl. If you will grant us this request, then we will provide you with thirty-three rills of brocade curtains every month for three years. We will also sponsor a myriad-light service on each of your festival days for three years, and we will have thirty thousand scrolls of sutras read aloud for you every month for that time as well."

Amazing to say, in the middle of the night Kannon appeared before Lord Kyōgoku and his wife where they slept. "Dear couple," he said, "I am touched by your desperate pleas. As an act of mercy, I will grant you your desire." He offered them a single golden die and then vanished without a trace.

Lord Kyōgoku and his wife awoke with a start. "What a wonderful boon!" they cried and bowed again in reverent supplication. They hurried back to their mansion, where the household all gathered to hear the news. Everyone was overjoyed. The wife soon found herself pregnant, and after suffering her ninth-month misery, she gave birth in her tenth month to a daughter like a jewel, simply dazzling to behold. The lord and his wife were pleased beyond compare. For a name, they chose Sayohime Gozen, "Lady Short-Night," after the season in which they had received their dream. Then, with a retinue of nannies and wet nurses, they raised her with the utmost care.

The world is an uncertain place, or so people say, and thus at this most splendid of times, when Sayohime was only four years old, Lord Kyōgoku caught a passing cold that gradually worsened into something severe. First his wife and then all his family and retainers visited him where he lay and sought to minister to his needs. Sensing that the end was near, the lord summoned his

---

3. A famous image of the bodhisattva Kannon near the southeastern edge of the Nara valley.

4. Thirty-three times for the thirty-three manifestations of Kannon.

A nurse presents Sayohime to her mother and father. From *Sayohime* (seventeenth-century *nara ehon*). (Courtesy of the Kyoto University Department of Literature)

spouse. "I may have a child," he said, weeping all the while, "but she doesn't really count because she's a girl. So the only thing that troubles me is who'll be my heir. Whatever you do, be sure to raise our daughter well. Find a boy who'll marry into the family and then bring him up to take my place."[5]

The wife sobbed and exclaimed, "How am I supposed to get you an heir with no one to rely on when you're gone? And me being a woman! I can only pray to join you under the moss." The lady writhed in anguish, but to no avail. The lord grew increasingly weak, and finally feeling that the end had come, he turned toward the west, pressed his palms together, and chanted "Hail Amida Buddha" four or five times. It must have pained him to die so young, but he slipped away like the morning dew, his days run out at the age of thirty-six. People clung to him from the left and right, wailing to the heavens and weeping on the ground, but their grief was for naught. With no other choice, they carried him to the cremation grounds, where a multitude of priests conducted services. Their weekly memorial rites were beyond the power of words to describe.

As the months and years passed, the household gradually exhausted its wealth, becoming ever more impoverished. The servants and retainers all scattered, never to return, until, alas, only the poor wife and child remained. In her despair, the mother hugged her daughter tight, smoothed back her stray locks, and said, "There, there, my unfortunate girl! If your father only had stayed with us until you were ten, we could have found you a husband and gotten a rich heir. But he died when you were little, and we've fallen on such wretched times! I wouldn't mind dying now, either, except that I'd worry about what would become of you." Thus they passed the days and months, forever wringing out their teary sleeves.

Sayohime was soon seven years old. She was an exceptionally clever girl; hearing one thing explained, she naturally grasped another ten. She had also become increasingly beautiful, like some heavenly being descended to earth. Wealthy men sent her notes and letters, but being ashamed of her poverty, she refused to give them any serious consideration. Rather, with no other means of supporting themselves in their gloomy, lonely home, Sayohime and her mother

---

5. In the 1661 and circa 1704 *Matsura Chōja*, the lord says nothing about an heir; rather, he simply instructs his wife to raise their daughter well. In the 1661 *Matsura Chōja*, he also gives his wife a copy of the Lotus sutra to pass on to the girl. See SNKS *Sekkyō shū*, 350–51, and SSS 1:183b.

preserved their fragile lives by plucking parsley from a marsh and gleaning rice from the village fields.

The years passed, and Sayohime turned sixteen. The thirteenth anniversary of her father's death had come, and although she desperately wished to sponsor a memorial service, there was nothing she could do. "The truth is," she reflected, "a child's debt to her parents is taller than the tallest mountain and deeper than the deepest sea. Children should engage services for the sake of their parents' enlightenment, even if they have to sell themselves to do so. Since I'm so poor, how could I think of doing otherwise? Even if I'm to be eaten by eagles, hawks, or bears, I'll sell myself and hold a service for my father's enlightenment!"

With no clear plan in mind, Sayohime left her mother and visited Kasuga Shrine.[6] "I want to sell myself," she prayed with all her might, "so that I can sponsor a service for my father's enlightenment. If there's someone who would buy me, then please let us meet!" Now around that time there was a holy man from Kōfukuji Temple who had come to the shrine to preach. Learning of his presence there, Sayohime went to hear him speak. "We should all sponsor rites for our parents' enlightenment," the holy man instructed, "even if we have to sell ourselves to do so." Listening until the end, Sayohime became all the more resolved.

There was a great lake in the Adachi district of Michinoku Province,[7] and in that lake there lived a giant old serpent. Being the tutelary deity of eight hamlets and eight villages, the serpent was worshipped in a variety of ways. But among the many rites performed on its behalf, there was one that was especially strange: once every year, a beautiful young girl was provided to it as a sacrificial offering. The responsibility for this ritual rotated among the residents of the eight hamlets and eight villages, and this year the duty had fallen to a wealthy village headman by the name of Gonga no Tayū. Lamenting his task, Gonga sadly said to his wife, "We've got only one daughter, so how are we supposed to feed her to the snake?"

"Listen, dear," the wife replied, "the deity will punish us terribly if you go on grieving like that about your sacred duty. And complaining won't do any good.

---

6. Kasuga Shrine is situated in the mountains on the eastern side of the Nara valley, near Kōfukuji Temple.

7. In the far north of the central Japanese island of Honshū.

Sayohime hears a holy man preach at Kasuga Shrine. From *Sayohime* (seventeenth-century *nara ehon*). (Courtesy of the Kyoto University Department of Literature)

We love our daughter as much as ourselves, so you know we can't give her up as an offering. You should visit the capital, buy some orphan girl, and bring her back here." Gonga was delighted. "What a wonderful idea!" he exclaimed, and he secretly set out for the capital.

Gonga made inquiries at all the inns along the way, but he was unable to find an appropriate girl. Upon arriving in the capital, he took lodging at the

Kikuya Inn near the corner of First Avenue and Ogawa Road, after which he began asking around the city. But he had no luck, despite quietly letting it be known that he would pay an excellent price for a beautiful young girl not yet touched by a man. As there was no one willing to sell, Gonga decided to search in the provinces of Yamato and Kawachi. Moving on to the old Nara capital, he took lodging in the Tengai quarter.[8] He made inquiries here and there, but no one wanted to sell. Thus, with no other choice, he put up a tall sign outside the Great Southern Gate at Kōfukuji Temple.

Poor Sayohime! Returning home from the sermon, she immediately noticed Gonga's sign. "What's this?" she thought, and took a closer look. "Top price for a young woman not yet touched by a man. Inquire at Gorō Dayū's Tsuruya Inn in Tengai." Reading the placard, her heart was filled with reverent joy. "How wonderful!" she thought. "This must be a message from the Kasuga deity!" Although she wished to sell herself right away, she remembered how sad her mother would be waiting for her at home, and she decided that first she would return to the Kyōgoku mansion to say good-bye.

Now Gonga no Tayū had set up his sign, but because no one had come to see him about it, he had given up hope. Thinking that he would search someplace else, he set out from his inn and wandered here and there, inquiring all the while. The Kasuga deity was struck with pity, and appearing as an eighty-year-old man, he walked up to Gonga and said, "Tell me, sir, what is it that you're trying to find?"

Gonga explained, whereupon the Kasuga deity said, "Just this side of that distant mountain, there's a place called Matsura Valley. A great rich man used to have his estate there. While he was alive, he owned myriad treasures and all the seven kinds of jewels, such that he wanted for nothing. But perhaps because he was such an evil man,[9] he died and all his vast wealth disappeared like foam on the water. His people were impoverished; his house went to ruin; and no one comes to call anymore. Only his wife and daughter live there now, and their days are sad indeed! I hear that it's his thirteenth death-anniversary this year and that his wife and daughter are always crying because they can't afford to pay for a memorial service. So the girl might be willing to sell herself.

---

8. The area around Tegai (also Tengai) Gate at Tōdaiji Temple.

9. According to the 1661 and circa 1704 *Matsura Chōja*, Lord Kyōgoku lost all his riches because he was excessively stingy. See SNKS *Sekkyō shū*, 356, and SSS 1:185b.

Who knows if you'll find anyone else." And with that, the deity vanished without a trace.

"What a strange encounter!" Gonga thought to himself. "It must have been the tutelary deity from home—it must have pitied me and come all this way to help!" Gonga bowed and prayed toward where the old man had been. Then he made his way to Matsura Valley.

Gazing off to the south, Gonga could indeed see what looked like the great rich man's former estate. There was a mansion with tall, gabled gates surrounded by a deep moat. But the gates lacked doors, and the fine mud wall had lost its mantle. The eaves and roofing tiles were falling down, and although water dripped and leaked inside, no one seemed to have paid it any mind. That a majestic house could fall into such ruin was moving indeed! Even for a heartless easterner like Gonga, it was a pitiful sight to see. With tears in his eyes, he crossed a pontoon bridge over the moat, entered the front gate, and circled around to the courtyard. "Excuse me!" he shouted, whereupon Sayohime emerged. "Who is it?" she asked.

"Don't worry, it's nothing to be alarmed about," Gonga began. "I come from the capital, near the intersection of First Avenue and Ogawa Road. Can you please tell me if there's a young woman around here who hasn't yet been touched by a man? I'd like to buy her for an excellent price." Sayohime instantly realized that this must be the man who had put up the sign. Concluding that the Kasuga deity had sent him, she replied, "Hello, sir, it is I myself whom you should buy. And I'll be happy to oblige." Gonga was overjoyed. "What a sad thing for you to say!" he declared. "But if that's how you feel, then how much shall I pay you?"

"I'll be selling myself to sponsor services for my father's enlightenment," the girl replied, "so it has to be enough to pay for rites. Other than that, I'll leave it up to you." And with these words, she broke down and cried as if to disappear.

"Well, you're an awfully kind child, aren't you?" Gonga said. "And because it's for your father's enlightenment, I won't skimp on the price. I'll give you fifty *ryō* in gold dust."[10] He took out the gold from inside his robe and handed it to Sayohime. Sad to say, the poor girl accepted it. "Please, master," she said,

---

10. In the late sixteenth century, one *ryō* of gold equaled two *kan* of coined currency, or enough rice to feed three or four people for a year. See SNKS *Sekkyō shū*, 357n.7.

weeping all the while, "allow me five days. I'm going to offer prayers for my father to my heart's content. Then, five days from now, in the evening, I'll go with you. Please come for me then."

Gonga, too, shed a tear. "In that case," he said, confirming their agreement, "I'll be back in the evening, five days from now. I'm staying at Gorō Dayū's Tsuruya Inn in Tengai. Let me know if you need me." And with that, he set out for his lodging.

Sayohime's mother was visiting the family buddha hall, sounding the sacred bell and drum, and reciting the *nenbutsu*.[11] Sayohime approached. "Hello, Mother, listen," she cried. "I just found some gold outside the gate! Here, take a look."

"How wonderful!" the mother exclaimed. "This gold must be something special. Even though you're a girl, you've been so concerned about your father in the afterworld and so anxious to give him the proper rites that heaven has granted you this gift! It's entirely due to your dear father's kindness." The mother was infinitely pleased. "So," she continued, "let's put on a fine anniversary service." Summoning their former retainers, Sayohime and her mother organized a grand ceremony with a multitude of priests to pray for Lord Kyōgoku's enlightenment. The priests' efforts were marvelous to behold.

After the day had ended, poor Sayohime turned to her mother and spoke: "I'm so happy that we've been able to carry out these diligent devotions for Father's enlightenment! There's just a little bit of gold left, so please use it to continue your observances for a while. There's something I have to tell you—I've sold myself to a trader, and when he comes for me, I'll be leaving for some far-off province. But even if I'm to be eaten by eagles, hawks, or bears, it will be for my father's sake, and I won't regret it in the least. As long as I'm alive, then no matter where I am, I'll be sure to write. There's nothing you can do about it now, so please just accept it and try not to grieve too much. That would make me happier than anything else. Still, it'll be hard to say good-bye!" And with that, Sayohime broke down and sobbed.

"Is this a dream?" the mother cried. "Can it be true? Have you really gone and done such a heartless thing? You may have offered prayers for your father's enlightenment, but you've still got a mother living in the world! Do you think it's filial to cause me such pain? Your dead father may be a parent, but isn't

---

11. The *nenbutsu* is the ritual invocation of the name of Amida Buddha.

your living mother one, too? Oh, you cruel girl!" The mother bawled in grief. And she was right to feel the way she did.

The appointed hour soon arrived, and Gonga no Tayū came to claim the child. He stood waiting outside the gate. "Listen, Mother," poor Sayohime said, "it won't do any good to cry now. Just think of it as my destiny from a previous life, and please don't grieve! Wherever I end up, I'll send a message right away. The trader has come already, so I'll say farewell now." Reluctantly, she headed outside.

The mother was overcome with sorrow. "What kind of awful karma is this?" she lamented. "Since losing your father I've been living this wretched, lonely life, only to be left by you! I've survived it all until now, but after you go, do you think I'll live for one more day or even another hour? You're a hateful child to mourn your dead father while torturing your living mother like this! Are there no gods or buddhas in the world? Wherever you go, dear, take me with you, please! How can I get along without you?" Clinging to her daughter, the mother wept and wailed as if she had lost her mind. It was a moving sight to see.

Sayohime spoke: "Please, Mother, don't cry like that! It'll be the death of you. You're right to be upset, but there's nothing we can do about it now. And even if you were to insist on coming with me, the trader wouldn't allow it. Please just accept it and let me go!" But the mother clung to her daughter all the more.

Gonga had been waiting outside the gate, and although a great deal of time had passed, the girl had yet to emerge. He was extremely annoyed. "This is a bad business," he fumed. "I paid an extremely generous price, and we made a deal! Now I'm waiting and waiting, and she's not here. What's the meaning of this?"

Gonga barged in through the gate and began to shout. But no one made the slightest sound, and that angered him even more. He stormed through a passageway and down a winding corridor. Then, when he stepped into the main house, he saw the mother and daughter flailing on the floor in a paroxysm of grief.[12] He glared at them and snarled, "Hey, little lady, why are you late? And how long am I supposed to wait? It's past time already and it's going to be dark soon, so hurry up!" He strode over to Sayohime, grabbed her by the wrist, jerked her to her feet, and marched her outside. It was a terrible sight to see!

---

12. In the 1661 *Matsura Chōja*, Gonga finds them chanting sutras in the family buddha hall. See SNKS *Sekkyō shū*, 360.

The mother stared. "You heartless master!" she screamed, weeping bitter, burning tears. "It's not the girl's fault! I'm the one who's been keeping her here. Let her go, please!"

"What a stupid thing to say!" Gonga retorted. "I bought her for an extremely generous price, so however much you cry, it won't do any good."

Poor Sayohime! Having resigned herself to her fate, she surrendered to the man.

The mother was beside herself with grief. "Oh, how cruel!" she thought. "Rather than stay here and suffer like this, I'll follow them wherever they go, for as long as I'm alive, until it kills me!" She ran outside in her bare feet and clung to her daughter. Gonga was enraged. "Listen, lady," he threatened, glowering at her ferociously, "if you follow us any farther, I'll give the girl a vicious beating."

"You heartless master!" the poor mother cried. "It's our final parting in life, so don't talk to me like that! If you don't want me to come along, then tell me where you're taking her. Tell me now, tell me!"

Gonga decided to lie. "It's like this, ma'am," he explained. "I'm from Michinoku in the north, and I'm adopting the girl so that I can have her married to some provincial lord. I'll be able to count on a son-in-law like that to support me. If it all works out, I'll send someone to fetch you right away. Now go home, quickly." Pushing the child ahead, Gonga set out for the capital.

The poor mother spoke through her tears: "Please, master, wait. I know it's pointless to plead anymore. If that's what you intend, then please take good care of my daughter on the road. She's still so young!" Gonga saw that the woman was relenting. "As I said," he continued, pretending to care, "I don't have any children of my own, so I'm planning to rely on her for my personal support. Please put your heart at ease."

PART 2

The poor mother accepted Gonga's explanation. "Listen, Sayohime," she said, "you have to think of Master Gonga as your father now and serve him well. But can this really be good-bye? Oh, how sad! I wonder if we'll ever meet again?" Seizing her daughter by the hems and sleeves, she wept as if to disappear. And she was right to grieve!

Gonga listened, and his blood began to boil. "This is uncalled for!" he declared. "The girl was expensive, and I bought her! What do you mean by

Gonga no Tayū beats Sayohime in front of her mother. From *Sayohime* (seventeenth-century *nara ehon*). (Courtesy of the Kyoto University Department of Literature)

crying so much when you've entrusted her to me, and when it's time for her to go? It's bad luck to carry on like that before such a long journey! I'll thrash her good!" Gonga raised his bamboo pole and struck Sayohime two and then three times on her snow-white skin. Her pathetic mother clung to his sleeve. "No, Master, please!" she cried. "I'll go now! Forgive me, please!"

Turning to her daughter, she said, "Oh, Sayohime! It breaks my heart to lose you! And sadder still, to see you suffer because of me! Wherever you end up, send word, please. It'll be what keeps me going. Oh, child, I almost forgot! That protective charm around your neck is a sutra left to you by your father. It's the Lotus, the most important of all the sutras that the Buddha preached over fifty years. Among its eight scrolls, the fifth contains the Devadatta chapter, which tells about buddhahood for women—how even the eight-year-old Dragon Girl was able to achieve salvation.[13] Women should honor and trust in it, for both this life and their next rebirth. Wherever you go, stay safe! As they say, it's the long-lived turtle that reaches Mount Hōrai.[14] We'll meet again someday! Oh, my daughter!"

Looking back all the while, Sayohime set out on her way. Her mother stood and watched. After her daughter had disappeared from sight, she returned to the mansion in a haze of tears. She collapsed in the buddha hall in an anguish of sorrow, and at sometime or other she lost her mind. Screaming and sobbing through the day and night, she cried herself blind. In her madness, she fled from the mansion to the old Nara capital, where children jeered at her as she dashed, pranced, wept, and grieved with her face shamefully exposed.[15] Her wretchedness was beyond words.

Sayohime and Gonga left the capital in the hours before dawn.[16] Crossing the white waves of the Shirakawa River, they came to the Gion Forest, where

---

13. According to the Devadatta chapter of the Lotus sutra, the eight-year-old daughter of the *nāga* dragon king heard the bodhisattva Mañjuśrī preach the Lotus sutra, whereupon, after presenting Shakyamuni Buddha with a priceless jewel, she attained instant and full enlightenment before the eyes of a group of doubting men.

14. Mount Hōrai is a legendary island of Daoist immortals in the ocean east of Japan.

15. As a woman of high social status, the mother would normally wear a veil in public.

16. The Kyoto capital, rather than the old capital of Nara. Unlike the 1661 and circa 1704 *Matsura Chōja*, which include descriptions of Gonga and Sayohime's trip from Nara to Kyoto, the Kyoto University *Sayohime* begins its *michiyuki* travel passage from the city of Kyoto.

flocks of crows arose like the feelings in Sayohime's heart. At Awataguchi, Sayohime wondered what further misery might await her at her unknown destination, while in the dark hills of Yamashina, crickets cried, "Who pines?" in the early morning light. At Shinomiya Shrine, Jūzenji Temple, and Ōsaka Barrier Shrine,[17] Sayohime bowed and prayed that the parting from her mother might not be their last; pressing on to Uchide Beach, she wept with the plovers that were crying on the strand. Traversing Seta Bridge, she sadly contemplated the long way ahead. She continued past Shinohara, her sleeves drenched with the dew and autumn rain, and pushed on to Moriyama. Bedraggled by travel, she felt ashamed to face Kagamiyama, "Mirror Mountain." She walked on to the Banba post station, where stormy winds blow fierce; awoke from her dreams at Samegai, the "Awakening Well"; trod the Narrow Road of Ono; and threaded her way through Surihari "Needle" Pass, where, looking back into the distance, she found herself cut off from her beloved Yamato Province by the faraway, spreading clouds.

Alas, poor Sayohime! Being still just a child and thus exhausted from the journey, distant beyond imagination, she collapsed along the way, weeping and moaning in pain. "You cursed girl!" Gonga railed. "After twenty days I might feel some pity, but we've only just set out! If you start crying like that now, then what are we supposed to do about the rest of the trip ahead?" He pulled Sayohime to her feet and forced her on for another two or three leagues, but his efforts were for naught. When the girl could not take another step, she clung to his sleeves, weeping as if to die. "I can't go any farther!" she cried. "Please let me stop for today!" Gonga was enraged. Deciding that it was useless to reason with a hateful woman, he simply yanked her to her feet and shouted, "Walk! Walk!" But try as he might, he could not make her go. He grabbed his pole and beat her savagely; yet even with a flogging, she still would not move. Thus, with no other choice, he let her rest for three days at the Yamanaka post station.

Setting out again on their way, Sayohime and Gonga came to the windswept Fuwa Barrier,[18] where Sayohime soaked her sleeves so fully with grief that the moon seemed to reflect in the fabric. Dew dripped from between the ceiling

---

17. The Ōsaka Barrier at Ōtsu at the southern tip of Lake Biwa marked an eastern entrance to the capital region. Jūzenji Temple and Shinomiya Shrine (Moroha Shrine) are farther west.

18. The Fuwa Barrier was in the southwest part of contemporary Gifu Prefecture.

planks of the ruined barrier house. Hearing that they were near Tarui, or "Dripping Well," Sayohime was indeed unable to stanch her tears. They reached Akasaka in the faint light of dawn, and passing through "flowering" Mino Province—are the blossoms there in bloom?—they came to the Kunze River and the Ōkuma riverbed, where the wind in the pines blows like the sound of a *koto*. Sayohime exclaimed at the name of the "Difficult post station," and pushing on into Owari Province, she felt that her end was near. She bowed and prayed at Atsuta Shrine;[19] passed by the Narumi Inlet, wondering what would become of her at last; and crossed into Mikawa Province. Approaching Mount Asuke, she heard a stag cry with longing for its mate. It reminded her of the Kasuga deer in her own home town, and she cried along with him as she walked.

The days passed, and eventually the travelers came to the famous Eight Bridges of Yatsuhashi.[20] Hoping to comfort his companion, Gonga said, "Listen, Sayohime, you're not the only girl who ever sold herself for the sake of her parents. In fact, these eight bridges were built by two children, six and two years old, who sold themselves to sponsor services for their parents' enlightenment. That's why this place is called Yatsuhashi, or 'Slave Bridges.'[21] So cheer up now and hurry along!"

The two travelers continued on their way. Wondering where the journey would end, Sayohime found herself in Tōtōmi Province. Fishing boats rode the evening tide into Hamana Lake, with no need to pole. Did the fishermen there long for their loved ones as they pulled on their oars? Gazing off toward the south, Sayohime saw trawling boats bobbing on the endless ocean. Wretchedly rowing across the horizon, they reminded her of herself. "How sad!" she exclaimed. The lake lay to the north, with encampments strung out along the shore. Hearing the wind in the pines and the sound of the waves, Sayohime sensed the true form of all things, and staring out afar, she saw it as a part of the Buddha's holy law.

Passing through this fleeting, illusory world, they came to the "Wretched post station" and marveled at its name; then to the "Living Fields" of Ikeda,

---

19. Atsuta Shrine is in the city of Nagoya in contemporary Aichi Prefecture.

20. A place where eight bridges are said to have spanned eight branches of the Aizuma River.

21. The name Yatsuhashi is typically written with the characters for "eight bridges" 八橋, but because *yatsu* (eight) is a homonym for "slave," the name can also mean "Slave Bridges."

Sayohime and Gonga no Tayū at the Eight Bridges of Yatsuhashi. From *Sayohime* (seventeenth-century *nara ehon*). (Courtesy of the Kyoto University Department of Literature)

barren in spite of their appellation; and on to Fukuroi. Following a long road through the paddies, they passed by Nissaka and ascended the famous slope of Sayo no Nakayama. Crossing the ridge, Sayohime was dejected to think that she might never climb it again. Sick with sorrow, she came to the Ōi River and then to Fujieda, "Wisteria Branch" of purple flowers. Having fallen into such a state, Sayohime wept into her sleeves all the way to the Okabe post station.

Awake or in a dream, the travelers came to Mount Utsu. Then, with heavy hearts, they pushed their way through the Narrow Road of Ivy,[22] past the villages of Mariko and Tegoshi. Crossing Mount Shizuhata on a long spring day, they heard warblers warbling a tapestry of sound. It made Sayohime miss her home even more, and whether sleeping or awake, she came to see visions of her mother's face. Skirting the Miho Pine Forest, they looked out on waves of treetops to their right. They passed Yui and the Kanbara post station, and gazing up at Mount Fuji, they saw this year's snow blanketing the mottled drifts of yesteryear. Smoke sadly rose from the white-mantled peak, reminding poor Sayohime of her own incessant, smoldering grief.

The waves lapped at Tago Bay, and the wind whipped up sand at Fukiage Beach, where the view of the pines was a lonely one indeed. Passing by the forlorn fields of Ukishima-ga-hara, Sayohime watched mandarin ducks frolic in the marsh, and she envied them their ability to fly off to wherever they pleased.

At Mishima in Izu, they wondered where Urashima Tarō opened that regrettable box, and they struggled up Mount Hakone beyond.[23] Leaving the Ashigara mountains behind her, Sayohime climbed with all her might, but before long she could not take another step, and she collapsed along the way. Gonga checked on her when she failed to arise. "Poor girl!" he thought to himself. "She's just a child, so it's only natural. But it won't do for me to show her any kindness." He therefore glared at her and said, "How can you lie there looking so pathetic? Don't you know that everyone's pointing and laughing?" It would have been easy for Gonga to have taken a break, but they were traveling on a schedule and there was no time to spare. "Hurry up!" he shouted, pulling her to her feet and forcing her to walk. Poor Sayohime, so mercilessly abused! The hem of her robe was soaked from the dew, while her sleeves were wilted with tears. Dripping blood from her feet, she stained the roadside grasses wherever she stepped.

Continuing ever onward, the travelers entered Sagami Province. Though beset by numerous hardships, they pushed past Oiso and the Sagami Plain.

---

22. The Narrow Road of Ivy was a stretch of road made famous in the classical *Tales of Ise* (episode 9).

23. An allusion to the legend of the fisherman Urashima Tarō, inspired by the name Hakone, the first two syllables of which can mean "box." In addition to being a place-name, Izu no Mishima (Mishima in Izu) can mean "on what island" (hence, "where"), allowing for a series of wordplays that defy translation.

With an eye on the Kamakura mountains to their right, they asked the way ahead on their seemingly endless trek through the Musashi fields, pressing on in a daze until they came to the Sumida River.[24] There, Sayohime marveled at the sight of Umewakamaru's grave, of which she had heard in tales of old.[25] Willows and cherry trees had been planted all around, and even the sound of the *nenbutsu* seemed to hang in the air. Recognizing that the boy's pitiful plight had been the same as her own, Sayohime thought about how she, too, had come so far while her mother grieved at home. And what if her mother were to follow her here and find her dead? What would become of her then? Overcome with sadness and blinded by tears, Sayohime stood frozen in place.

Seeing the girl's distress, Gonga said, "We're almost there, Sayohime. Come on, now, quickly!" At the break of dawn they passed through the Shirakawa Barrier, also known as the Two-Site Barricade.[26] They walked on by Bald Peak at the Aizu post station, longing to see their loved ones, and after several more days they arrived at the Adachi district of Michinoku Province. The feelings in Sayohime's heart were miserable beyond compare.

Gonga no Tayū stepped inside his mansion. His wife and children crowded around him, cheering, "Oh, what a surprise!" Turning to his wife, Gonga said, "Well, it was a long hard trip, but not in vain! I bought a beautiful young lady and brought her back here with me. She's a top-notch girl, so the deity ought to be pleased. Come out front and meet her, and then see to her needs." The wife stepped outside. "Oh, you poor darling!" she declared. "You must be worn out from such a long journey! Come this way, please." She led Sayohime to a rear reception room and treated her with the utmost care.

Alas, poor Sayohime! Creeping into an adjoining room, she surveyed the house's interior. Then, she pressed her sleeve to her face and sobbed. "Curse this wretched world!" she mumbled as she cried. "My father's mansion in Tsubosaka in Yamato Province was grander than this! I can still remember how it

---

24. Today, the Sumida River runs through the eastern part of metropolitan Tokyo.

25. According to the nō play *Sumidagawa* and other sources, the boy Umewakamaru was kidnapped from the capital when he was only twelve years old. His captors brought him north, but he died at the Sumida River. His mother followed him there, distraught with grief. She found his grave planted with willows, and while chanting the *nenbutsu* through the night, she was able to speak with his ghost.

26. Located in the southern part of contemporary Fukushima Prefecture, the Shirakawa Barrier marked the entrance to the far northern province of Michinoku.

used to be . . ." Weeping torrents of tears through the day and night, she was a sad sight to see.

"You hateful girl!" Gonga roared. "I can see why you'd be upset along the road, and I felt sorry for you when you were, but what could be the matter now that we're taking such good care of you? I'll give you something to cry about!"

"Wait, dear, listen," Gonga's wife interrupted. "From her looks and her bearing, you can see that she's no ordinary girl. In fact, she doesn't look at all like someone who would put herself up for sale! Are you sure you didn't kidnap her someplace? It makes me wonder . . ." Gonga was enraged. "How dare you! She had her reasons, and I bought her! And if I had stolen or kidnapped her, she wouldn't have come along with me, would she?"

Later, Gonga instructed his retainers to clean the house. He had them purify one of the rooms and adorn it with seven strands of sacred ceremonial rope, coarse ceremonial matting, and the like, which they spread on the floor, and twelve wooden wands with holy paper streamers. Then Gonga declared that this would be Sayohime's room. "Now let's purify the girl," he said, and he had her perform seven sets of hot, cold, and saltwater ablutions for a total of twenty-one rounds of ritual cleansing. Afterward, he moved her into her new quarters.

Poor Sayohime had no idea that she was to be sacrificed to the deity. "What's going on around here?" she wondered to herself. "Back in the capital, I never even heard about things like this. These easterners have some strange customs."

"Excuse me, ladies," Sayohime asked her attendants, "but is this kind of thing a tradition in these parts? It seems odd." The women wept and replied, "So you don't know, then, do you? How sad! We weren't going to say anything, but there are no more days left now, and you should be prepared. We have a peculiar ritual in our district. Eight *chō* to the north of here is a lake known as the Sakurai Abyss.[27] It's three leagues around, and a great snake lives in it. The serpent is our god, and once every year the people of the eight hamlets and eight villages hold a festival in which they take turns feeding it a beautiful young girl as a living human sacrifice. This year the responsibility fell to our own Master Gonga, which is why he traveled to the capital and bought you. Just think of it as your karma from a previous life and try to focus on the world to come."

Hearing the women's words, Sayohime wondered whether she was dreaming or awake. Pressing her sleeves to her face, she wept as if to disappear. "You

---

27. One *chō* equals approximately 119 yards, so eight *chō* is slightly more than half a mile.

see," she said, speaking between her sobs, "when I sold myself for my father's sake, I knew that I'd be coming to this unknown eastern province. But I miss my home anyway, and when I think about how brokenhearted my mother must be, I feel so sad that I can hardly stand it! Even if I were to live at the edge of some faraway land like this, as long as I'm alive I could at least take a little comfort in the thought that I might see her again someday. But not if I'm going to be eaten by a giant snake tomorrow! Still, I feel sorrier for my mother than I do for myself. She doesn't even know what's going to happen. She's probably waiting desperately for some news, crying all the while. Oh, my poor mother!" The girl spoke haltingly, shedding bitter, burning tears. All those who saw or heard her had to wring the sorrow from their sleeves.

Gonga's wife listened to Sayohime's laments, and she thought that she was right to grieve. Weeping, she approached the girl and spoke: "Listen, Sayohime, I can see why you're upset. It's perfectly reasonable. What province does your mother live in and in what town? I'll be going on a pilgrimage to Kumano in the spring of next year to fulfill a long-standing vow,[28] and I can take something for you then. Why don't you write her a letter? I'll be sure to deliver it."

Gonga happened to overhear his wife. Glaring at her furiously with wide, angry eyes, he shouted, "What's going on here? How can you carry on like that beside our sacrifice-girl? We're offering her in prayer for the prosperity of our house and community!"

"Listen, dear," the wife replied in tears, "let's offer our own daughter instead. It couldn't be any sadder than this! It breaks my heart to imagine what the girl must be feeling or the depth of her mother's grief!" Gonga thought that she had a point, but he angrily countered, "Well, if you think we should sacrifice our own child, then I don't know why I had to go all the way to the capital to buy someone else's!" And with that, he slammed the sliding paper door and retreated inside.

PART 3

Following precedent, Gonga no Tayū thought that he would inform the residents of the eight hamlets and eight villages about the upcoming ceremony.

---

28. The three-site Kumano shrine complex on the Kii peninsula, southeast of the capital.

The weather being fine, he set out on a sturdy mount with a large retinue of retainers. He rode from place to place, immediately announcing throughout the entire district that he, Gonga no Tayū, would be sponsoring the rite this year and that the same as always, everyone should attend. The people were overjoyed. "How wonderful!" they all exclaimed.

Upon hearing the news, the locals built a viewing stand beside the lake, and everyone gathered together, clamoring to see the spectacle. As the day had finally arrived, Gonga sidled up to Sayohime and spoke: "Hello, girl, listen. Since a long time ago, it's been an annual ritual here to present our deity with a living human sacrifice. It's also customary for the responsibility for the ceremony to rotate among the eight hamlets and eight villages. This year it's my turn, but because I have only one daughter, I couldn't bear to give her up. I traveled to the capital, and among all the people who were selling themselves there, I happened to find you! It's a sad situation, but since it's entirely the result of karma, there's no point in crying. Just try to accept it. It breaks my heart to see you mourn, so I'd like you to send home a keepsake. I'll have it specially delivered; you won't have to worry about it at all. Just hurry up and get something ready. What do you think?"

"Oh, Master Gonga," Sayohime calmly replied, "as I said at the start, I sold myself in order to hold a service for my father's enlightenment. So any hardship that I meet is for his sake, and there's no reason to grieve. But as you saw for yourself in Tsubosaka, I tried to comfort my mother when she was distressed by saying that wherever I might end up living, I'd be sure to write. That's how I left her, and she's probably been waiting desperately for some news. Poor Mother! But even so, it won't do any good to cry about it now. Yes, I would like you to take her something for me." Gonga was a man like a demon, but even he shed a furtive tear. And everyone who saw or heard tell of it likewise soaked their sleeves with dew.

Thinking that she would compose a farewell letter, Sayohime called for paper and an inkstone. But when she tried to write, she was blinded by tears. If only she could see where to set her brush to the paper! When her characters came out in a muddled disarray, she threw away the brush with a clatter and began to sob, pitiful beyond description.

After a while, she pulled herself together. She cut a lock of hair from her temple and rolled it up in the letter, which she carried to Gonga's wife. "Please take this for me," she requested in a faltering voice. The wife wept with Sayohime and replied, "I'll make sure that it's delivered. You can put your heart at ease."

Seeing Sayohime with his wife, Gonga was elated at how calm the girl was. Because the time had come to leave, he had her get dressed in the appropriate attire. Then he hung a sacred ceremonial rope around a plain wooden palanquin and placed her inside. The weather being fine, Gonga's entire household set out in a boisterous procession, marching eighteen *chō* to the edge of the lake.[29] A vast crowd of rich and poor had gathered there to watch. There were three splendid boats bobbing near the shore: one for the district overseer and other provincial officials, one for Gonga's household, and one that was decked out with a sacred ceremonial rope and wooden wands with holy paper streamers.

The Shinto priests, the lake guardians, and Gonga no Tayū, because he was the designated sponsor, put Sayohime inside the covered cabin of the third vessel and gaily rowed out on the lake. They drew up to an island with a three-tiered platform festooned on all four sides with sacred ceremonial ropes and wooden wands with holy paper streamers. As the sacrificial offering, Sayohime was placed on the upper tier. The middle tier was for the priests, who took up the wooden wands, bowed twice in supplication, and pronounced a ritual invocation. Gonga ascended to the lower tier, where he prayed that all his wishes might be fulfilled.

After they had finished their invocation, the priests pressed their heads to the floor, rubbed their rosary beads with a scraping sound, and earnestly addressed the deity, saying, "Gonga no Tayū presents this girl to you as a votive offering for the prosperity of his house and district. Please accept his gift and appear here now!" Having completed the ceremony, the men all scrambled for the boat, terrified that the great serpent might suddenly appear. They took to the oars in a panic and rowed away from the island. Upon finally reaching the beach and climbing the bank, Gonga and the priests felt as if they had tread on a tiger's tail or stroked the whiskers of some poisonous snake. They sat in a row on the shore and began to wait in eager anticipation. But strange to say, although they waited for one and then two hours, the deity failed to appear.

Meanwhile, having been left alone on the platform, Sayohime was overcome with hopeless tears. But she soon decided that there was no point in crying anymore, and abandoning all thought for the present world, she took out the

---

29. Eighteen *chō* is approximately one-and-a-quarter miles. Previously, Sayohime's attendants described the lake as being eight *chō* away from the mansion.

fifth scroll of the Lotus sutra and began to chant the Devadatta chapter with perfect concentration. "If I am to be devoured by the great serpent," she prayed in her heart, "then by the power of this scripture, please allow me to attain enlightenment as an immediate result."

Gonga and the priests and all the other people who were lining the shore began to wonder what was happening. "Our offering this year is the best and most beautiful we've ever had," they whispered among themselves. "We were sure that the serpent would accept it. But it doesn't come, so something must be wrong. Who knows . . . maybe it was displeased with the priests' invocation? What should we do? If it's offended, then the eight hamlets and eight villages are doomed! Even if there's no escape, let's get away from here. We can all pray for forgiveness on our own!"

The people fled for their houses in a mad rush. Young and old collapsed here and there, falling into ditches and wailing in a way that was pitiful to hear. Upon finally reaching their homes, all the villagers locked themselves inside, barred their doors, and waited silently in anxious dread.

After a while, the sunny sky clouded over. Thunderbolts crashed amid a fury of wind and rain. The lake roiled, and the great snake emerged. It was thirty yards long, with eyes that shone like the sun and moon. It had 99,000 scales and 14,000 bristling fins. Spitting flames from its mouth and flicking its crimson tongue, it slapped the water with its tail, splashing up waves like tall, snowy peaks. Seeing Sayohime, it slithered up to the island and rested its head on the platform's second tier, ready to devour the girl at once.

Poor Sayohime! Having already accepted her fate, she was not agitated in the least. Raising a mighty voice, she said, "Listen carefully, snake! I come from Yamato Province. I lost my father when I was young, and I've been without his support ever since. My mother raised me over the months and years. It's the thirteenth anniversary of my father's death this year, and although I wanted to hold services for his enlightenment, I couldn't afford to. So I decided to sell myself and use the money to pay for rites. I happened to meet Gonga no Tayū, who comes from this land, and he brought me here. Now, strangely, I am to be your sacrificial offering. But because it's for my father's sake that I'm going to give up this fleeting life of mine, I don't wish you any harm. My only sorrow is for my mother, who's still living in this world, and for my own enlightenment. There's no use in grieving for my mother, but please allow me a little time to read a sutra scroll. I want you to listen to it, too. By the power of this scripture, the eight-year-old Dragon Girl received the prophecy to attain enlightenment

Sayohime reads the Lotus sutra to the great snake. From *Sayohime* (seventeenth-century *nara ehon*). (Courtesy of the Kyoto University Department of Literature)

as Heavenly King Thus Come One.³⁰ I therefore command you, too, to attain buddhahood with me!"³¹

The serpent hung its head and retracted its tongue, seemingly lost in thought. Feeling encouraged, Sayohime raised her voice again and recited from the fifth scroll of the Lotus sutra: "*Unga nyoshin, sokutoku jōbutsu.* As a woman, how could you quickly become a buddha?"³² With all her heart, she dedicated the merit of her reading to the snake.³³ "You too shall become a buddha!" she cried. She read aloud the famous passage about how "gods, dragons, and others of the eight kinds of guardians, humans and nonhumans, all from a distance saw the Dragon Girl attain buddhahood,"³⁴ and she struck the great snake on the head with the sutra scroll. Wondrously and miraculously, all its twelve horns fell free and shattered. Shouting, "Uphold the Buddhist law, uphold the Buddhist law!" Sayohime stroked the monster's body with the Lotus sutra from head to tail. Its 14,000 fins and 99,000 scales fluttered and fell away, scattering like blossoms in a gale.

The serpent was overjoyed. "How wonderful!" it exclaimed. "Thanks to the power of this sutra, I am sure to become a buddha and obtain release. What shall I offer you in return?" With that, the creature slid back into the lake. After a while, it reappeared as a seventeen- or eighteen-year-old girl, faced Sayohime, and spoke: "Dear lady, something happened to me in the past, and because of it, I've been living in this lake for 999 years. During that time, I have devoured more than eight hundred sacrificial victims. But until now, I've never

---

30. According to the Devadatta chapter of the Lotus sutra, it was actually Devadatta who was prophesied to attain enlightenment as Heavenly King Thus Come One. See Burton Watson, trans., *The Lotus Sutra* (New York: Columbia University Press, 1993), 184.

31. In medieval Japan, snakes and dragons were considered to be closely related species.

32. This question is posed by Shariputra in the Devadatta chapter. The Dragon Girl answers by attaining enlightenment before his very eyes. See Watson, trans., *Lotus Sutra*, 188.

33. In the 1661 *Matsura Chōja*, Sayohime dedicates the merit of the first scroll to her father, the second scroll to her mother, the third scroll to the members of her former household in Nara, the fourth scroll to Gonga and his wife, and the fifth scroll to herself. The 1704 *Matsura Chōja* is similar, except that Sayohime dedicates the merit of the fifth scroll to the serpent, rather than herself. See SNKS *Sekkyō shū*, 378, and SSS 1:194a.

34. Again, Sayohime quotes from the Devadatta chapter. Translation adapted from Watson, trans., *Lotus Sutra*, 188.

encountered anyone as magnificent as you. I'll confess my karmic obstructions on this joyful day, become a buddha, and obtain release.

"First, I am not from around here. I come from Futami Bay in Ise Province. My mother died when I was young, and since my stepmother hated me, I wandered away from home with no place to go. I was tricked by a slave trader and sold from place to place until a man named Kurihara no Jūrō, who was famous in these parts, bought me and took me in. In those days, the lake was just a little river. But the people couldn't bridge it, no matter how they tried. They held a meeting to decide what to do, and someone suggested that they ask a diviner. Everyone agreed, and when the diviner divined, he told them to offer a beautiful young woman as a pillar sacrifice.[35] It was therefore decided that all the local beauties would draw lots to see who should be drowned. I drew the losing one, whereupon they dragged me to the river's edge, saying that I was to be their pillar sacrifice. I couldn't believe it! Out of all the girls in the eight hamlets and eight villages, they were going to drown me? It was infuriating! In fact, I was so angry that I transformed into a giant serpent, thirty yards long, and became the guardian of the river.

"It seems like just the other day, but it was 999 years ago. So I've been worshipped as the district deity for almost a thousand years. I may look like I'm enjoying it, but I suffer constantly from the Three Burning Torments.[36] Yet thanks to the power of that sutra just now, as you can see, my horns and scales have fallen away, and I have escaped the suffering of my serpent form. I will soon be reborn in the Heavenly Realm,[37] where I'll establish a karmic link to enlightenment. In return for your sutra offering, I will grant you this: a wish-fulfilling jewel, the greatest treasure of the Dragon Palace.[38] It will allow you

---

35. A pillar sacrifice was a living human sacrifice for the construction of castles, bridges, levees, and the like. According to the *kōwakamai Tsukishima*, the twelfth-century Taira no Kiyomori ordered that thirty men and women be drowned as a pillar sacrifice for the construction of an artificial island near Fukuhara.

36. The Three Burning Torments are the three agonies that snakes and dragons are said to suffer in the Animal Realm. According to the 1661 *Matsura Chōja*, the serpent was infested with 99,000 insects under its scales, which caused it further indescribable pain. See SNKS *Sekkyō shū*, 382.

37. The Heavenly Realm is the highest of the six realms of nonenlightened existence, just above the Human Realm.

38. The Dragon Palace is the underwater palace of the Dragon King, a home of serpents and dragons.

to achieve your every desire." The deity presented Sayohime with the wish-fulfilling jewel. "Now, since you've told me where you're from, I will be happy to return you there myself. You can put your heart at ease."

"Tell me," Sayohime said, "are you speaking the truth? If not, then don't make me lose my concentration. Just hurry up and kill me. How about it, snake?"

"You are right to be suspicious," the deity replied. "But demons and gods aren't prone to deception. You can put your heart at ease."

"What wonderful news! In that case, please take me back to Yamato Province. But first, take me to the shore. I need to say good-bye to Gonga no Tayū, the man who bought me." The deity agreed and immediately delivered Sayohime to the bank.[39] The girl made her way to Gonga's mansion, and when the people there saw her, they could hardly believe their eyes. "How strange!" they marveled. "She must be a god or a buddha for the serpent to have saved her!"

Sayohime explained everything to Gonga and his wife, from beginning to end. "What a fabulous young lady you are!" the couple declared with boundless joy. "If it weren't just as you say, the deity would have surely accepted our offering. We'd like to keep you here with us somehow or other. Won't you please stay?"

"I wish I could," Sayohime said, "but I'm worried about my mother in Yamato. So I'll take my leave now." Sayohime set out from the mansion with Gonga and his wife seeing her on her way. Naturally, everyone in the eight hamlets and eight villages came out to pay their respects. People say that from that day forward, the province of Michinoku was blessed with peace.

Sayohime stared into the water at the edge of the lake. "Great snake," she called, "please keep your promise to carry me home! Great snake!" The serpent rose from the depths. "Yes," it said, "I'll carry you home. Just step over here." Accepting the girl on its head, the creature dove down to the bottom of the lake. By its supernatural powers, it instantly surfaced in the famous Sarusawa Pond in the Nara capital in Yamato Province. "This is as far as I'll take you. Farewell." The deity soared up into the sky on a white cloud and disappeared. It is said that the pond there has been called Sarusawa, "Leaving Marsh," ever

---

39. According to the seventeenth-century *Matsura Sayohime*, the deity changed back into a giant serpent before taking Sayohime to the shore. See Sakaguchi Hiroyuki, "Tōyō Bunko-bon *Matsura Sayohime*: Shōkai to honkoku," *Jinbun kenkyū* 34, no. 4 (1982): 41b.

since.⁴⁰ People say that in its original form, the serpent was actually the Tsubosaka Kannon of Yamato Province.⁴¹

Sayohime returned to her hometown. She searched the old family mansion for a while, looking this place and that, but her mother was gone. The house had fallen utterly into ruin, so that only foxes and owls lived there now. Taking in the sight, Sayohime lamented the cruelty of her fate. She strayed back outside and questioned one of the locals. "It's like this," the person explained. "After you went away, your mother was so upset that she lost her mind. She left the mansion and wandered around from place to place. Then she cried herself blind! She was an awful sight to see, stumbling about in a daze. I hear that she's in Nara now."

Sayohime was stunned. In her horror, she rushed to Nara and searched here and there for her mother. Perhaps because of the mysterious bond between parent and child, she soon found her. The poor woman was being teased by a crowd of urchins who were calling her "the madwoman of Matsura" and shouting, "Come over here! No, go over there!" When Sayohime saw what was happening, she ran to her mother's side, weeping, and cried, "Oh, how horrible! Mother, it's me, Sayohime! I've come back!"

"You children!" the mother spat. "Back when I lived in Matsura Valley, I had a daughter named Sayohime, but she was tricked by a slaver and taken off to who-knows-where. That's why I went crazy like this! So don't mock me like that! You know, you can't blame a blind woman for whacking you with her stick!" She snatched up her bamboo staff and flailed the air all around. Sayohime stared. Stifling her tears, she took out the wish-fulfilling jewel that the giant serpent had given her and pressed it to her mother's eyes. They were instantly restored, whereupon parent and child stood face to face, reunited as few have ever been. Sayohime and her mother embraced, sobbing and wondering whether this was not too good to be true. It was surely a case of "weeping for joy."

"What's there to cry about like that now?" Sayohime chided as she returned with her mother to Matsura Valley. She used the wish-fulfilling jewel to

---

40. The name of the pond is usually written with the characters for "monkey marsh" (Sarusawa 猿澤), but the *Sayohime* author puns on a homonym, calling it "Leaving Marsh" (Sarusawa 去澤).

41. A famous statue of the bodhisattva Kannon at Tsubosaka Temple in Nara Prefecture.

Sayohime finds her mother. From *Sayohime* (seventeenth-century *nara ehon*). (Courtesy of the Kyoto University Department of Literature)

summon showers of wealth, which she freely bestowed on her former servants and retainers and everyone who had ever shown her any kindness. She built a new mansion where the old one had been and flourished there again as her family had before. All the former members of her household flocked back on their own without having to be asked. The magnificence of Sayohime's wealth and position exceeded her father's, beyond words to describe.

Sayohime sent a messenger to Michinoku Province to summon Gonga no Tayū and his clan. She granted him numerous treasures, to his boundless delight. Later, she married the governor of Yamato Province and bore him many children. She possessed eternal youth and immortality, and exhibiting various wondrous signs, she manifested as the goddess Benzaiten of Chikubushima Shrine in Ōmi Province.[42]

Chikubushima Island is also known as Chirihōsan, "Jewel Mountain, Free from Earth," because it floats unattached to the land in all eight directions. It first appeared in the night, which is why it is also called Akezu-ga-shima, "Isle Without Dawn." And because three stalks of bamboo sprouted there in the night, it is called Chikubushima, "Isle of Sprouting Bamboo." The island's greatest treasure is its wish-fulfilling jewel. Even now in this Latter Age of the Dharma, all those who visit Chikubushima even only once will be graced with excellent good fortune. There are many examples of this from the past, so you should never doubt it at all. It was because of the goddess's profound filial devotion that such marvelous events occurred. Blessed indeed, blessed indeed!

---

42. On Chikubushima Island in Lake Biwa. According to the 1661 *Matsura Chōja*, Sayohime achieved rebirth in Amida's Pure Land at the age of eighty-five, after which she was worshipped as the Benzaiten of Chikubushima Shrine. See SNKS *Sekkyō shū*, 388. Likewise, according to the late-sixteenth- or early-seventeenth-century *Sayohime no sōshi*, Sayohime's mother manifested as the Yakushi Buddha of Hōraiji Temple in Mikawa Province at the age of eighty-three. See SSS 3:461b. The seventeenth-century *Matsura Sayohime* also reports that Sayohime's father was an incarnation of the Buddhist guardian deity Bishamonten of Kurama Temple and that Sayohime and her husband ascended to the heavens at the age of 120. See Sakaguchi, "Tōyō Bunko-bon *Matsura Sayohime*," 45.

Aigo-no-waka

ACT 1

On careful reflection, we can see the importance of embracing moral principles, revering the emperor, showing compassion for the people, and upholding the five lay precepts in the practice of government.[1] Our seventy-third human sovereign was a ruler named Emperor Saga.[2] In the age of his reign there was a noble in the flowering capital by the name of Second Avenue Chamberlain Kiyohira, former minister of the left. His wife was a daughter of First Avenue Chancellor Munetsugu, and people said that she was beautiful beyond compare.

Among the treasures passed down to Kiyohira from former generations were a special *yaiba* sword,[3] a Chinese saddle, and riches rained from heaven.

Translated from the circa 1670 *Aigo-no-waka*.

1. The five lay precepts are prohibitions against killing, stealing, lying, drinking alcohol, and sexual misconduct.

2. Saga (r. 809–823) is actually counted as the fifty-second human emperor, not the seventy-third.

3. *Yaiba* refers to a method of hardening steel in cold water; in this case, the term seems to be used to indicate a kind of magical sharpness. See SNKS *Sekkyō shū*, 301n.8.

Once when the emperor was seven years old, the imperial mother fell ill. After graciously setting Kiyohira's Chinese saddle on a two-year-old horse and strapping the *yaiba* sword to his waist, the emperor paraded to the Shishinden Ceremonial Hall and back again. The demon king of the sixth heaven was stuck with fear, and the imperial mother revived. Recognizing the rarity of Kiyohira's treasures, the emperor showered him with boundless favor.

Kiyohira's retainers included a certain Araki no Saemon Chikakuni, a resident of Negoro in Kii Province—a man who deeply revered his lord. In fact, everyone everywhere was awed by the power of Kiyohira's authority.

After the first and second months of the year had passed, the emperor decreed that his ministers hold a contest of treasures at the Shishinden Ceremonial Hall in order to liven up the snowy days. After receiving their sovereign's command, the emperor's attendants all spread the word. The chancellor, the minister of the right, the minister of the left, and everyone else brought their most prized possessions and piled them on the white gravel of the Shishinden yard. After examining the objects, the emperor declared with deep admiration that there was no treasure greater than Kiyohira's *yaiba* sword and Chinese saddle.

Reveling in his supremacy, Kiyohira addressed the Sixth Avenue lord: "Well, sir, I can do without any big talk from a wretched pauper like you every day! Isn't that so?" The poor Sixth Avenue lord crept out of the palace hall without making the slightest reply. A row of seated nobles stood up as one and also took their leave.

Later, the Sixth Avenue lord seethed with indignation. He summoned his sons and spoke: "Hello, boys, listen up! There was a contest of treasures at the palace today, and because we're poor, Second Avenue Chamberlain Kiyohira insulted me for no good reason. I was ready to take him on and die, but since we were in the palace, I couldn't do a thing. I'm going to stage an attack and go down fighting. A night assault would be best, I think. You're my heir, Yoshinaga—what do you say?"

Yoshinaga took in his father's words. "You've got a point," he replied. "But if we attack without cause, we're bound to be judged for it later. Kiyohira has no children, so there's no future to his glory. You should ask the emperor to hold a 'contest of children' next time. If he refuses, we'll launch an attack against Kiyohira, cross swords, and die. What could be the problem then, Father?" The Sixth Avenue lord smiled. "In that case," he said, "I'll speak to the emperor." And with that, he hurried off to the palace.

The emperor (*upper-left corner*) oversees a contest of treasures at the palace. From *Aigo-no-waka* (ca. 1670 woodblock-printed edition). (Courtesy of Osaka University Library)

The Rokujō lord explained his idea at the palace hall. The emperor considered: In the tenth month, the blustery winds would scatter the mountain brocade of autumn leaves, leaving the maples to await the spring. Being a boring season, it was well suited to a contest of children.

The emperor's attendants all spread the word, and when the time arrived, the head of every noble family in the capital came to present his progeny at the palace. Among them, the Sixth Avenue lord paid his respects with his five sons at his left-hand side. Taking in the sight, the emperor declared with the utmost admiration that there was in fact no treasure greater than a child. In addition, he named Yoshinaga governor of Etchū Province.

Dazzled by his son's appointment, the Sixth Avenue lord approached Chamberlain Kiyohira. Pulling him to his feet, he said, "You know, Kiyohira, there's no future for a man without children, and there's no place for him in the palace! So get out, now!"

"What's going on here?" the surrounding nobles and ministers clamored, pushing the two men apart. Then they all took their leave. The Sixth Avenue lord left, too, with his five sons in tow. "So much for my grudge!" he exclaimed, happily heading back home.

But poor Kiyohira! Upon returning to his mansion, he summoned his wife and spoke: "Listen here, dear. There was a contest of children at the palace today, and since the Sixth Avenue lord had five sons, he ran me out of the reception hall. I've never been so mortified! I was ready to fight, but because we were in the palace, I couldn't do a thing. And now I've come home without taking my revenge. I'm going to slit my belly. I want you to live on and pray for me in the world to come." Kiyohira looked ready to do himself in. His wife clung to him and cried, "Oh, you're so right, so correct! And it's all because we have no children!" She wept as if to disappear.

The wife spoke between bouts of tears: "Listen, dear, I hear that if we pray to the buddhas and gods, they'll give us a child. Let's pray to the Kannon of Mount Hase.[4] Then, if we still don't have a child, I'll kill myself with you and we can cross the Great Sanzu River hand in hand.[5] How does that sound, dear?" The wife clutched her husband's sleeves and wept bitter, anguished tears. Kiyohira agreed, so with a multitude of retainers, they set out for Mount Hase.

At the temple, they purified themselves by rinsing their mouths and hands. Then they rattled the sacred summoning bell and made their earnest request: "Hail most merciful Kannon! We ask that you please give us a child, either a boy or a girl." They ensconced themselves in the temple for seven days, whereupon the marvelous Hase Kannon appeared before them where they slept. "Dear Kiyohira," he said, "although there are more children in the world than there are stars in the heavens, for you and your wife there are none. Go home now, quickly!" The supplicants awoke, and the bodhisattva disappeared.

Kiyohira and his wife jumped up with a start. "What a heartless blessing! If you won't give us a child, then take our lives instead!" Having spoken thus, they stayed inside the temple for another three days. Again, the marvelous Kannon appeared before them where they slept. "Although I had no child for

---

4. The statue of the bodhisattva Kannon at Hase Temple, in the mountains on the southeastern side of the Nara valley.

5. The Great Sanzu River is a mythical river on the way to the court of King Enma, judge of the afterworld.

you," he explained, "I am moved by your desperate pleading at the risk of your lives. When the child turns three, I will come for either you or your wife. How about that, Kiyohira?" Dreamily, the wife said, "Take my life in the morning if I can have a child tonight! But please give me a child, either a boy or a girl." Hearing her promise, the bodhisattva granted her wish and vanished without a trace.

The couple jumped up with a start. "Oh, thank you!" they cried, and bowed down three times in grateful supplication. Then, with their many retainers, they set out for the capital. The joy in Kiyohira's heart was beyond the power of words to describe.

ACT 2

The Sixth Avenue lord summoned his retainer Takeda no Tarō and spoke: "Hello, Takeda, listen up! Second Avenue Chamberlain Kiyohira insulted me at the palace when he was full of the emperor's favor, and then he never gave it a second thought. What's more, people say that he's scheming and plotting against me now! It'll be our downfall if we let him continue. I hear that he's made a little prayer request at Mount Hase in Yamato Province and that he'll be leaving there today. And it just so happens that he's got a woman slowing him down! It's the chance we've been waiting for. We'll lie in ambush at the Katsura River and cut him down there. What could go wrong?"

With Takeda and a force of more than three thousand riders, the Sixth Avenue lord rushed to the Katsura River with his heir, the governor of Etchū. Kiyohira soon arrived. Catching sight of him there, the waiting warriors raised a clamorous cry. When their voices had died down, Araki no Saemon stepped forward and shouted, "Who's making all that ruckus? Give me your name—I'm listening!"

A single rider stepped forward from the attacking army. Standing tall in his stirrups over the bridge of his saddle, he announced himself in a booming voice: "Who do you think I am, this great general who confronts you now? Sixth Avenue Lord Yukishige, that's who! Kiyohira, you once ran me out of the reception hall at the palace and then never gave it a second thought! What's more, I hear that you've been scheming, slandering me to the emperor, and plotting against me! How about it, Kiyohira? You're caught in heaven's net, and there's no one who can save you! Go ahead and slash your belly!"

"So, you're the lousy Sixth Avenue lord!" Saemon bellowed. "And you've come all this way? It may be pointless addressing all you villains like this, but you've got no beef with my master. Whether or not it's true, I hear the Sixth Avenue lord doesn't venerate the Buddha, the Dharma, or the Sangha![6] His robes are thin, and people say that when he's starving, he goes out pillaging and pirating! Rather than facing me like this, running off your mouths and looking to get hurt, you should all just go home."

The Sixth Avenue lord was enraged. "Slandering knave!" he roared, turning to his men. "Cut him down!" His warriors charged forward, attacking as if the day were their last. Suddenly, the Nara priest Tokkōbō ran between the two forces. Looking to his left, he saw the banner design of the Sixth Avenue lord's assaulting army—a one-wheeled cart, beset by waves—and to his right, which he had come to defend, he saw the crest of Second Avenue Chamberlain Kiyohira: a circle cut by two lines over a *mokkō* flower emblem. "As all of you know," he shouted, "I am Tokkōbō of Nara! Do you disturb the peace because of some order of the emperor or because of a personal grudge? Speak up now, I'm listening!"

Araki no Saemon stepped forward and explained the situation. "Foolishness!" Tokkōbō declared. "If any of you men continue brawling, the emperor will be hard pressed to forgive either Chamberlain Kiyohira or the Sixth Avenue lord. He'll settle your disagreement for you, I think. How about that?" The two sides gave up their ire and returned to the capital. Everyone was amazed at the depth of Tokkōbō's wisdom.

ACT 3

Meanwhile, the bodhisattva seemed to have answered Kiyohira's prayers because his wife soon found herself pregnant. After enduring her seventh-month suffering and her ninth-month misery, she loosened her birthing sash in her tenth month and delivered a child. When Kiyohira and his wife picked up the baby for a look, they beheld a young master like a jewel, which is why they named him Aigo-no-waka, or "Little Aigo."[7] Providing him with a bevy of nurses and attendants, they cherished him to no end.

---

6. The Three Jewels of Buddhism: the Buddha, the Buddhist teachings, and the Buddhist monastic order. Saemon accuses the Sixth Avenue lord of irreligiosity.

7. His name is written with characters meaning "dearly protected child."

Tokkōbō and his disciples break up a fight between Kiyohira and the Sixth Avenue lord. From *Aigo-no-waka* (ca. 1670 woodblock-printed edition). (Courtesy of Osaka University Library)

The young master grew by leaps and bounds, like a bamboo shoot that sprouts in the evening and thrives on the midnight dew. He was soon five, ten, and then thirteen years old. With nothing to weigh on his heart, he passed his days within his eight-, nine-, and single-layered curtains, reveling in the pleasures of his painted screens. Masterfully executed, they depicted the four seasons before the boy's very eyes. Spring showed a flowering cherry tree beside a rough-woven fence; summer showed a cuckoo in a patch of sunflowers, spiritedly chirping for the first time of the season against the rush of a cool mountain stream; autumn showed colorful chrysanthemums blooming with a rare and lovely fragrance; and winter showed snow falling in a pure white valley with a small frozen stream. Everyone envied the splendor of the boy's daily life.

One day, in her idleness, Kiyohira's wife spoke: "Hey, everybody, listen. Back when we received our Little Aigo from the Hase Mountain Kannon, the bodhisattva said that when the child turned three, either Kiyohira or I would be in mortal danger. But he's thirteen now, and still nothing's happened! It just goes to show that even the gods and buddhas are liars. So it's only right that people should lie to get by in this world. How about that, everyone?" People say that with these words, the wife's luck ran out.

It may be a long way to Mount Hase, but the bodhisattva heard her there. Summoning his pestilence demons, he said, "Go and kill the Second Avenue chamberlain's wife!" and immediately set them loose. Taking the form of an evil wind, the demons blew into the Second Avenue estate, seized the poor lady, and began to tear away her spirit. Alas, the poor wife! Unable to remain in the reception hall, she withdrew to her bed where she lay down, dying. Kiyohira and Little Aigo tried to help her however they could, but because she suffered from a divine punishment, their efforts were for naught.

In the moments before her death, the wife sat up with some assistance and said, "My dear husband, I'm on my way now to the afterworld. I'm entrusting you to look after our one and only son. And you, Aigo—please understand that after I'm gone, your father will need a new wife, whatever anybody says. You should treat her like a parent and serve her well. Oh, Kiyohira, it's so hard for me to say good-bye! And to leave you, Little Aigo—that's even harder still!" These were her final words. Thus, at the age of thirty-three, the lady passed away. Kiyohira and the boy could only cry, "How can this be? How can this be?" weeping as if to disappear.

The young master was especially affected. "Oh, Mother," he whimpered, sobbing bitter, burning tears, "there isn't anyone—not anyone—who can escape death. But this parting is unbearable! If you have to go, then please take me with you!" But because there was nothing that Kiyohira or the boy could do, they eventually carried her corpse to the cremation grounds, where she disappeared in a wisp of smoke.

On the way home, Little Aigo offered flowers and incense and intoned a sutra for his mother's salvation. "By the power of the ten *rakshasa* daughters described in this scripture," he declared, "may you quickly attain buddhahood![8] Hail the Three Jewels in this fleeting world of sorrow!" Then he wept as if to die. His grief was beyond description.

---

8. A *rakshasa* is a kind of flesh-eating demon. According to the Dharani chapter of the Lotus sutra, ten *rakshasa* daughters made a vow to Shakyamuni Buddha to protect everyone who accepts and recites the Lotus sutra.

Elsewhere, the extended family gathered to discuss the situation. "Whatever anybody says," they observed, "Kiyohira will need a wife." Araki no Saemon stepped forward and asked, "How about the daughter of the Eighth Avenue lord?" Everyone agreed that this was an excellent idea. They immediately sent a messenger, who visited the Eighth Avenue estate and presented their proposal. Several of the people at the meeting also traveled to Eighth Avenue to make their case. The Eighth Avenue lord was favorably inclined, and quickly granting his approval, he sent the messenger back to Second Avenue. Then, without waiting to choose an auspicious day, he sent his daughter there as well.[9] Upon arriving, she and Kiyohira became husband and wife, like birds that fly with wings as one or like trees with branches entwined.

The days passed, but the young master was more pitiful than before. Word of his father's marriage reached him in the family buddha hall. "How unfeeling!" he exclaimed. "It's been only a few days since my mother died—hardly any time at all. But it's the way of the world that all things change, and now my father's gone and done this in the blink of an eye, without even leaving any time to mourn! It may be what he wants, but it's terribly cruel. And it makes me long for my dear mother even more!" Pulling his robe up over his head, he collapsed in a paroxysm of weeping.

That night, too, gave way to the dawn. Little Aigo tearfully left his bed and visited the hillside orchard. Approaching a cherry tree in riotous bloom, he thought to himself, "My mother used to adore these blossoms! How unkind of them to bloom in her absence." And in an excess of emotion, he composed the following verse:

aruji naki	Who will lament
niwa no sakura no	the aimless scattering
itazura ni	of cherry blossoms
sakite chiru wo ya	in a garden
tare ka oshiman	without a mistress?

Reciting his poem, the young master felt better for a little while. He played with his monkey, Tejiro, and then returned to the buddha hall.

---

9. In the 1708 *Aigo-no-waka*, the Eighth Avenue lord does in fact choose an auspicious day before sending his daughter to Kiyohira. See SSS 2:130b.

Now at just this most pitiful time, the new wife, Kumoi-no-mae, happened to catch a first glimpse of Little Aigo, and it threw her heart into a tumult of love. Taking to her sickbed, she looked as if she were about to die. Her maid, Tsukisayo, approached her where she lay. "My lady," she said, "please tell me what's on your mind."

"What could I have to hide anymore?" the wife replied. "Ever since I saw that boy playing with his monkey in the hillside orchard yesterday, my heart's been filled with love. Please do something, Tsukisayo—anything you can!" And with that, she sank back down into her bed.

"My lady," Tsukisayo blurted, "this is all too rash! That child is Master Aigo, Lord Kiyohira's heir! What you're saying is outrageous! Still, even if it meant my death, how could I disobey your command? So please stop thinking such things!"

The poor wife! To her utter surprise, she saw that Tsukisayo would be no help at all. Concluding that there was now nothing left to live for, she gave up eating and seemed to teeter on the brink of death. Tsukisayo took in the sight. "My poor lady!" she thought to herself. "What a disgrace it would be for her to die! I'll see if I can ease her heart this one time." Drawing near her pillow, she spoke: "My lady, if it means that much to you, then write the boy a note. But it'll be hard to deliver, I think."

The wife jumped up with a start. "Oh, how wonderful!" she exclaimed. "So you'll take a letter for me? Even if things don't work out and I end up dying, I'll never forget what you just said—not in all the worlds to come!" The wife took out some paper and an inkstone and composed a message in an exceptionally beautiful hand. "Tsukisayo," she called, "here it is."

Having received her charge, Tsukisayo withdrew from her lady's presence and hurried to see the young master in the buddha hall. She rapped softly on the sliding paper door. "Who is it?" the boy asked. "It's strange for someone to come here so quietly."

"Oh, it's nothing to be concerned about," the maid replied. "I am Tsukisayo, a servant of the new wife. I was on a seven-day pilgrimage to the eastern hills when I found this mysterious message. I've come here to show it to you. Will you please open the door?" Little Aigo opened the sliding paper door, whereupon Tsukisayo presented him with the letter. Unaware that it was a trick, he began by examining the outer wrapping.

"What beautiful handwriting!" he declared. "I don't know who wrote it, but when people speak of 'doing someone in with a letter,' this must be what they mean." He untied the fastening cord and looked inside, wondering what it could be. "It's written in the language of *Genji* and *The Tales of Ise*,"[10] he observed, "and the phrasing is quite refined. It says, 'Having seen a blossom beyond imagination, I'll disappear, grief-stricken, like the dew. Today, these days, in the garden—there's a saying that violets and garden cherries yield to a lover's pull. I may not be the autumn stag,[11] but I pine for you and waste away. The sight of you swells my passion, like a clear mirror thoroughly clouded in this fleeting, floating world. I might as well be a ship anchored in the offing, I am so pitifully sunken in love, alone, with you unaware. Despising this weary world and bewailing my fate, I languish on a sumptuous brocade bed of desire, my pillow soaked with terrible tears. When might I speak to you about my love?'

"There's a drawing of a single stalk of eulalia grass," the boy explained, "which perhaps means 'when will it go to seed, coming together in rampant disarray?' The picture of hail falling on dwarf bamboo—we should read it, 'fall to the touch of a flowery sleeve.' Here, love is divided into seven parts: what's known as seeing love, hearing love, speaking love, meeting love, parting love, secret love divided by walls, and unattainable love connected by a bridge of cloud, broken in the middle. Wait, this is an unexpected postscript! 'The person who loves is the new wife, and the one she loves is Aigo.'

"Oh, how awful! A stepmother falling in love with her stepson! It's unheard of! To consider a love like this—it's like what people call 'gazing into an abyss' or 'treading on thin ice.' Think of the shame if word were to get out! Who knows where it would lead?" Little Aigo tore the letter into two and three parts and threw them away. The distress in his heart was beyond all description.

ACT 4

The poor young master recited sutras in the buddha hall. Meanwhile, Tsukisayo hurried back to her mistress, humiliated. She explained all that had occurred. The wife was stirred to even greater longing. "Damn the consequences!" she cried. "Get me an inkstone and some paper!" The wife wrote and wrote, sending

---

10. *The Tale of Genji* and *The Tales of Ise* are literary works from the early tenth and early eleventh centuries.
11. The stag is known in poetry for its plaintive cries of love.

the boy seven letters in a single day. After receiving the seventh, Little Aigo said, "Look, Tsukisayo, if my father gets a glimpse of this, he'll have you tortured for sure. What do you think about that?" And he withdrew inside his rooms.

Tsukisayo was stunned. She hurried back to her mistress and related what the boy had said. The wife was put out. "If Lord Kiyohira hears of this," she said, "we're certain to lose our lives. I'll break into the buddha hall tonight, stab Little Aigo to death, and then kill myself, too! I can get over it in the course of my future lives. How about it, Tsukisayo?"

"Yes, indeed," Tsukisayo replied. "But I have a plan. The *yaiba* sword and Chinese saddle are family treasures. I'll steal them tonight, tell my husband to dress up as a peddler, and then have him hawk them at Sakura Gate.[12] Lord Kiyohira is bound to investigate, and when he does, we'll tell him that Little Aigo of Second Avenue put them up for sale. That way, the peddler won't be punished, and since the *yaiba* sword and Chinese saddle are so incomparably precious, the boy will be put to death."

The wife took in her servant's words. "A single wicked thought can bring countless *kalpas* of suffering,"[13] she replied, "in birth after birth and age after age. But even if it dooms me to five hundred lives of torment, including the pains of serpent incarnations, I can't stand the thought of simply leaving my love unfulfilled! Oh, the cruelty of that boy's hateful heart! Slander him well, Tsukisayo." Although until that morning the wife had relished the slightest breeze from her stepson's direction, her feelings now had changed, and such gusts caused her only pain. Thinking such thoughts, she retreated behind her blinds.

Tsukisayo summoned her husband and told him of their plan. Later receiving the two treasures, he headed out from the Second Avenue estate. He hurried on his way, and soon arriving at Sakura Gate, he set about selling the *yaiba* sword and Chinese saddle in a thunderous voice. Word reached Kiyohira, who sent for the peddler; when the man arrived, he presented Kiyohira with the two treasures. Kiyohira pounded his fist and demanded, "Where did you get these?"

"Little Aigo of Second Avenue wishes to sell them because he's starving and exhausted," the man explained.

---

12. Cherry Tree Gate. There are no historical records of such a gate in the capital.

13. A *kalpa* is typically described as the length of time necessary for a heavenly being to wear away a 40-*ri* (100-square-mile) rock by brushing it with its silken sleeve once every hundred years.

"Beat the peddler and throw him out!" Kiyohira cried.

"Yes, sir," his men replied, and they thrashed him severely. After that, the battered peddler disappeared to who-knows-where.

Kiyohira later returned to the Second Avenue estate with a company of men. The poor young master was reciting sutras in the buddha hall. He was surprised to hear his father return, considering that his ten days of palace service had not yet passed. "He must have lost a wager in the first linked-poetry contest of the year—a hundred verses in a thousand, or ten in a hundred—and now he's come home to ask my advice." With this thought in mind, Little Aigo set out to meet his father at the carriage porch, just as he always did.

Kiyohira watched him approach. He beat the poor boy mercilessly and then went inside.

Alas, the poor young master! Thoroughly pummeled, he stood up and thought to himself, "Oh, how cruel! When I came out to the carriage porch after my mother died, Father picked me up and placed me in his same carriage. He brushed back my hair and said, 'My poor boy! How sad you must be to lose your mother.' And the two of us wept together! But everything changes, and now that he's blinded by his new sweetheart, how cruel of him to wish me dead. Oh, how I miss my mother!" And in a haze of tears, he went back inside.

Kiyohira was enraged. "Aigo," he said, "even if you had sold the treasures, I wouldn't have been so angry if you had sold them in Yamato, Kawachi, Iga, or Ise Province. But how could you hawk them at Sakura Gate? To cast that kind of shame on your father—it's unheard of!" Kiyohira had the poor boy's arms twisted and tied behind his back, after which he had him suspended from the branches of an old cherry tree. In his rage, he decreed that anyone who undid the boy's bonds would be banished from the house. Then he hurried back to the palace.

The poor young master! "My nurses and maids," he called in a thin, faint voice, "aren't any of you there in the mansion? Please tell Father that I didn't do anything wrong!" The boy wept as if to die. Kumoi-no-mae and Tsukisayo laughed, and no one undid his bonds.

Little Aigo's beloved monkey, Tejiro, was overcome with grief at the imminent loss of his master. He climbed the old cherry tree and loosened the lower knots, but being just an animal, he could not untie the upper ones, and the child suffered all the more. The poor boy's eyes dimmed and his heart grew weak. Blood trickled from his mouth, staining his body red. It appeared that his end was near.

Elsewhere, in the afterworld, there was no one as pitiful as Little Aigo's mother. Weeping, she pressed her pure head to the ground in front of King Enma.[14] Wringing her saintly fingers, she spoke through her tears, pleading, "You know, sir, I have a darling child back in the human world. His stepmother has slandered him, and because of that, he's about to die. Please let me return for a little while to save his life!"

"Not lamenting your own suffering . . ." the king reflected. "When people speak of parents wandering lost in darkness on account of their children, it must be to people like you that they refer!"[15] Turning to his spying eyes,[16] he said, "Go see if there's an available corpse in the human realm." Receiving their command, the eyes set out, ascending eighty thousand *jō*.[17] They took stock of the great three-thousand-fold universe in a single glance and immediately returned to the king. "Many have been born today," they reported, "but no one has died. There's only the body of a weasel that's been dead for three days."

The king addressed the mother: "Will you take the form of a weasel?"

"I don't mind at all," the mother replied, overjoyed at the prospect of seeing her son. "Let me go now, please!"

"Very well!" the king declared, and he clapped his hands. The mother changed into a weasel, and in an instant, she found herself at the Second Avenue estate. She made her way to the hillside orchard, where she scrambled up the old cherry tree and quickly chewed through the boy's ropes. The monkey held him from below and set him down.

The weasel jumped to the ground. Tugging at the hem of the boy's robe, it began to speak: "Hello, Aigo, I bet you never heard of a talking weasel! I'm

---

14. King Enma is the judge and ruler of the dead. He also appears as a character in *Oguri*.

15. King Enma alludes to a poem attributed to Fujiwara no Kanesuke (877–933) in *Gosen wakashū*. According to the tenth-century *Yamato monogatari* (*dan* 45), Kanesuke composed it out of concern for his daughter's fortunes at court:

hito no oya no	Though a parent's heart
kokoro wa yami ni	may not be mired
aranedomo	in darkness,
ko wo omou michi ni	one still wanders lost
madoinuru kana	on paths of love for a child.

16. Supernatural demon spies in the service of the king.

17. Eighty thousand *jō* is pproximately 800,000 feet, or 151 miles.

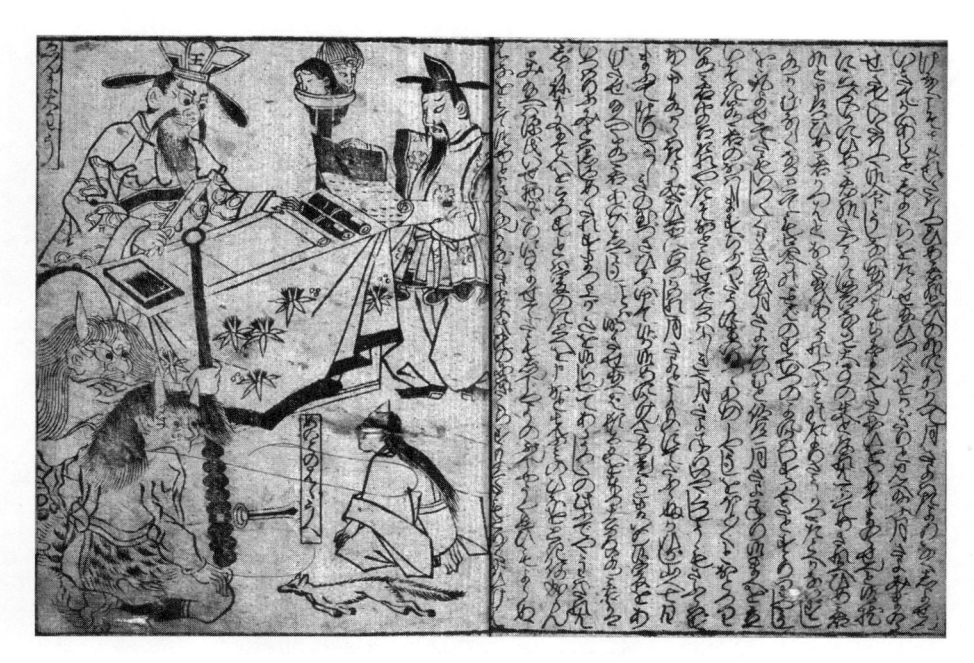

Little Aigo's mother (*lower right*) pleads with King Enma in the afterworld. From *Aigo-no-waka* (ca. 1670 woodblock-printed edition). (Courtesy of Osaka University Library)

your dead mother. I was so sad to see you dying because of your stepmother's lies that I asked King Enma to let me come back for a little while. I turned into a weasel and came all the way here! When I think about it now, your father is just too cruel. Even if I'm not alive anymore, it's heartless of him to treat you so unkindly. He's been blinded by his new sweetheart and become a demon inside. How sad it is to see him abuse you! If you stay here, he'll kill you for sure. You should run away to Saitō Kitadani on Mount Hiei. The Reverend Sotsu Ajari there is my brother.[18] He's your uncle, so ask him to give you the tonsure. Then recite a sutra for me in the next world. Even people in other countries hate letting go of the things they're accustomed to, so how much worse it is for parents and their children! I'd never get tired of being with you, no matter how long we were together. Oh, what grief! The envoys of the afterworld are pressing me

18. *Ajari* is a monastic title. Mount Hiei lies at the northeastern edge of the Kyoto valley; it is the site of Enryakuji Temple, headquarters of the Japanese Tendai Buddhist sect.

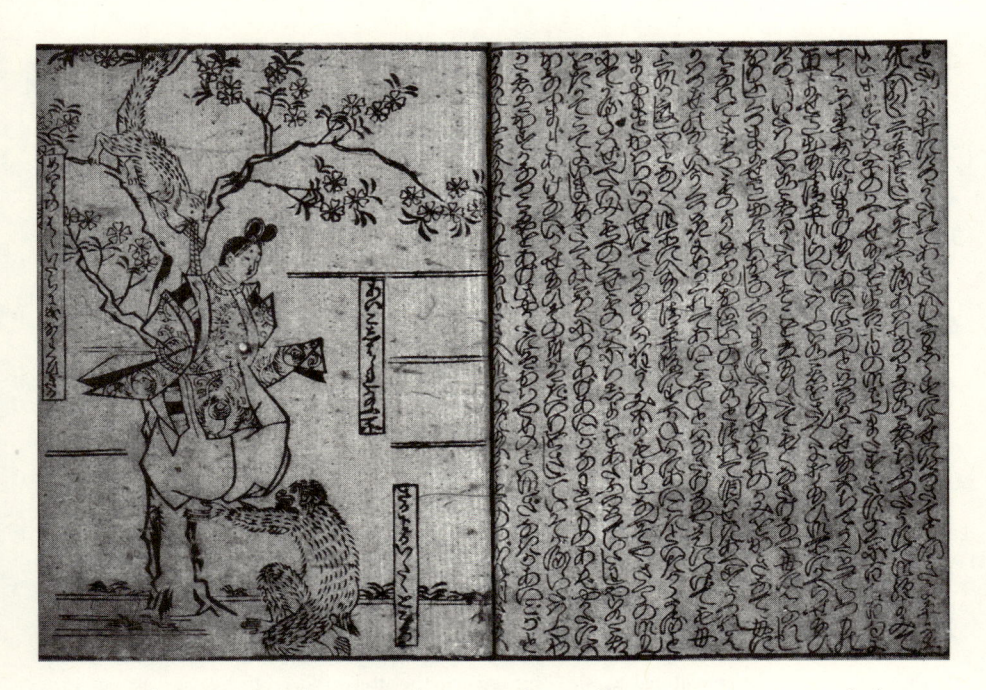

Reincarnated as a weasel, Little Aigo's mother rescues her son from a tree. From *Aigo-no-waka* (ca. 1670 woodblock-printed edition). (Courtesy of Osaka University Library)

to leave. I have to go now, Aigo." Shedding yellow tears, the weasel ran into a clump of grass and disappeared.

The poor young master! Frantically searching the grass all around, he cried, "Wait, Mother! Even if you've lost your body, just speak to me one more time!" He wept as if to disappear. But because it was an impossible request, he eventually stood up, tottering like a plucked bird. Since he could not very well go on sobbing, he decided to follow his mother's instructions and climb Mount Hiei. Awaiting the night, his appearance was wretched beyond words.

ACT 5

Following his mother's advice, the poor young master set out from the Second Avenue estate and began climbing Mount Hiei. The night was especially dark and rainy. Unsure of the way ahead, he gazed toward the south, where he saw a faint light in the distance. He followed it downhill to a far, humble cottage. Knocking softly on the brushwood door, he sobbed and said, "I am from the capital, and I've lost my way. Please put me up for the night."

Together with his wife, the artisan who lived there burst through the door with a spear in his hand. "Who is it?" he shouted.

The poor young master! "Please don't be so alarmed," he replied, weeping all the while. "What do I have to hide? I am Aigo-no-waka, heir of Second Avenue Chamberlain Kiyohira. I was on my way up Mount Hiei because of my stepmother's lies. But the darkness is so dark and the rain so hard, I didn't know which way to go. If you have any pity, then please put me up for the night!" And with that, he wept as if to disappear.

The artisan threw down his spear. "So you're the son of the Second Avenue lord!" he exclaimed. "Forgive me, please." He immediately invited the boy inside. He placed a plank on a mortar, spread a rough straw mat on top, and offered it to his guest. Then taking out some rice, he purified it seven times in the flowing waters of the Kamo River, placed it in an unglazed earthen vessel, and presented it to the boy. It was from this time that people began spreading rough straw mats as a way to purify the vicinities of gods.

"The bells of dawn have already rung," the artisan later said. "Let's go now, quickly." With the artisan helping him along, Little Aigo set out from the Fourth Avenue riverbed. And through what places do you think they passed? Skirting Sanjūsangendō and Gion Shrine,[19] they gazed far to the south, puzzling at the sight of Inari Forest and taking in a view of Takeda, Yodo, and Toba in the Fushimi district. Longing for his mother, Little Aigo made his way through Awataguchi, where the smoke of funeral pyres never ceases to rise. Climbing and descending with an anguished heart, he quickly passed Yamanaka, Obara, Shizuhara, and the Seryō settlement, bringing him to the village of Yase, where old men grow gaunt from love. When the road was bad, the artisan took the lead, helping the boy whenever he could. Thus floundering forward through a succession of distant places, they eventually arrived at Fukiagematsu, the Windswept Pine.[20]

---

19. Sanjūsangendō, the Hall of Thirty-Three Bays, actually lies to the south, in the opposite direction of Mount Hiei. As a *michiyuki* travelogue, the following passage contains a series of puns on prominent place-names in and around the capital.

20. Fukiagematsu is an unknown site, presumably at the foot of Mount Hiei.

The artisan spoke: "Young master, take a look at those placards. The first one says 'Entrance Forbidden to Women'; the second one says 'Entrance Forbidden to Lepers'; and the third one says 'Entrance Forbidden to Artisans,' which includes me.[21] I'm afraid I can't accompany you any farther. I'll have to take my leave."

"But the sign's not so important," the boy pleaded, beginning to cry. "And if you say that you're going to see Sotsu Ajari, then I doubt if anyone will blame you. Please, sir, please come with me up the mountain."

"I'm sure you're right," the artisan replied. "But I'm only a lowly craftsman, so I'll just say good-bye."

The poor young master! "Are you leaving me already?" he whimpered. "Oh, how I miss the capital, because my father's there! But my evil stepmother's there, so I hate it, too! Oh, how I'll miss you!"

"And I'll miss you too, master," the artisan replied. Staring into each other's eyes, the man and the boy wept a torrent of tears before finally parting ways, endlessly forlorn. Then the artisan returned to the capital.

Approaching the foot of the Windswept Pine, the poor young master sobbed and complained in a way that was moving to hear! "Who in the world bothered to write that sign, 'Entrance Forbidden to Artisans'? It's just too cruel!" Weeping all the while, he proceeded up the mountain, infinitely downhearted. Crossing mountain streams and traversing craggy ridges, he pushed his way through the leafy brush. Monkeys screeched at the mountain peak, pheasants cried, and Little Aigo cried along with them, his sleeves without a chance to dry.

Because he hurried on his way, he soon reached Saitō Kitadani, arriving after the sun had set on that very same day. He walked up to Sotsu Ajari's gate and softly knocked. "The gate's closed!" someone shouted. "Who's out there knocking in the middle of the night?"

"It's nothing to be alarmed at," the boy replied, speaking through his tears. "I am Aigo, heir of Second Avenue Chamberlain Kiyohira in the capital. Please tell your master that I've come to see him." The guard relayed the boy's message to Sotsu Ajari, just as he was told.

"Aigo from the capital . . ." the master mused. "Since it's his first time to the mountain, go see how many carriages and riders he's brought." "Yes, sir," the

---

21. Because many artisans worked with leather, they may have been considered ritually impure.

guard replied, and he went back out, pushed open the temple gate, and looked all around. There was only a twelve- or thirteen-year-old boy standing dejectedly by himself. The guard returned to his master and relayed what he had seen. Sotsu Ajari was enraged. "Then it's the Great Tengu of the Northern Valley," he cried, "or the Little Tengu of the Southern, who's come here to steal my ascetic powers![22] We can't let him in. Drive him away from the gate!"

Several priests rushed outside and thrashed the poor boy mercilessly. The pitiful young master! Severely beaten, he quickly withdrew. "You people," he whimpered, weeping as if to disappear, "he's my uncle! And am I not his nephew? So don't hit me like that!" Mumbling through his tears, he complained in a way that was moving to hear! "Rather than dying at the hands of some lowly stranger," he decided, "I might as well return to the capital and let my father do me in." Wondering when he would ever pray at his uncle's temple, he gave it a good last look. Then, though it pained him to leave, he headed back down the mountain.

But the poor young master! Losing his way on the mountain path, he came and he went and he went and he came, repeatedly tracing and retracing his steps. Brambly bushes and withered trees tore at his robes until he resembled a disordered thicket. He wandered lost in the mountains for three days, whereupon he came to the Shiga Pass at dusk. Taking a tree root for his pillow, a patch of moss for his mat, and a boulder for his bedside screen, he lay down and slept, utterly dead to the world. The feelings in his heart were moving indeed!

Elsewhere, Tabata no Suke and his brother Senjo from the Awazu estate were traveling to the capital on business. Coming across Little Aigo, they shouted, "Are you some wandering, shape-shifting monster? Identify yourself!"

The boy jumped up with a start. Weeping, he cried, "Excuse me, sirs, but I'm from the capital. I've been wandering around like this because of my stepmother's lies."

"Who's your father?" Senjo demanded.

"What do I have to hide?" the boy replied. "I am Aigo-no-waka, heir of Second Avenue Chamberlain Kiyohira." He told them everything that had happened and then wept as if to die. The brothers shed a tear and said, "Oh, you poor child! We've heard of Second Avenue Lord Kiyohira, but we've never actually seen him. So you're his son, are you? If you've been in the mountains for

---

22. The Northern and Southern Valleys (Kitadani and Minamidani) on Mount Hiei. *Tengu* are a kind of supernatural demon-bird-men known for deceiving Buddhist priests.

three days, you must be famished." The brothers divided their cooked millet-rice on an oak leaf and offered it to the young master. It was from this time that people began to speak of "wrapping your affection in tree leaves."[23]

The young master stared. "Please, sirs," he said, "tell me what this food is called."

"It's sometimes known as *kyosu* rice," Senjo explained.[24] The boy thought to himself, "Whatever it is will be fine. I'll never forget this kindness, not in all my lives to come." He threw the oak leaf into the Awazu River.

"We'd like to accompany you," the brothers said, "but we're on our way to the capital to fulfill our tax obligations. Perhaps we'll see you again." The brothers wept and set out for the city. People say that their compassion was unusually deep.

The pitiful young master pulled up a young pine and planted it on Shiga Pass. Then he addressed it, saying, "If I meet with success in this world, you shall be called the Thousand Pines of Karasaki, with branches sprouting from the tips of your branches. And if I die, you shall be called the Single Pine of Shiga Karasaki—with just a single trunk and a lone leaf."[25] Then with tears in his eyes, he set out for Anō Village.

It was near the end of the fourth month. The young master saw some early peaches on a tree beside a hedge, and they were almost perfectly ripe. Admiring one, he thought, "What a fine piece of fruit!" An old woman stepped outside and shouted, "You little imp, how dare you! I don't even pick those peaches!" She wanted to beat him, and since she lacked a staff, she picked up an invalid's stick and flogged him with that.[26] The poor young master must have felt ashamed, because he ran into a patch of hemp to hide. But when an unseasonable gust of wind revealed his location, the old woman cried, "It's bad enough that you steal my peaches! How dare you trample my hemp, too!" She beat him repeatedly and then disappeared.

The poor young master! "Peaches," he declared, "may you never again grow in Anō Village! And though people might plant it, may hemp never grow here,

---

23. This expression is akin to the English "thought that counts." It means that even the slightest present—even one wrapped in leaves—is a fine gift if the giver's intention is true.

24. The meaning of *kyosu* is unknown. As the son of a noble, Little Aigo may have been unfamiliar with a humble grain like millet.

25. Karasaki lies beyond Shiga Pass, in contemporary Ōtsu City on the shore of Lake Biwa. The Karasaki Pine is now said to stand inside the grounds of Karasaki Shrine.

26. A cane used by lepers and the like, compounding the boy's humiliation.

either! And may violent winds never blow!" From that time on, though the local peach trees blossomed, they never again bore fruit. And although people planted hemp, it never grew there, either. After all, this floating world is like no more than a vision in a dream.

The boy soon came to Kiryū Falls, where the late-blooming cherry blossoms were then at their peak. Taking in the sight, he imagined that the blossoms at the Second Avenue estate were at their peak now, too. An unseasonable gust of wind blew down a cluster of unopened buds, which landed on his sleeve. "Oh, these blossoms are enlightened!" he exclaimed. "The scattered ones are like my mother; the blooming ones are like my father; and the unopened ones are like me. How I'd like to write about my grief!"

Having no paper or inkstone, the young master bit open one of his left fingers and collected the blood in the hollow of a boulder. Taking a stalk of willow for his brush, he slipped off his small-sleeved robe and inscribed it with all the bitterness in his heart. Then he composed a poem:

kamikura ya	On Mount Kamikura,
Kiryū ga taki e	"Storehouse of the Gods,"
mi wo naguru	I'll throw myself into Kiryū Falls.[27]
kataritsutaeyo	Tell it to the world,
sugi no muradachi	you standing grove of cedar.

Reciting this verse, the young master turned toward the west, pressed his palms together, and prostrated himself in prayer: "Hail Amida Buddha of the Western Land! Please allow me to be born on the same lotus pedestal as you." Then, at the age of fifteen, he threw himself into Kiryū Falls, where he finally met his end. Everyone was moved to hear of the boy's death; they all said that it was the saddest thing in the world.

ACT 6

"Hey, did that boy just throw himself into the falls?" some nearby monks exclaimed. They took the young master's small-sleeved robe from the branches of a cedar tree and hurried back to the central Buddha hall. Ringing the temple

---

27. Kiryū Falls are not actually on Mount Kamikura; they are a short distance away.

Upper right, An old woman chases Little Aigo from her peach tree; *lower right*, Little Aigo addresses a young pine; *left*, Little Aigo throws himself into Kiryū Falls. From *Aigo-no-waka* (ca. 1670 woodblock-printed edition). (Courtesy of Osaka University Library)

bell and pounding on a drum, they quickly assembled all the temple acolytes, but found none of them missing.

The monks hurried off to see Sotsu Ajari and show him the robe. Examining the garment, he said, "This is Second Avenue Lord Kiyohira's crest. So that boy last night really was Little Aigo! You should take this to the Second Avenue lord." Replying that they understood, the monks withdrew and immediately set out for the capital.

Upon arriving at the Second Avenue estate, the monks related everything that had occurred. Kiyohira's retainers accepted the robe, and the monks returned to the mountain. The men presented the small-sleeved robe to their lord, who picked it up and wept bitter, anguished tears. "How awful, how awful!" was all that he could say.

Later mumbling between his sobs, Kiyohira complained in a way that was moving to hear! "Whenever the softest breeze blew," he said, weeping bitterly, "I wondered in despair if it weren't bringing back my Little Aigo. But now to see this souvenir instead—it's beyond belief! And how cruel to learn that even my women and retainers scorned him—this child that I spurned! Oh, give me back my boy!"

In his grief, Kiyohira examined the lower hem of the small-sleeved robe, where he found his son's indignant message. "Father," the boy had begun, "it's only natural that you wouldn't know. I didn't know it either when your wife set her heart on me. But because she couldn't fulfill her lascivious desire, she hatched a no-good plot and slandered me to you, which is why I couldn't stay at home. I climbed Mount Hiei, but my heartless uncle, the priest, said he didn't have a nephew in the capital, and he had me badly beaten. Still, in all my lives to come, how could I ever forget the kindness of the Fourth Avenue riverbed artisan and his wife or the compassion of Tabata no Suke and his brother? Please forgive them their tax obligations." The message was signed "Aigo-no-waka." Kiyohira stared. "What kind of compassion did Tabata no Suke and his brother show to my son?" he wondered. "Summon them here!"

The brothers appeared before Kiyohira. Meeting with them personally, the master said, "Please, you two, tell me about Aigo's final hours. Tell me, please!" He wept as if to disappear. Crying all the while, Kiyohira issued the brothers an official seal exempting them from their taxes. "Thank you, sir," the brothers replied in awe, after which they took their leave. But poor Kiyohira! "To think that Aigo's enemy was here before my eyes," he raved, "and I never even knew it! So what shall I do for my son in his grave?"

Kiyohira's retainers received their command. They rolled Kumoi-no-mae up in a reed mat, seized and bound Tsukisayo, and placed the two women in a cart. After pulling them through the capital, they drowned Kumoi-no-mae in the Inase Pool.[28] As for Tsukisayo, they cut her into pieces and threw them away.

Afterward, Kiyohira hurried to Kiryū Falls, where he noticed something strange. Although his son's body had been seen floating in the waves, it had now sunk and disappeared. Kiyohira sent a messenger to Mount Hiei. Sotsu Ajari was astonished at the news, and he set out for Kiryū Falls with a number of his disciples. Kiyohira met with him and tearfully explained the situation.

---

28. The Inase Pool is a stretch of water at the confluence of the Kamo and Katsura Rivers, immediately to the south of the capital.

Sotsu Ajari had a *goma* prayer altar brought down from the temple.[29] He burned two sacred wooden sticks, but to no effect. Then he rubbed his rosary beads with a scraping sound and prayed: "To the east, Mantra King Gōsanze; to the south, Mantra King Gundariyasha; to the west, Daiitoku; to the north, Kongōyasha.[30] First, Kongara; second, Seitaka; third, Kurikara; fourth, Keika Dōji.[31] It is done, it is done."

Miraculously, the water in the lake began to shudder and shake, and dark clouds descended to the north. A 150-foot serpent rose from the depths with Little Aigo's corpse on its head, and it placed it on the prayer altar. "Ah, how humiliating!" the creature cried. "I lightly set my heart on the boy, but now, at last, I have fulfilled my desire! The holy man's ascetic powers are strong, so I'll return Aigo's body now. Please pray for me in the next life." And with that, the giant snake disappeared beneath the surface. It was enough to make a man's hair stand on end.

Poor Sotsu Ajari and Kiyohira clung to the boy's corpse and cried, "How can this be? How can this be?" bawling as if to disappear. "Give me back my boy!" Kiyohira shouted between sobs. "And give me back my nephew!" the holy man howled. Weeping and wailing, they were a pitiful sight to see.

"It won't do any good to go on crying like this," Kiyohira declared in his grief. "I'm going to go with my son!" Embracing the dead boy's body, he jumped into the lake and drowned. Sotsu Ajari jumped in after him, whereupon all his disciples threw themselves in as well. The old woman from Anō who had begrudged the boy a peach threw herself in, and when Tabata no Suke and his brother came to Kiryū Falls, they drowned themselves, too. The monkey Tejiro ran off into the valley. The artisan said to his wife, "Since the Karasaki Pine stands in memory of the young master, we might as well drown ourselves here." "You're absolutely right!" the wife agreed, and they also died. Counting from Sotsu Ajari, 108 people of higher and lower rank are said to have drowned.

Word reached the major archbishop of Minamidani. "It's a remarkable story," he said, "unheard of in ages past," and he worshipped Little Aigo as the

---

29. A *goma* prayer altar is used in esoteric Buddhist fire rites.

30. In esoteric Buddhism, these are four of the Five Great Mantra Kings (*godai myōō*). The fifth is Mantra King Fudō, who occupies the center.

31. The divine boys Kongara and Seitaka are two attendants of Fudō; Kurikara is a dragon-king manifestation of Fudō; and Keika Dōji is otherwise unknown.

Little Aigo rises from the waves on a giant serpent's head. From *Aigo-no-waka* (ca. 1670 woodblock-printed edition). (Courtesy of Osaka University Library)

Great Sannō Gongen.³² On the second day of the monkey in the fourth month of every year, three thousand monks from Mount Hiei, three thousand monks from Mii Temple, and the parishioners of twenty-one villages, including Heitsuji and Upper, Middle, and Lower Sakamoto, began holding a festival to invigorate the deity. Throughout this land of ours in which the emperor's grace is as far-reaching as a climbing vine, there was not a single person of any rank who was not moved by these events.

---

32. The deity of Hie Shrine at the eastern foot of Mount Hiei. *Gongen* is a term for a buddha or a bodhisattva in its Japanese manifestation as a Shinto deity.

Amida's Riven Breast

ACT 1

There was once a vast realm on the outskirts of India known as the Land of Bishari.[1] In a place called Katahira Village in the Enta district, there was a great wealthy man by the name of Kanshi Byōe. Among his many riches, Kanshi Byōe possessed seven special treasures: first, he owned nine gold-gushing mountains; second, he owned seven silver-streaming mountains; third, he owned two demon-ridding swords; and fourth, in his south-facing garden, he owned a single *otowa* pine. The pine was a wondrous tree. When a gentle breeze blew through its branches on an eighty- or ninety-year-old man or woman, that person would be instantly restored to seventeen or eighteen years old. The pine was Kanshi Byōe's number-one treasure, which is why he included it in his top four. Fifth, he owned a Kantan "prosperity

---

Translated from the 1651 *Amida no munewari*, supplemented by the Urokogataya *Amida no munewari*.

1. Bishari is a Japanese name for Vaiśāli, in the north-central part of India.

pillow";[2] sixth, he owned twelve water-springing urns; and seventh, he owned five fragrant musk dogs. In addition to his seven treasures, Kanshi Byōe had two children, a daughter and a son. His daughter was named Tenju, and she was seven years old. His son was named Teirei, and he was five. There was thus nothing in the world that the rich man lacked.

In his splendid magnificence, Kanshi Byōe once summoned his wife and spoke: "Hello, dear, listen. It seems to me that people pray for salvation in the next life because they won't be around when the future buddha Maitreya will appear in this world. But since we have the *otowa* pine, when we get old we can rejuvenate ourselves with the breeze through its branches. There's no way we'll die before the final age! So what use is it to pray for the life to come? If it's all the same, let's be wicked and have some fun." "Good idea!" the wife replied, and they did terrible things to no end. As inferiors tend to imitate their superiors, Kanshi Byōe's servants, retainers, and neighbors all took after his example and began to perform the most heinous evil deeds as well.

Kanshi Byōe burned down all the stupas and temple halls that people had built since the distant past, and he neither floated ships on rivers nor built bridges over streams. He sponsored no services for the Buddha, the Dharma, and the Sangha,[3] and he spurned the holy practice of bestowing alms. He envied others their good fortune and rejoiced in their hardships, such that it quickly became known that Kanshi Byōe of Katahira Village in the Enta district in the Land of Bishari in India was a stingy, greedy man.

Now around this time Shakyamuni Buddha was on Mount Dandoku,[4] and word reached him there about Kanshi Byōe. "Outrageous!" he cried. "It's already hard enough to get people to do good, what with their natural tendency toward evil. If I leave that man alone there, everyone in the four directions will fall into wicked ways. If that's the way it's going to be, then right or

---

2. A "prosperity pillow" is a magical pillow that produces wealth in dreams. According to a Tang Chinese story that circulated in medieval Japan, a young man once received such a pillow from a sage in the village of Kantan, which allowed him to experience more than fifty years of worldly success in a short nap before dinner.

3. The Buddha (Shakyamuni), the Dharma (the teachings of the Buddha), and the Sangha (the monastic community) are the Three Jewels of Buddhism.

4. Dandoku is a Japanese name for Mount Dandaka, in the Gandhāra region of Pakistan. Shakyamuni is said to have performed bodhisattva practices there in his former life as Prince Sudana.

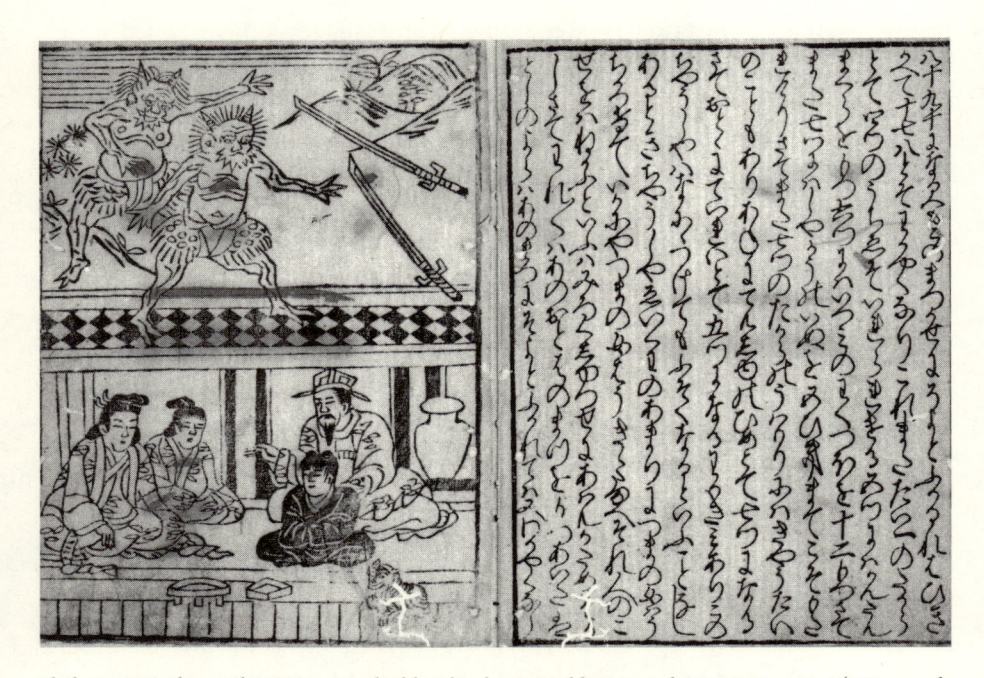

Shakyamuni's demon kings are attacked by the demon-ridding swords. From *Munewari* (1651 woodblock-printed edition). (Courtesy of Tenri University Library)

wrong, I'll have to do something about it." Calling on the demon kings of the sixth heaven, Shakyamuni said, "You demon kings, go put a stop to that Kanshi Byōe for me."

The demon kings hurtled headlong into Kanshi Byōe's mansion, whereupon the man's demon-ridding swords flew out and about, slashing with all their might. Defeated, the demons made a hasty retreat.

Seeing what had occurred, Shakyamuni said, "Well, then, I'll send some pestilence deities instead!" Consenting to their task, 98,000 pestilence deities pushed their way into Kanshi Byōe's mansion. But although they sought to put an end to the rich man's mischief, the demon-ridding swords flew out as before, slashing heaven and earth in all four directions, and the deities, finding no way to succeed, fled.

Shakyamuni thought that there must be something he could do to make Kanshi Byōe pay. He called together his disciples and spoke: "I want you all to go to hell and bring back some demons, quick!" "Yes, sir," the disciples replied. Among them, Ānanda, Kāśyapa, Subhūti, Maudgalyāyana, and some others

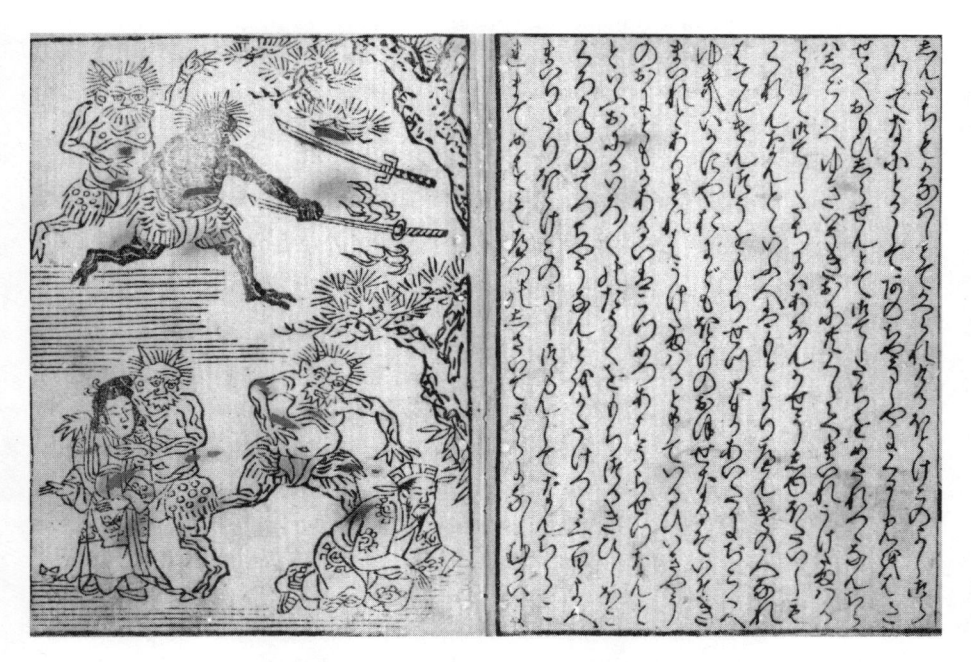

Shakyamuni's demons kill Kanshi Byōe and his wife. From *Munewari* (1651 woodblock-printed edition). (Courtesy of Tenri University Library)

were themselves avatars of buddhas and deities, and thus possessing supernatural powers, they traveled to hell in an instant. "Hello, demons!" they shouted. "The Buddha commands you to come at once." Murmuring their assent, a motley crew of more than three hundred demons, including ox- and horse-headed monsters and *abō* and *rasetsu* fiends, made their way from hell. They shouldered a variety of weapons, such as swords, spears, pikes, and iron maces.

Beholding the demons, Shakyamuni spoke. "I haven't summoned you here for anything special," he said. "It's just that that Kanshi Byōe over there is so stingy and greedy, I want you to grab him and kill him for me. And be sure to make him suffer." "Yes, sir," the demons replied. Pouring helter-skelter into Kanshi Byōe's mansion, they sought to put an end to his evil, but again the demon-ridding swords flew out and about, slashing with all their might. Among the attackers was a fiend named Great Flame. Spitting fire from his hands, he seized the two swords, melting them in his grasp.

Kanshi Byōe's treasures disappeared like foam on the water. In their triumph, the demons ripped apart and devoured all the servants and retainers.

But they took their time killing Kanshi Byōe and his wife. They boiled a pot of molten iron and then poured it down the couple's throats, burning up their five and six internal organs. Then they dropped them into hell.

Shakyamuni watched. "Don't kill the children," he said. "I have other plans for them, so keep them safe." "Yes, sir," the demons replied, and sparing the sister and brother, they all returned to hell. The feelings in those poor children's hearts were truly beyond compare!

ACT 2

Now what could be more pitiful than those two little siblings? Suddenly separated from their father and mother, and without the slightest means of getting by in the world, they set out for their neighbors' houses to beg. The sister led her brother by the hand, and the brother clung to his sister. Watching them come, the neighbors said, "Take a look at that! Until yesterday, they were admired as a rich man's heirs. But today's another day, and the poor things beg!" Others scorned the children and refused to let them in, saying, "You've lost your parents at the ages of seven and five! It means that all the buddhas have abandoned you. You're disgusting! Keep away from our house. And don't stand at the gate!"

Berated and abused, the children returned the way they had come. Sometimes they slept in deserted fields and sometimes in patches of towering eulalia grass. With homelessness their home, they passed the days and months for naught, constantly suffering in their hearts. As they had nothing to eat, they picked parsley on the marshy plains and gathered fallen grains of rice in the village paddies, thereby extending their evanescent lives. Except for the barking dogs in the fields, no one addressed them at all.

One time, the brother approached his sister, Tenju, and spoke: "Listen, sister, I have something to say. Children of the world hold services for their parents' enlightenment as an act of religious charity, one of the six bodhisattva practices.[5] They float ships on rivers and build bridges over streams, read a

---

5. Charity is the first of six religious practices (*roku haramitsu*) on the bodhisattva path to enlightenment. The other five are rectitude, forbearance, exertion, meditation, and wisdom.

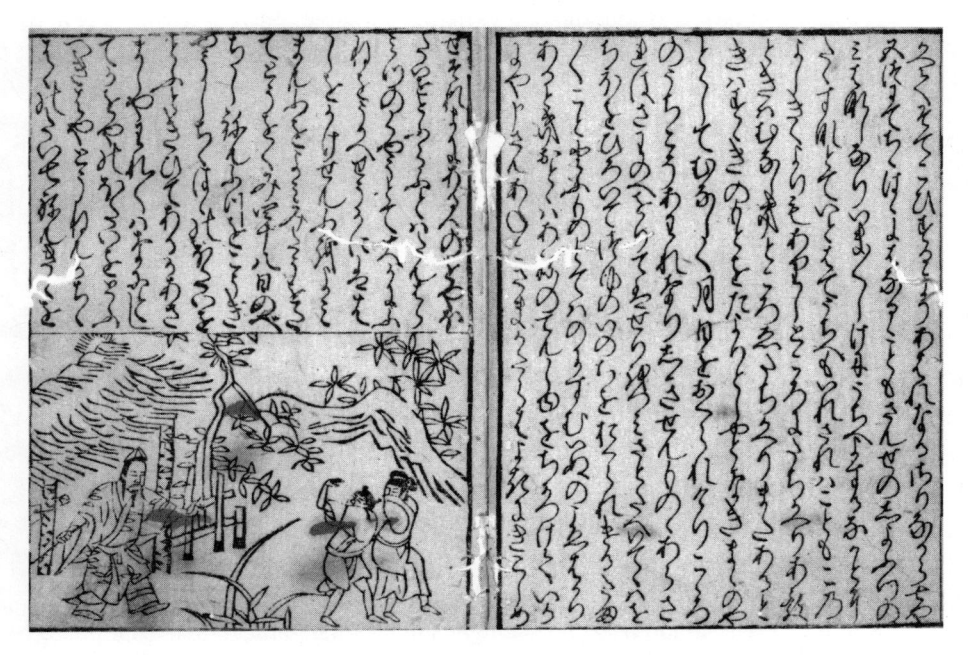

A neighbor chases Tenju and Teirei away from his home. From *Munewari* (1651 woodblock-printed edition). (Courtesy of Tenri University Library)

thousand and ten thousand sutras, erect stupas and construct temple halls, and sponsor forty-eight-day recitations of the *nenbutsu*, all for the sake of their father's and mother's enlightenment, or so I've heard. But tell me, how are we to do these things for our own parents' enlightenment? It's already the seventh anniversary of their death this year! Even if we should become food for eagles and hawks, let's sell ourselves somewhere and use the money to sponsor services for their enlightenment. What do you think, sister?"

"How kind of you!" Tenju exclaimed. "I should have been grown-up enough to suggest it myself. It must be because you're a boy! Yes, let's go someplace and sell ourselves so that we can hold services for our father and mother's enlightenment."

Hand in hand, the children set out. Sleeping in the fields and on the mountains, they walked on and on until, on the ninth day, they came to the Arara district in the Land of Haranai, famous throughout all of India.[6] This Arara district

---

6. Haranai is a Japanese name for Vārāṇasī, in the north-central part of India.

boasted some forty thousand houses in the four directions, but to the sister and brother's repeated cries of "People for sale!" and "Buy us, please!" not a single person replied.

Looking around, the children saw a large temple hall dedicated to Amida Buddha. In front of the building there was a clear waterfall, and the sister and brother purified themselves in its cold cascade. Then they composed a poem:

asagao no	So very quickly
itsushika hana wa	the morning glory petals
chirihatete	scattered all away—
ha ni kienokoru	and the sadness of the dew
tsuyu zo mono uki	that remains on the leaves!

The children wept and visited the temple hall. Rattling the sacred summoning bell, they earnestly prayed: "Hail, Amida Buddha of the West! We wish to sell ourselves so that we might hold services for our father and mother's enlightenment. We ask that if there's anyone here who would buy us, that you please let us meet." The children spent that night supplicating in the temple hall.

Just as they had hoped, Amida Buddha appeared before them in the dark of night. Shining 84,000 rays of light, awesome to behold, he stood beside the sister and brother where they slept. "Dear children," he said, "how moving that you wish to sell yourselves for the sake of your parents' enlightenment! As it turns out, there is no one around here who will buy you. However, there is a great wealthy man by the name of Ōman Chōja in Oki Village in the Yume district, deep in the mountains and far away from here. He is certain to buy you without a fuss." Having spoken thus, Amida caressed the children from top to bottom and bottom to top, two, three, four, and five times and then vanished without a trace. The children awoke.

ACT 3

In their gratitude, the siblings bowed thirty-three times in obeisance.[7] Then as it was beginning to grow light, they tearfully set out from the Amida hall, the

---

7. Perhaps thirty-three times for the thirty-three manifestations of Kannon, Amida's attendant bodhisattva.

fatigue of their long journey lifted. Following Amida's instructions, they hurried on their way.

At around this time in Oki Village, there was a rich man named Genta Byōe. He had repeatedly requested that Ōman Chōja's son, Matsuwaka, be married to his daughter, but in the end Ōman Chōja refused to consent. Genta Byōe was enraged. Summoning a retainer by the name of Kagetsu no Jirō, he told him of his thwarted plans and asked his opinion. "It's truly hateful!" Kagetsu replied. "Make me your general and I will bring you your enemies' heads! I'll see to it that you achieve your aims." Genta Byōe was enormously pleased. "Well spoken, Kagetsu!" he cried. "Then you shall confront my foe." And with that, Genta awarded Kagetsu a force of more than three hundred riders.

Kagetsu quickly led his men against Ōman Chōja. Upon arriving at their opponent's mansion, they surrounded it on three sides and raised a battle cry. After the men's shouts had died down, the brothers Seigan no Samanosuke and Tōboku no Umanojō emerged from within the compound and bounded up the forward turret. "Who are you, making such a ruckus?" they demanded. "Identify yourselves!"

In a thunderous voice, Kagetsu replied: "The attacking general is I, Kagetsu no Jirō, servant of Genta Byōe! I have come here today to achieve my lord's long-held desire. You might as well go ahead and slit your bellies now!"

"What a bunch of nonsense!" the brothers declared. "We'll show you a thing or two!" Striding into the enemy horde, the two men fought as if the day were their last. They cut down fifty strong riders with their own hands, and they sent the remaining attackers flying in the four directions. Kagetsu thought, "This is awful! I'll have to achieve my master's desire some other time," and he set off toward home. But the brothers chased him down, and after twisting and tying his arms behind his back, they brought him before their lord.

"Damn it all!" Kagetsu quietly fumed. "But even if I am a prisoner now, I'll be the roaring thunder when I'm dead and fulfill my master's wishes before I'm done!" He glared furiously at his captors, his large eyes contorted with rage. Taking in the sight, Ōman Chōja said, "Shut him up." The men immediately cut off Kagetsu's head, whereupon it rose into the sky of its own accord. The men all curled their tongues with dread. Needless to say, Kagetsu's expression was terrible beyond description.

Ōman Chōja had won the battle, but his only son, Matsuwaka, fell ill with a mysterious ailment and took to his bed, dying. In his sorrow, Ōman Chōja summoned a diviner. "Tell me, doctor," he said, "what illness afflicts my child? And what is the cure? Divine for me, please." As the man was an able seer, he nimbly set eighty-one divination blocks on a sixty-one-space calendar and began to read the signs. "Oh, how interesting!" he said. "Let me explain. You must buy a girl who was born at the exact same time of the same year as your son was born and then extract her living liver. Wash and cleanse it seventy-five times in the wine known as Longevity Water, and then give it to your son as medicine. If you do, his illness will be cured straightaway."

"That's easy enough!" Ōman Chōja exclaimed, and he proceeded to put up placards in the Indian foothills. The placards read:

Wanted for Purchase: Twelve-Year-Old Girls, Best Price Paid

As this was India, more than 350 girls came to see Ōman Chōja about his signs, saying, "I'm twelve years old" and "I'm twelve years old, too." Ōman Chōja invited them inside, but when he compared them with his son, he found that even though they all were alike in being twelve years old, some were born in a different month than Matsuwaka had been, and those who were born on the same day were born at different hours. Thus in the end there was not a single girl who was born at the exact same time as Ōman Chōja's son, and they all went home.

ACT 4

Now what could be more pitiful than our two little siblings? As the dawn had already broken, the sister called her brother to her side and spoke: "How about it, Teirei? Let's go sell ourselves, just as Amida instructed." And thus they set out, hand in hand. Approaching Ōman Chōja's mansion, the sister shouted, "People for sale!" and the brother cried, "Buy us, please!" Ōman Chōja sent his ladies out to greet them. The women invited the children inside, where they served them an assortment of wine, delicacies, and local sweets.

After a while, Ōman Chōja wished to see his guests. Swaggering into his reception hall, he beheld a girl so lovely that she seemed to illuminate the entire room. "You beautiful girl!" he exclaimed. "Tell me, why do you wish to sell yourself? How old are you? Where do you come from, and where do you live?"

"Master," the sister replied, "I am the child of a lowly man from Katahira Village in the Enta district in the Land of Bishari, far away from here. I lost my parents when I was small. I would like to sponsor services for their enlightenment, but I lack the means, which is why I am seeking to sell myself. As for my age, I am twelve years old.[8] Please buy me and let me serve you, sir, even if only as a wretched water girl."

Ōman Chōja took in the sister's words. "So you are twelve years old," he said. "At what hour of what day of what month of what year were you born?"

"How specific!" the sister replied. "I was born early in the hour of the dragon on the sixth day of the third month of the *mizunoto-tori* year."[9]

"Wonderful!" Ōman Chōja thought to himself. "Our Matsuwaka was also born early in the hour of the dragon on the sixth day of the third month of the *mizunoto-tori* year. This girl is a perfect match! I'll buy her as medicine for our son." Withdrawing from the reception hall, Ōman Chōja summoned his wife and spoke: "Hello, dear, listen to this! That girl here is a perfect match! Go take a look! We'll buy her, whatever the cost."

"Really?" the wife replied. Approaching the reception hall, she beheld a child so lovely that she seemed to illuminate the entire room. "What a beautiful girl!" the wife thought. "She's surely no ordinary human being. She must be a god or a buddha in disguise! If we buy her and then trick her and kill her, we're bound to suffer heaven's wrath."

Deciding that she must tell the girl a bit about their plan, the wife spoke: "Hello, little lady. We, too, have a child, but he has contracted a mysterious illness and is afflicted now to the point of death. In our sorrow, we have assembled the greatest priests of India and offered prayers to the god of Mount Tai,[10] but so far to no effect. We summoned a trusty diviner from a particular place and asked him to divine. 'If you buy a girl who was born at exactly the same time as your son,' he said, 'and then extract her living liver, wash and cleanse it seventy-five times in the wine known as Longevity Water, and then feed it to your son, he is sure to be cured.' 'That's easy enough,' we thought, and we erected

---

8. There is an inconsistency in the text. Tenju is said to have been seven years old before her parents died and to have set out for the Land of Haranai near the seventh anniversary of their death. So she should be thirteen or fourteen years old.

9. The hour of the dragon is from 7:00 to 9:00 A.M. *Mizunoto-tori* is the tenth year in the cyclical sexagenary cycle.

10. Mount Tai in China's Shandong Province. The god of Mount Tai is celebrated as an arbiter of human life and death.

Tenju and Teirei meet Ōman Chōja and his wife. From *Munewari* (1651 woodblock-printed edition). (Courtesy of Tenri University Library)

placards in the foothills. This being India, more than 350 girls approached us about the signs, saying, 'I'm twelve years old' and 'I'm twelve years old, too.' We compared them with our son, but even though they all were alike in being twelve years old, some were born in a different month. Some others were born in the same month, but on different days, and some others who were born on the same day were born at different hours. In the end, there was not a single girl who was a perfect match. But you were born at the same hour of the same month of the same year as our son! If we buy you, then right or wrong, you'll have to give us your liver. So if you begrudge your life or despise our plan, then there's nothing we can do about it and you should leave here at once."

Tenju listened. Then, without making the slightest reply, she hung her head and cried. After a while she spoke: "Dear sir and madam, it is not for my own life that I mourn. Since this little boy and I lost our parents at the ages of five and seven, we have had only each other to rely on as we made our sad home in the fields. So if I give my life to you in the evening, who will be his sister in the morning? Who will raise this little boy? I felt so sorry for him just now that I was overcome with tears." The girl pressed her sleeve to her face and wept anew. Ōman Chōja and his wife took in the sight. "How right of her to cry!" they exclaimed, and they wept together with her.

ACT 5

Tenju spoke through her tears: "I will sell myself to you. However, I want to be paid while I'm still alive. I won't desire a lot of treasure after I die, so I want you to construct a gilded buddha hall now, for the sake of my parents' enlightenment. It should be four sided and seven *ken* square.[11] Then, if you will carve and install an Amida triad as the principal image,[12] I will gladly give you my living liver."

"That's easy enough," Ōman Chōja replied. He assembled carpenters and blacksmiths from all over India, and in twenty-one days he had built a gilded buddha hall, four sided, and seven *ken* square. He presented it to Tenju.

"There is now nothing that weighs on my mind," Tenju said, taking in the sight. "But I do worry that this little boy will be an obstacle for me in the world to come. I am entrusting him to you, sir. If you like, please keep him on as Master Matsuwaka's attendant or page. Or if not that, then employ him as a lowly garden boy. But please, sir, raise him well."

"Little lady," Ōman Chōja replied, "fortunately for you, I have no child except for Matsuwaka. I will think of this boy as my second son, and I will leave him half my fortune."

"There is now truly nothing that weighs on my mind," Tenju said, and she entered the buddha hall to pray. "Hail, Amida Buddha triad!" she declared. "I offer you this buddha hall, which I have built at the cost of my life. Even if our karmic transgressions run deep, through the power of this offering please save me and my parents and allow us to be reborn on a single jeweled lotus pedestal

---

11. One *ken* equals approximately 3.95 square yards, or 3.31 square meters. Seven *ken* is an area of about 83 square feet, or 23 square meters.

12. The triad consists of statues of Amida and his two bodhisattva attendants, Kannon and Seishi. The "principal image" (*honzon*) is the central object of worship in a temple or buddha hall.

in the upper grade, upper rank of Pure Land rebirth."[13] Then taking out a copy of the Lotus sutra, she assigned the merit of her recitation by proclaiming, "I will read the fifth scroll for my father; the sixth scroll for my mother; the seventh scroll for my brother, Teirei, for his future salvation; and the eighth scroll for myself."

Teirei approached his sister and spoke. His complaint was moving to hear! "Dear sister," he began, "when we left our village, you said that we would sell ourselves together for the sake of our parents' enlightenment. But now we've come to this unheard-of faraway land, and you've gone and built a big buddha hall for our parents' enlightenment without me! Why didn't you let us be bought together? Oh, sister!" Overcome with emotion, the brother could only cry.

"If I explain that I haven't sold myself," Tenju thought to herself, "but that I've exchanged my life for this buddha hall, then he'll beg me to take him away somewhere, and that will be too hard to bear." Tenju therefore decided to tell a little lie: "Listen, Teirei. Ōman Chōja thinks that I'm beautiful, and he's going to make me his daughter-in-law. He has given me enormous wealth, and because I wanted to do something for our parents' enlightenment, I built this buddha hall for them. You should become a temple priest. You can dedicate your years to picking fragrant flowers and praying for Mom's and Dad's salvation." Being the small child that he was and knowing nothing of the world, Teirei believed what his sister said. He pillowed his head on her knee and fell fast asleep. It was moving to behold!

Stroking the stray locks of her sleeping brother's hair, Tenju lamented piteously: "Ever since this little boy and I lost our parents at the ages of five and seven, we've always depended on each other. I've tried to protect him from everything! As for this hair of his, I dressed it five times a day—never only three. So if I give my life tonight, who will be his sister from tomorrow? Who will dress his hair? My poor little boy!" Again, Tenju pressed her sleeve to her face and wept without restraint.

ACT 6

As dawn broke on the following day, Matsuwaka was suffering horribly from his disease. Ōman Chōja summoned five fierce warriors. "Good morning, men,"

---

13. The Visualization sutra (Kanmuryōjukyō) explains that there are three grades of Pure Land rebirth (higher, middle, and lower), each of which is divided into an additional three (higher, middle, and lower), for a total of nine grades of Pure Land rebirth.

he said. "I want you to go to the buddha hall and get me that girl's living liver."
"Yes, sir," the warriors replied, and they quickly set out.

Arriving at the buddha hall, the warriors shouted, "Hello, young lady! We've been sent here to remove your liver. There's nothing you can do about it, so quit your crying and come right out."

Tenju heard the men's calls. "There's no use in grieving," she thought, and with a curt reply, she stepped outside. The early morning darkness was shattered by a blaze of light, but whether from the brilliance of Tenju's beauty or the glimmering of the gilded buddha hall, the warriors could not tell. Dazzled by the girl's loveliness, the men were at a loss where to strike. They cried out in grief, fearless fighters though they were. "Don't carry on like that," Tenju said, taking in the scene. "You'll make me lose my concentration. It's for my parents' sake that I'm giving up my life, and I don't begrudge it in the least. But it won't do to spill blood here in the precincts of the buddha hall, so come with me to the foothills village." Tenju and the men set out together.

When they reached the foothills, Tenju turned toward the west, pressed her palms together and prayed: "Hail, Amida Buddha of the West! Even if our karmic transgressions run deep, please save me and my parents and allow us to be reborn together on a jeweled lotus pedestal in the upper grade, upper rank of Pure Land rebirth." Then, she chanted a verse in four lines:

sho gyō mu jō	All things are impermanent,
ze shō metsu hō	as that which arises will also expire.
shō metsu metsu i	When arising and expiring themselves have expired,
jaku metsu i raku	that silent extinction produces joy.[14]

"You warriors," Tenju said, "it's a delicate matter, removing a woman's living liver. I'm sure you don't know how to do it, so I'll instruct you. First, wrap a short sword so that only half the blade is exposed. Then, jab it into my left side and rip across to the right. If you do it that way, you won't have any trouble."

Replying that they understood, the men wrapped a short sword so that only half the blade was exposed, just as Tenju had instructed. Then they plunged it into her lovely left side, ripped across to the right, and pulled out her

---

14. A famous verse in Heian and medieval Japan. According to the Nirvana sutra, Shakyamuni agreed to feed himself to a ravenous demon in order to learn its second half. The term "silent extinction" (*jakumetsu*) is a Chinese translation of the Sanskrit word "nirvana."

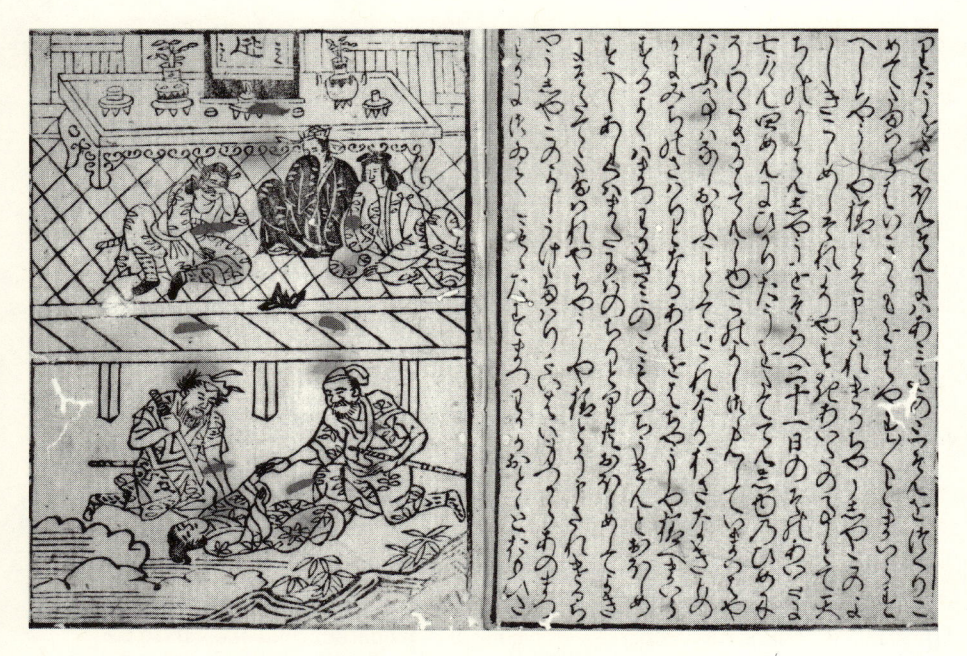

Ōman Chōja's men cut out Tenju's liver. From *Munewari* (1651 woodblock-printed edition). (Courtesy of Tenri University Library)

living liver. They returned to Ōman Chōja's mansion, where they washed and cleansed the organ seventy-five times in the wine known as Longevity Water, just as the diviner had said. When they fed it to Matsuwaka, he hopped out of bed in the middle of the night, his illness cured.

Ōman Chōja was overjoyed to see his son restored. Moved at the thought of Tenju's selflessness, he set off for the foothills to tend to the girl's bodily remains. Yet despite looking here and there, Ōman Chōja could find no body—only a pool of crimson blood. Thinking this strange, he proceeded to the buddha hall, where he found the girl and her brother lying arm in arm, sound asleep.

Ōman Chōja approached the buddha altar. Opening the altar doors and peering at the Amida triad inside, he saw that the central image was split open at the breast. Crimson blood spilled from the gory wound. "Look at that!" his men exclaimed. "The buddhas all pity filial children, and Amida gave himself for the girl!" "Put your hands together and pray!" others cried, and everyone did.

"What shall we do with such a wonderful girl?" Ōman Chōja inquired. He took her as his daughter-in-law, making her Matsuwaka's wife. The brother, Teirei, became a priest in that same buddha hall. Everyone said that such events were exceedingly rare, and there were none who did not pray.[15]

---

15. According to the Urokogataya *Amida no munewari*, Tenju and Teirei's parents were saved in the afterlife as a result of their daughter's Buddhist merit. See SSS 3:141a.

Goō-no-hime

ACT 1

Yoshitsune was studying hard at Kurama Temple.[1] He thought to himself, "It's already the thirteenth anniversary of my father Yoshitomo's death this year. I'd like to honor him by having a priest perform some services, but the Taira rule the land now and the Minamoto are in decline. I think I'll sneak out and ask Master Hōnen at Shinkurodani to say some prayers."[2]

Translated from the 1673 *Goō-no-hime*.

1. Yoshitsune was the youngest son of the late Minamoto no Yoshitomo (d. 1160), one of two leaders of the failed Heiji uprising against Taira no Kiyomori in 1159. Although spared execution, from the age of seven Yoshitsune was placed under a kind of house arrest at Kurama Temple in the mountains north of Kyoto. He would have been thirteen years old (or fifteen years old, by Japanese count) on the thirteenth anniversary of his father's death. As one of the great heroes of medieval and early modern fiction and drama, Yoshitsune would have been well known to seventeenth-century audiences of *Goō-no-hime*.

2. Hōnen (1133–1212) was the founder of the Pure Land school of Buddhism. He established the Shirakawa Zenbō (Konkai Kōmyōji Temple) in what came to be known as Shinkurodani (or simply Kurodani) in eastern Kyoto in 1175.

The young lord crept out of Kurama Temple in the dark of night and quickly made his way to Shinkurodani. Because he hurried, he soon met with the holy man. "Excuse me, master," he said, "I'm just a lowly boy from the east. It's the thirteenth anniversary of my father's death this year, and I would like to ask you to dedicate ten *nenbutsu* invocations to him in the afterworld." Hōnen agreed and immediately conferred the invocations.

Yoshitsune took his leave. He was about to return to Kurama Temple when he remembered hearing that his father's tomb was in the vicinity of the Gongen Buddha Hall at Seventh Avenue and Shushaka Street. Thinking that he would pay it a visit, he set out for Seventh Avenue.

At his father's grave, Yoshitsune took out the Devadatta chapter from the fifth scroll of the Lotus sutra and recited, "*Issha-fu-toku-sa-bon-ten-nō ni-sha-tai-shaku san-sha-ma-ō shi-sha-ten-rin-jō-ō go-sha-butsu-shin un-ga-nyo-shin-soku-toku-jō-butsu*."[3] Then, after reciting the sixth scroll for the future salvation of his mother, Tokiwa, who was still living in this world, and the seventh and eighth scrolls for Evil Genda and Minamoto no Tomonaga,[4] Yoshitsune set out for home. But before he had proceeded beyond a shabby block of Seventh Avenue row houses, the sky began to pour rain.

Off to the west, Yoshitsune saw a mansion behind an imposing gate with a gabled roof. When he approached it for a closer look, he saw that the gate had no doors and that the fine mud wall enclosing the estate had lost its mantle. Everything was in a terrible state of disrepair. Nevertheless, he took shelter there from the blowing, driving rain.

After a while, a sixteen- or seventeen-year-old girl emerged from inside the mansion. But when she saw Yoshitsune in all his handsome appeal, she turned on her heels and went back indoors. The girl ran to her aunt, who was a nun, and spoke: "Dear Aunt, when I had a look outside the front just now, I saw a young man from who-knows-where standing and waiting for

---

3. "First, a woman may not be reborn as a brahmā god king; second, as Śakra; third, as Māra; fourth, as a wheel-turning king; and fifth, as a buddha. How, then, may a woman swiftly attain buddhahood?" These are the five obstructions, the five forms of rebirth listed in the Lotus sutra as prohibited to women. Yoshitsune recites the passage in Chinese, the language of the sutras in Japan.

4. Evil Genda (Minamoto no Yoshihira) and Minamoto no Tomonaga were Yoshitsune's half brothers by his father. Both lost their lives in the Heiji uprising of 1159.

the rain to pass. He looks like he was raised in the capital. His face is lightly made up, and his eyebrows are shaved and painted high on his forehead. His teeth are blackened, too. He's wearing an underrobe woven of gold Chinese thread, and a trouser-skirt made from a heavy sky-blue fabric daubed with single strokes of bluish yellow and embroidered in seven places with ten-, eight-, and five-colored thread. And the elegance of his cuffs! He's hiding a pair of long and short swords with gold-plated fittings at his left side, and he has a panpipe, a flute, and two other kinds of wind instruments in a sandalwood case tucked into his robe at his right. Oh, Auntie, he's grander than the greatest general!"

"If that's the case," the old nun replied, "then hurry up and invite him inside." The girl was overjoyed—her name was Goō-no-hime—and rushing outside again, she called to Yoshitsune and beckoned him indoors.

Yoshitsune was pleased. Although he did not know the identity of his host, he quickly went inside. As soon as the old nun saw him, she said, "Hello, traveling sir! Our house is in a terrible state, but do come in." She showed him to a wide reception hall, where she served him wine, local sweets, and an assortment of delicacies from the mountains and sea. After they had been drinking for a while, the old nun turned to Yoshitsune and said, "Won't you play us a tune on that flute at your waist?"

"I do have a piece of cheap bamboo with holes in it," Yoshitsune replied, "but as for playing music, I don't know the slightest thing. Please forgive me."

"I've forgotten all about it now," the old nun said, "but it seems to me that in the year that Kūkai and Mañjuśrī were having their battle of wits in the Oki district in India,[5] there was a shaft of especially fine bamboo growing there. Kūkai thought it was marvelous, and he cut it down and tossed it into the ocean. The bamboo drifted to Byōbu Bay in Sanuki Province in this very land. Kūkai found it again when he returned to Japan, and still thinking it marvelous, he broke it into three pieces and made the flutes Green Leaf, Little Branch, and Broken Cicada. People say that those three instruments survive to this day. Yours is one of them, I guess. So won't you please play us a tune?"

---

5. Kūkai (774–835) was the founder of the Shingon sect of Japanese Buddhism; Mañjuśrī (Monju) is popularly known as the bodhisattva of wisdom. For an account of their battle, see *Karukaya*.

Yoshitsune and Goō-no-hime take shelter from the rain. From *Goō-no-hime* (1673 woodblock-printed edition). (Courtesy of Osaka University Library)

Impressed by the old nun's savvy, Yoshitsune acquiesced. He took out that very same Broken Cicada, and after moistening the blow hole and seven finger holes with the dew from a China pink, he blew a note straight to the heavens. Then, softening his tone, he performed a melody called "Blue Ocean Waves."

"What a lovely sound!" the old nun exclaimed. "You must stay here until tomorrow. We'll have twelve ladies perform on wind and string instruments, and you shall play the flute!" Everyone in the household agreed, and they all sought to keep him on. Yoshitsune's feelings were beyond compare!

ACT 2

The young lord was unused to traveling, and whether from the strain of the journey or some other cause, he fell desperately ill and was soon unable to arise from bed. Elsewhere, the Taira general Kiyomori was shocked to hear that Yoshitsune had disappeared from Kurama Temple. Appointing Kagekiyo his lieutenant,[6] Kiyomori sent him out to find the boy. And where do you think he looked? In Ōtsu, Sakamoto, Daigo, and the provinces of Kawachi, Settsu, and Tanba. But search as he might, Kagekiyo could not find him anywhere. Eventually, Kagekiyo erected signs at the seven entrances to the capital and waited for someone to bring him information.

Back at Seventh Avenue, the old nun approached her niece and spoke: "Hello, dear. As people say, 'Be kind to travelers, and be caring in life.' So please take good care of our guest." Goō-no-hime was thrilled to be entrusted with the young man's health, and she visited him where he lay. "How are you, young sir?" she inquired. "People say that when strangers seek shelter in the shade of a single tree or scoop water from the same stream, it's because they share a karmic bond from a previous life. So for me to be tending to you in your illness—how much deeper must our own connection be! Where do you come from, sir? Please tell me your name."

Yoshitsune drew a painful breath and replied, "I come from the east."

"Oh, indeed, I forgot!" the girl exclaimed. "I've heard that when you ask people about their families, you should tell them about your own first. Who do you think I am? It embarrasses me to speak of myself, sir, but I am Goō-no-hime, the younger sister of Kamata Byōe,[7] a retainer of that Yoshitomo who lost his life at Numa no Utsumi in Owari Province."

Yoshitsune thought that he must be dreaming. He slowly lifted his head and said, "So you are Goō! I am Yoshitsune from Kurama Temple. I had heard that my father's tomb was around Seventh Avenue, and I wanted to pay it a visit, which is why I'm here. I'm so happy to meet you! The bonds of former lives are strong indeed. But the Minamoto are in decline and the Taira rule the land now, so please don't tell anyone who I am."

Weeping for joy, Goō-no-hime bowed to Yoshitsune three times. To meet the young lord of the house that her own family had served for generations—it was as rare and excellent as a one-eyed turtle happening on a floating log in the vast, empty ocean! She imagined how pleased her aunt would be to hear the news, and she hurried off to tell her.

---

6. Fujiwara no Kagekiyo (d. 1195) was a famous Taira loyalist in the Genpei War.

7. Kamata Masakiyo (1123–1160) was the son of Yoshitomo's wet nurse and one of Yoshitomo's most trusted retainers.

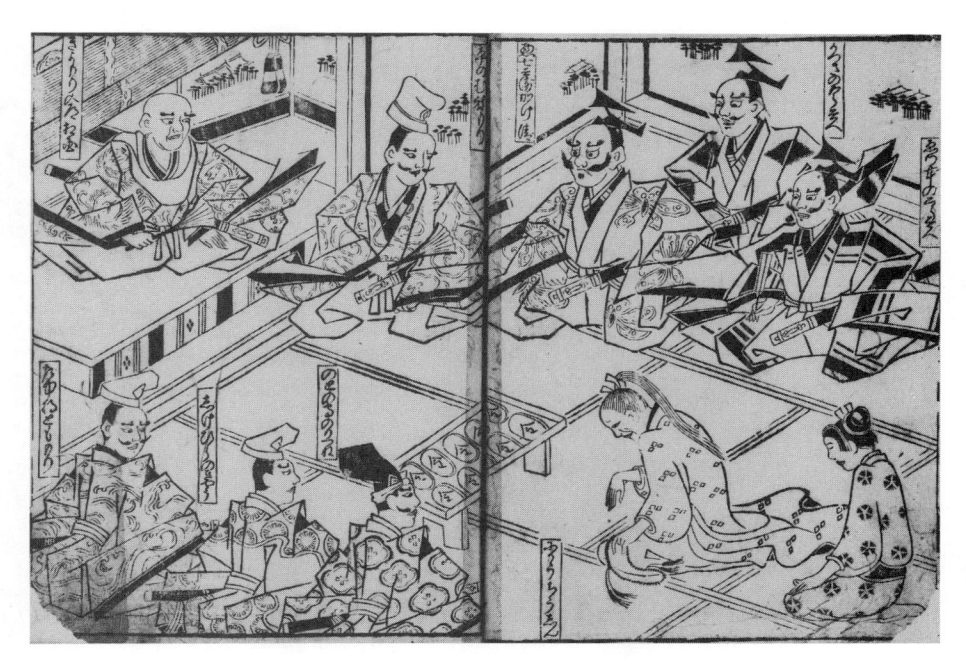

The old nun reports to Kiyomori. From *Goō-no-hime* (1673 woodblock-printed edition). (Courtesy of Osaka University Library)

Upon learning the identity of their guest, the old nun rapped her fan on the reed-mat floor and blurted out, "Is it true, dear? He's really Yoshitsune? There are signs up saying that Kiyomori will pay a bounty to anyone who catches the boy, dead or alive. I'll visit Kiyomori's headquarters at Rokuhara and tell him myself! He'll pay me the reward, and then instead of being called 'that shabby old row-house nun,' people will refer to me as 'the rich reverend!'" With that, she slicked back her three strands of gray hair, blackened her two front teeth, and scurried off to Rokuhara.

Soon arriving at her destination, the old nun meekly announced, "That Yoshitsune you've been looking for is staying at my house. Please send some men to kill him, quickly." Kiyomori was delighted. "You've done well to bring us this information!" he cried. "I'll send a force right away," and he dispatched a large group of men. Everyone at Rokuhara despised the old nun for the avarice in her heart!

ACT 3

Poor Goō-no-hime! Seeing that her aunt had sped away, she moaned to herself, "Oh, how terrible! What shall I do?" Her breast was in a flutter, but since there was no time to lose, she approached the young lord where he lay and, weeping all the while, explained to him what her aunt had said and done.

"Don't cry like that, Goō-no-hime," Yoshitsune said. "As the Buddha says, 'those who are born will surely perish, just as those who meet are sure to part.' Is there anyone alive who won't die someday? Since that's the way of the world, I'm not going to wait here to perish—I'll storm Rokuhara and get revenge on Kiyomori with a single strike! After that, I'll cut open my belly and take my own life!" Placing a hand on the hilt of his sword, Yoshitsune struggled to rise. But being as sick as he was, his limbs and joints refused to obey. He could only flail about on his bed, pushing first with his left hand and then with his right.

Goō-no-hime took in the sight. "Young sir," she said, "since the ancient past, people have said that it's the long-lived turtle that survives to see Mount Hōrai.[8] So please wait here for a while. I'll go find my uncle at Upper Daigo.[9] He's the holy man Shōshinbō, and he's served your family for generations. I'll get his help, but I'll have to leave you here first. If Kiyomori's men come before I return, you should slip out through the bamboo grove at the back." Goō-no-hime hurried off toward Daigo with tears in her eyes.

It was the twenty-eighth day of the fourth month of Angen 4 (1178),[10] and there was no moon at all. The road was veiled in gloom like the long night of spiritual darkness, and buckets of rain poured from the sky. And although Goō-no-hime had heard about Daigoji Temple, she had never actually been there herself—she only knew that it was to the east.

Traveling on foot, the girl soon came to the Toribeno charnel ground. It was a terrifying place, with dogs and wolves barking and howling and dead bodies scattered all around. In her despair, she intoned a single poem:

---

8. In other words, good things come to those who live. Mount Hōrai is a legendary island of Daoist immortals to the east of Japan.

9. The site of Daigoji Temple in the Fushimi district of Kyoto.

10. There is an inconsistency in the text. Because Yoshitomo was killed in the first month of 1160, 1178 would have been the eighteenth, rather than the thirteenth, year since his death.

Toribeno ni	When I hear the howls
arasou inu no	of the dogs vying for flesh
koe kikeba	at Toribeno,
kanete wagami no	I know that for me, too,
okidokoro nashi	there will be no place to rest.

Continuing on, Goō-no-hime came to the foot of Mount Daigo. But what sorrow! Having heard that the upper reaches of the mountain were closed to women, she had no idea how to proceed. Utterly confounded, she broke down and cried.

Shō Hachiman, the patron deity of the Minamoto clan, was struck with pity for the girl. Manifesting as an eighty-year-old priest, he approached her in scented robes and a quilted stole. Fingering an elegant crystal rosary and leaning on a staff, he said, "Hello, child. Women are forbidden from climbing the mountain. Who are you, and whatever is the matter?"

"I have some business with the priest Shōshinbō," Goō-no-hime replied, "which is why I've come, but women are barred from the mountain and I don't know what to do." And with that, she wept anew.

"If that's the case," Hachiman said, "then please write him a letter. I'll deliver it for you." Goō-no-hime was overjoyed. She wrote a detailed message and entrusted it to the priest, who immediately climbed Mount Daigo and presented it to Shōshinbō.

Shōshinbō was much surprised, and descending the mountain straightaway, he met with Goō-no-hime. "What's going on?" he asked, whereupon the girl grabbed his sleeves and told him what had occurred. Shōshinbō was aghast. "Is it true?" he exclaimed. "Then this really is a problem! But don't worry, dear, I'll save him somehow or other."

With two young monks in tow, Goō-no-hime and her uncle sped on their way. They soon arrived at the Toribeno charnel ground, where, strange to say, they saw a single funeral casket. Thinking it odd, Shōshinbō paused for a closer look. There was a message stamped on the casket from Shō Hachiman and the deity Bishamonten of Kurama Temple: "We entreat you, master. Help Yoshitsune escape." Encouraged by this portent and pleased that his luck was so strong, Shōshinbō had the two monks carry the coffin as they raced toward Seventh Avenue. The master's determination was truly beyond description!

ACT 4

Because he hurried, Shōshinbō quickly came to the mansion among the row houses. He approached Yoshitsune's pillow and spoke: "Hello, young sir. I am the priest Shōshinbō from Daigoji Temple. Please get into this casket, now!" Yoshitsune was relieved, and he climbed inside.

Goō-no-hime took in the sight. "Uncle," she cried, "how dare you place our lord in a coffin! We've served his family for generations."

"No, no, child, it's not like that," the holy man explained. "People say that the character for 'casket' is written as an 'open carriage,' so this coffin will serve splendidly. Please put your mind at ease." He draped a white silken shawl over Goō-no-hime's head to indicate mourning. Then, with heavy hearts, they all hurried off toward Mount Daigo.

Meanwhile, a force of more than three hundred riders had set out from Rokuhara under Kagekiyo's command. As they pressed on their way, they suddenly encountered Shōshinbō and his funeral procession. Taking in the sight, Kagekiyo realized that Yoshitsune might in fact be playing dead in order to escape. He grabbed Shōshinbō by the sleeve and said, "Hold on, you look suspicious. I'm going to open up your casket and have a look inside. I've got my reasons."

Shōshinbō was not shaken in the least. Raising a mighty voice, he shouted, "What did you say, young samurai? 'I'm going to open up your casket and have a look inside? I've got my reasons?' I am an independent priest, and I walk the capital collecting corpses! I take them to the fields for cremation and pray for their enlightenment. That's my religious practice! Now it just so happens that I came upon a dead child this evening as I was passing along Seventh Avenue. I picked him up, and now I'm taking him to the fields. If you have a heart, then let me pass!"

There was a man among Kagekiyo's warriors named Kenmotsu no Tarō Yorikata. Upon hearing the holy man's explanation, he spoke up, saying, "Listen, everyone! It's good luck to meet a corpse on your way to kill an enemy! We're wasting time here questioning this stupid priest. Let's be done with him and go." "Yes, right!" the men all cried, and the more than three hundred riders slipped away to the left and right, allowing Shōshinbō to pass. The master was exceptionally pleased. Feeling as if he had tread on a tiger's tail or escaped the bite of some poisonous snake, he hastened on toward Daigo.

The group soon arrived at the foot of Mount Daigo. Goō-no-hime clutched the shafts of Yoshitsune's casket-palanquin. Their final parting was a sad one!

Shōshinbō and his party encounter Kagekiyo and his men. From *Goō-no-hime* (1673 woodblock-printed edition). (Courtesy of Osaka University Library)

"My lord," she said, "I have brought you this far, and now you will embark on your glorious reign! I'll say good-bye here. I'm sure to be arrested by Kiyomori as punishment for helping you escape. No doubt I'll be tortured and killed. He'll probably twist off my ten fingers in ten days and smash my twenty parts in twenty. Shōshinbō, if it comes to that, then please pray for me in the afterworld. Good-bye." Thus, with tears in her eyes, Goō-no-hime set out on her return. The strength in her heart was greater than that of two people combined!

The girl proceeded to the house of one of her serving women, Midori, who lived at Third Avenue and Abura Lane, and she hid there. Meanwhile, the Taira warriors came to the mansion among the Seventh Avenue row houses. They encircled the estate with two and three rows of men while fresh forces took turns searching inside. But Yoshitsune was nowhere to be found. Declaring their mission a futile waste of time, the warriors returned to Rokuhara, where they reported to Kiyomori all that had occurred. For Yoshitsune, it had been a close call indeed!

ACT 5

Kiyomori heard the news. "If that's the case," he declared, "then the old nun came here to deceive us! Kagekiyo, have her arrested!" "Yes, sir," Kagekiyo replied, and he had the woman seized, bound, and imprisoned.

The pitiful old nun spoke from inside her cell: "Oh, how cruel! Why would I lie? But wait—I remember now! There was a girl by the name of Goō-no-hime, and she must have helped him escape! Summon her here and ask!" Kagekiyo suspected that this was true, and he made inquiries throughout the capital. However, no one knew where the young woman had gone.

Unaware of all this, Goō-no-hime visited the Kiyomizu Kannon in order to perform a seven-day prayer vigil for Yoshitsune.[11] Kagekiyo happened to have his own reason for visiting Kiyomizu just then, and he crossed paths with the girl as she was leaving. Being the quick-witted fellow that he was, Kagekiyo realized that this was the very person he had been trying to find. He rushed at the poor child and trussed her up, twisting her arms painfully behind her back. Then, in his joy, he returned to Rokuhara.

Goō-no-hime appeared before the general. "Are you Goō-no-hime?" Kiyomori asked.

"Yes," she replied.

"Then why did you let Yoshitsune escape? Tell me exactly what happened. If I get the slightest sense you're lying, I'll have you tortured to find out."

"How should I know where my lord went?" Goō-no-hime snapped. "You should ask the old nun!"

Kiyomori turned to Kagekiyo. "She's not likely to break like any ordinary woman," he said. "Try seven or eight of your interrogation techniques. Question her under duress." "Yes, sir," Kagekiyo replied.

Withdrawing from the general's presence, Kagekiyo led Goō-no-hime to a broad courtyard. As his first interrogation technique, he tied her to a ladder with nine rungs for the cold water torture.[12] "Give in!" he shouted, "Give in!" Goō-no-hime thought to herself, "What cruelty! There are 136 hells in the world to come, and people say that among them is a freezing hell in which sinners

---

11. The statue of the Eleven-Headed, Thousand-Armed Kannon at Kiyomizu Temple in Kyoto.

12. A method of simulating drowning by pouring water into the mouth and nose.

Kiyomori questions Goō-no-hime. From *Goō-no-hime* (1673 woodblock-printed edition). (Courtesy of Osaka University Library)

are sealed in the ice of the Great Crimson Lotus with no chance to escape.[13] But because I am already suffering that punishment here, I am sure to be reborn in Amida's Pure Land in the next life." And she replied, "Master Kagekiyo, I do not know where my lord has gone."

As his second interrogation technique, Kagekiyo employed the boiling water torture. "Give in!" he shouted as he scalded her fourteen and fifteen times, "Give in!" Goō-no-hime thought to herself, "I've heard that in the world to come there is a place called the Hell of No Respite where people are tormented like this.[14] But because I am already suffering this punishment here, I will surely attain buddhahood in the next life." And she replied, "I do not know where my lord has gone."

---

13. Daiguren Jigoku, "Hell of the Great Crimson Lotus," is named for the splotchy red appearance of its inhabitants' frostbitten skin.

14. Muken Jigoku (in Sanskrit, Avīci) is the deepest and worst of the Eight Burning Hells.

As his third interrogation technique, Kagekiyo screwed arrows into each of Goō-no-hime's joints. "Oh, how cruel!" Goō-no-hime thought. "In the Barren Women's Hell in the world to come,[15] women are forced to shoulder enormous boulders and to dig up bamboo shoots with limp lamp wicks. But because I am already suffering like this here, I'll surely be saved in the next life." And she replied, "I do not know where my lord has gone."

As his fourth interrogation technique, Kagekiyo studded a pinewood plank with a multitude of ten-inch nails and demanded that Goō-no-hime walk across it. Because she had no choice, she complied. Blood dripped from the soles of her feet in a crimson cascade. Poor Goō-no-hime! "In the world to come," she thought to herself, "I've heard that people cross a place like this called the Mountain of Swords.[16] But because I am already suffering that punishment here, I am sure to be reborn in Amida's Pure Land in the next life." And she replied, "Master Kagekiyo—" The feelings in her heart were moving beyond compare!

ACT 6

Now as his fifth interrogation technique, Kagekiyo used a short sword to cut out Goō-no-hime's twenty nails. "Oh, how vicious!" Goō-no-hime thought to herself. "I've heard that in the world to come there is a place called the Hell of Eternal Carnage where those who take up arms without due cause are tormented like this.[17] But because I am already suffering that punishment here, I will surely become a buddha in the next life." And she replied, "I do not know where my lord has gone."

As his sixth interrogation technique, Kagekiyo buried Goō-no-hime up to her waist and afflicted her with snakes. "Give in!" he shouted, "Give in!" Goō-no-hime thought to herself, "Even ordinarily, women are deeply sinful beings, marked by the five obstructions and the three obediences.[18] In particular, those

---

15. Umazume Jigoku is a special hell for women without children.

16. Tsurugi no Yama is a mountain of swords and daggers that barefoot sinners are forced to climb.

17. Ashura no Jigoku (Ashura-dō) is a place of constant battle.

18. The five obstructions are five forms of rebirth listed in the Devadatta chapter of the Lotus sutra as prohibited to women. The three obediences constitute a woman's duty to obey her father, her husband, and, finally, her son.

Goō-no-hime is interrogated. From *Goō-no-hime* (1673 woodblock-printed edition). (Courtesy of Osaka University Library)

who experience the seven-day monthly obstruction or who die within seventy-five days of giving birth will fall into the Blood Pool Hell in the world to come.[19] The Blood Pool is forty thousand *yojanas* deep and wide,[20] and it is spanned by an iron bridge thinner than a thread. Demons shout, "Cross it! Cross it!" The sinners have no choice, and so shedding tears of blood, they try to traverse to the other shore. When they look down, they see a mass of great poisonous snakes, like a writhing woven lattice. I've heard that sometimes a woman will make it across but that hordes of birds then flock to her and peck her brains out. Because I am already suffering that punishment here, I will surely be reborn in Amida's Pure Land in the next life." And she replied, "I do not know where my lord has gone."

    19. The "seven-day monthly obstruction" refers to menstruation. The Blood Pool Hell (Chi no Ike Jigoku) is another special hell reserved for women.
    20. One *yojana* equals seven or nine miles, depending on the interpretation.

Goō-no-hime is interrogated and saved after death. From *Goō-no-hime* (1673 woodblock-printed edition). (Courtesy of Osaka University Library)

As his seventh interrogation technique, Kagekiyo carried charcoal embers into the courtyard and used a great fan to rouse them to a raging heat. Then, after binding Goō-no-hime's arms and legs, he harrowed her with the so-called bird-roasting torment. "Give in!" he shouted, "Give in!" Dizzy from the pain, Goō-no-hime wished to surrender at last. But because she knew that to do so now would achieve nothing, she decided instead to berate her enemies before she died. "Master Kagekiyo," she said, "I'll tell you where my lord went. But there's no one here with enough sense to understand. So take me to Kiyomori." Kagekiyo was overjoyed, and he dragged her to the general.

Kiyomori glared at the girl. "If you had something to say, then why didn't you say it at the start? I would have given you many treasures. But now I can pay you only with prayers for the next life. So how about it?" All of the attending samurai listened closely, thinking that now at last they would learn where their foe had fled.

The old nun is put to death. From *Goō-no-hime* (1673 woodblock-printed edition). (Courtesy of Osaka University Library)

"As for my lord," Goō-no-hime began, "he has neither ascended to the heavens nor burrowed underground. Go find him in the sixty-six provinces of Japan! He will attack you from Michinoku in the north, cut off your head, and hang it on the prison gate. And as for you, Kagekiyo, he will torture you as you've tortured me! I'll be watching from my grave, and I'll be oh so pleased! How about that, Kiyomori?"

The general was enraged. "If she won't tell," he shouted, "then change the punishment!" And with that, he stormed inside his mansion.

As his eighth interrogation technique, Kagekiyo dangled an iron chain from the branch of a withered pine. He attached the chain to a rope around Goō-no-hime's neck so that when he hoisted her up she strangled, and when he let her down she gasped for air. Poor Goō-no-hime! Deciding that she was now ready to die, she turned toward the west, pressed her palms together in her mind, and recited "Hail Amida Buddha!" Then, having spoken these final words, at the age of seventeen, she bit off her tongue and expired like the morning dew. A mysterious fragrance wafted through the air, and blossoms rained from the sky as a host of twenty-five bodhisattvas appeared with baldachins in hand to carry her away to the Pure Land.

Kiyomori took in the sight. Impressed by the girl's loyalty to her lord and wishing to preserve it as a model for future generations, he built a shrine above the waterfall at Kiyomizu Temple and consecrated it "Goō Shrine." Later he summoned the old nun. "I will grant you a domain," he declared. "Would you like a large province or a small one?" The old nun smiled and said, "A large one, please." "If that's the case," Kiyomori replied, "then you shall have the Land of the Dead!"

Kiyomori's men bound the old woman, set her on a cart, and paraded her through the narrow streets, from First Avenue at Yanagibara to the Seventh Avenue riverbed. They fastened one of her legs to a horse and the other to an ox, and then spurred the two animals in opposite directions so that the old nun was ripped in half. The sky suddenly clouded over and poured with rain, whereupon a demon grabbed the old woman's body and fled. Among all the people there—high and low alike—there were none who did not despise her for what she had done.

APPENDIX 1

Major *Sekkyō* Chanters

The *sekkyō* chanters mentioned in this book include

Higurashi Kodayū 日暮小太夫　Active in Kyoto around the mid-seventeenth century. Muroki Yatarō suggests that he was the chanter of the 1661 *Aigo-no-waka*.[1] Likewise, Yokoyama Shigeru suggests that he was the chanter of the 1675 *Oguri Hangan* because the 1675 *Oguri Hangan* was published by Shōhon-ya Gohei of the Kamigata (Kyoto–Osaka) region, and Higurashi Kodayū was so famous in Kyoto that few of the Kamigata *shōhon* published at that time were *not* attributed to him. Yokoyama also cites evidence that Higurashi Kodayū performed *Oguri* around 1665 and that the work may have been a standard in his repertoire (SSS 2:314b–15a, 493b). Asai Ryōi's *Kyō suzume* (1665) includes a drawing of his theater in Kyoto.[2] According to *Biyō kejō jishi* (preface dated 1782), Higurashi Kodayū performed *Gosui Tennō*, *Sanshō Dayū*, *Aigo-no-waka*, *Karukaya*, *Oguri Hangan*, *Shintokumaru*, *Matsura Chōja* (*Sayohime*), *Ikenie*, and *Kozarashi monogatari* at a theater in Nagoya in 1665.[3] Extant *shōhon* include the 1662 *Yuriwaka Daijin* (SSS 2:211–26), the 1669 *Ōshōgun* (SSS 2:227–47), and an undated *Oguri* excerpt (*nukihon*) titled *Oguri Terute yume monogatari* (*Oguri and the Story of Terute's Dream*), published by Tsukuri-honya Hachibei 作本屋八兵衛 (SSS 2:492–95).

Osaka Yoshichirō 大阪与七郎　Active in Osaka in the first half of the seventeenth century. According to Fujimoto Kizan's *Shikidō ōkagami* (1678), Yoshichirō was the first *sekkyō* chanter to use puppets in his performances.[4] Shinoda Jun'ichi argues that he usually performed at Shitennōji (Tennōji) Temple in Osaka;[5] Nishida Kōzō argues that he may have established a theater in the Edochō district of Osaka.[6] Extant *shōhon* include the circa 1639 *Sanshō Dayū* (translated here), attributed to Tenka-ichi Sekkyō Yoshichirō (Yoshichirō, the Greatest Sekkyō Chanter Under Heaven), and, possibly, the 1631 *Sekkyō Karukaya* (also translated here), the fragmentary *Sekkyō Oguri* (published in the Kan'ei period, 1624–1644), and the 1661 *Matsura Chōja*.

Sado Shichidayū 佐渡七太夫　Active in Osaka around 1648 to 1658. Moved to Edo around 1661, where he was sometimes known as Osaka Shichidayū 大阪七太夫.[7] Extant *shōhon* include the 1648 *Sekkyō Shintokumaru* (translated here), the 1651 *Shintokumaru* (cited in SSS 1:452a), the 1656 *Sekkyō Sanshō Dayū*, and the Urokogataya *Shintokumaru* (published ca. 1681–1688), in which he is variously identified as Tenka Musō Sado Shichidayū (The Incomparable Sado Shichidayū), Tenka-ichi Sekkyō Sado Shichidayū (Sado Shichidayū, the Greatest Sekkyō Chanter Under Heaven), and simply Osaka Shichidayū. He also is the attributed chanter of an undated *Oguri* excerpt (*nukihon*) titled *Shinpan Oguri Hangan* (*Oguri Hangan, Newly Published*) and subtitled *Terute-no-hime, shimizu no dan* (*Terute-no-hime and the Pure Water Episode*) (SSS 2:491–92).

Sado Shichidayū Toyotaka 佐渡七太夫豊孝　Active in Edo in the early eighteenth century. His connection to Sado Shichidayū is unknown. Extant *shōhon* include the 1713 *Sanshō Dayū*, the circa 1711 to 1736 *Oguri no Hangan*, the 1719 *Kamata Hyōe Masakiyo* (*Fushimi Tokiwa*, SSS 3:26–54), the circa 1718 *Kumagae senjin mondō* (SSS 1:230–47), the circa 1718 *Hōzōbiku* (SSS 2:190–210), the circa 1718 *Shida no Kotarō* (SSS 3:73–96), and an undated *Gosuiden* (SSS 1:149–62).

Tenma Hachidayū 天満八太夫　Active in Edo in the second half of the seventeenth century. Beginning in the twelfth month of 1661, he was also known as Iwami-no-jō 石見掾; between around 1660 and 1692, he was the leading *sekkyō* chanter in Edo. Although some sources report that Tenma Hachidayū died around 1708, Shinoda Jun'ichi argues that he ceased performing around 1691/1692 and died shortly thereafter.[8] Asai Ryōi's *Edo meishoki* (1662) includes a drawing of his theater in the Negichō district of Edo, and a placard outside the building advertises a performance of *Oguri*.⁹ *Yakusha-e zukushi* (ca. 1688) includes a drawing of what may have been his later theater in the Sakaichō district of Edo.¹⁰ Extant *shōhon* include the Urokogataya *Amida no munewari*, the circa 1704 *Amida no munewari*, the Urokogataya Magobei *Karukaya Dōshin*, the 1687 *Mokurenki* (SSS 2:157–73), the 1690 *Kamata Hyōe Masakiyo* (also known as *Fushimi Tokiwa*, SSS 3:3–25), *Shaka no go-honji* (SSS 1:196–211), *Kumagae senjin mondō* (SSS 1:212–29), *Daifukujin Benzaiten no go-honji* (SSS 1:297–315), *Kasadera Kannon no honji* (SSS 1:271–96), *Hōzōbiku* (SSS 2:174–89), *Bishamon no honji* (SSS 3:168–83), *Ronzan Shōnin no yurai* (SSS 3:142–67), *Hyōgo no Tsukishima* (SSS 2:248–64), *Ishiyama-ki* (SSS 2:283–304),¹¹ and, possibly, the circa 1661 *Karukaya Dōshin*, the circa 1670 *Aigo-no-waka* (translated here), the circa 1704 *Matsura Chōja*, and the 1708 *Aigo-no-waka*.

Tenma Magoshirō 天満孫四郎 Active in Edo in the second half of the seventeenth century; also known as Edo Magoshirō 江戸孫四郎. He seems to have been a student of Tenma Hachidayū, from whom his name is derived, and to have operated his own theater in the Sakaichō district of Edo from at least 1682 (SSS 3:550a, 551a). *Yakusha-e zukushi* (ca. 1688) includes a drawing of one his puppet performances,¹² although which one is unclear. Extant *shōhon* include the undated Urokogataya *Karukaya Dōshin*, and the circa 1685 *Kōchi Shōnin* (SSS 3:224–46).

NOTES

1. Muroki Yatarō, "Kaisetsu," in SNKS *Sekkyō shū*, 421.
2. Reproduced in *Kyō suzume*, Kinsei bungaku shiryō ruijū: Kohan chishi hen (Tokyo: Benseisha, 1979), 4:284. See also figure 3.
3. Cited in Muroki Yatarō, *Zōtei katarimono (mai, sekkyō, ko-jōruri) no kenkyū* (Tokyo: Kazama shobō, 1981), 313.
4. Shinpan Shikidō ōkagami kankōkai, ed., *Shinpan Shikidō ōkagami* (Tokyo: Yagi shoten, 2006), 235.
5. Shinoda Jun'ichi, "Kinsei shoki no katarimono," in *Ko-jōruri, sekkyō shū*, SNKBT 90:569–70.
6. Nishida Kōzō, "Sekkyō jōruri to ko-jōruri: Toshika, gekika," *Kokubungaku: Kaishaku to kanshō* 70, no. 12 (2005): 114–16.
7. Shinoda, "Kinsei shoki no katarimono," 571.
8. Shinoda Jun'ichi, "Tenma Hachidayū zakkō," in SSS 3:599b, 600b.

9. Reproduced in *Edo meishoki*, Kinsei bungaku shiryō ruijū: Kohan chishi hen (Tokyo: Benseisha, 1977), 8:252. See also figure 2.

10. Reproduced as frontispieces 2 and 3 of SSS 3 (unnumbered pp. 2–3). Although *Edo meishoki* of 1662 and *Edo suzume* of 1677 locate Tenma Hachidayū's theater in Negichō, two maps from 1681 and 1684, as well as *Edo kanoko* of 1687, locate it in Sakaichō. See SSS 3:591; and Yasuda Fukiko, *Ko-jōruri: Tayū no zuryō to sono jidai* (Tokyo: Yagi shoten, 1998), 147, 153, 156.

11. Yasuda Fukiko suggests that the last two of these works may actually be by Tenma Hachidayū II, whom Shinoda Jun'ichi identifies as Iwami-no-jō Fujiwara Morinobu Tenma Hachidayū 石見掾藤原守信天満八太夫 and who, according to a 1676 entry in *Moriyama go-nikki*, was Tenma Hachidayū's son. See Yasuda, *Ko-jōruri*, 154–56; and Shinoda, "Tenma Hachidayū zakkō," 601a.

12. Reproduced as frontispiece 1 of SSS 3 (unnumbered p. 1).

Appendix 2

Works in This Volume

Aigo-no-waka

My translation is based on the annotated edition of the circa 1670 *Aigo-no-waka*, in SNKS *Sekkyō shū*, 301–44, and Tōyō bunko 243:163–98.

Some *Aigo-no-waka* texts that are available in photographic or modern typeset editions:

Aigo-no-waka あいごの若 (1661)   An illustrated and incomplete woodblock-printed *shōhon* in six acts. Published by Yamamoto Kuhei 山本九兵衛 of Kyoto in the first month of Manji 4 (1661). Several pages have been lost. The chanter is unknown; Muroki Yatarō suggests that it was Higurashi Kodayū (SNKS *Sekkyō shū*, 421). Typeset in SSS 2:108–25, in which the missing pages have been replaced by the corresponding passages in an undated six-act text from the former Koshidō bunko 古梓堂文庫 archive. Illustrations reproduced in SSS 2:527–29.

Aigo-no-waka あいこの若 (ca. 1670)   An illustrated woodblock-printed *shōhon* in six acts. The chanter is unknown; Richard Lane and Muroki Yatarō suggest that it was Tenma Hachidayū (Tōyō bunko 243:331; SNKS *Sekkyō shū*, 421).

Published in Edo around Kanbun 10 (1670). Formerly owned by Yokoyama Shigeru (Akagi bunko archive); currently in the possession of Osaka University Library. Typeset and annotated in SNKS *Sekkyō shū*, 301–44, and *Tōyō bunko* 243:163–98. Photographically reproduced at the Akagi bunko *ko-jōruri* Web site of Osaka University Library.[1] Two of its illustrations are also reproduced as a frontispiece to SSS 2 (unnumbered p. 36).

Aigo-no-waka あいこの若 (1708)   An illustrated woodblock-printed *shōhon* in six acts, subtitled *Hiyoshi Sannō matsuri* (*Festival of Hiyoshi Sannō Shrine*) and *Karasaki no hitotsumatsu no yurai* (*On the Origins of the Single Pine of Karasaki*). Attributed to the chanter Tenma Hachidayū. Muroki Yatarō surmises that this was in fact Tenma Hachidayū II, rather than the original Tenma Hachidayū.[2] Published by Urokogataya Sanzaemon 鱗形屋三左衛門 of Edo in the first month of Hōei 5 (1708). In the possession of the National Diet Library. Typeset in SSS 2:126–40. Cover and illustrations reproduced in SSS 2:531–33. Facsimile reproduction in *Kinpira-bon zenshū* (Osaka Mainichi shinbunsha, 1926).

Amida's Riven Breast (Amida no munewari)

My translation is based on the annotated edition of the 1651 *Munewari*, supplemented by several pages from the Urokogataya *Amida no munewari*, in SNKBT 90:387–411. *Amida no munewari* also has been translated in C. J. Dunn, *The Early Japanese Puppet Drama* (London: Luzac, 1966), 112–34, from which I have borrowed the English title *Amida's Riven Breast*.

Some *Amida no munewari* texts that are available in photographic or modern typeset editions:

Amida no munewari 阿弥陀胸割 (movable type)   An illustrated and untitled *kokatsuji-ban* text. Published in the late Keichō or Genna era (1596–1615 and 1615–1624). Recently rediscovered. Photographically reproduced at the Web site of the National Institute of Japanese Literature (accession number 99–91).[3]

Munewari むねわり (1651)   An illustrated *tanrokubon* in six acts. Two volumes bound into one. Published by Sōshiya Kahei 草紙屋賀兵衛 of Kyoto in the ninth month of Keian 4 (1651). Shinoda Jun'ichi argues that Kahei used the blocks from an *Amida no munewari* text published around the Kan'ei period

(1624–1644) but that at the end of the first and second volumes (end of the third and sixth acts), he substituted newly carved blocks containing highly condensed versions of the corresponding sections. For this reason, the 1651 *Munewari* is unnaturally abbreviated in those two places.[4] Typeset in Yokoyama Shigeru, ed., *Ko-jōruri shōhon shū* (Tokyo: Kadokawa shoten, 1964), 2:45–56. Typeset and annotated in SNKBT 90:387–411. Photographically reproduced in TTZS 9:309–38. Facsimile reproduction by Yoneyamadō (1932); photographically reproduced in SKFS 15:65–98.

Amida no munewari 阿弥陀胸割 (ca. 1704)   An illustrated woodblock-printed *shōhon* in six acts, attributed to the chanter Tenma Hachidayū and published by the Murataya 村田屋 publishing house of Edo. Subtitled *Shakuson fushigi no hōben* (*Shakyamuni's Mysterious Buddhist Ways*). Yokoyama Shigeru suggests that it was published around the end of the Genroku period (1688–1704; SSS 3:520a). Typeset in Yoshida Kōichi, ed., *Sekkyō jōruri shū 2*, Koten bunko (Tokyo: Koten bunko, 1959), 145:59–85. A copy with handwritten notes by the *gesaku* author Ryūtei Tanehiko (1783–1842) is photographically reproduced at the Akagi bunko *ko-jōruri* Web site of Osaka University Library;[5] facsimile reproduction in *Kinpira-bon zenshū* (Osaka Mainichi shinbunsha, 1926). The cover slip (*daisen*) and first page of an alternative copy from the former collection of the *gesaku* author Shikitei Sanba (1776–1822) are reproduced as frontispiece 7 in SSS 3 (unnumbered p. 7).

Urokogataya *Amida no munewari* 阿弥陀胸割   An illustrated woodblock-printed *shōhon* in six acts, attributed to the chanter Tenma Hachidayū. Subtitled *Shakuson fushigi no hōben* (*Shakyamuni's Mysterious Buddhist Ways*). Published by Urokogataya Magobei 鱗形屋孫兵衛 of Edo. Yokoyama Shigeru proposes that like the circa 1704 *Amida no munewari*, it was derived from a lost Urokogataya *Amida no munewari shōhon* published around the Jōkyō era (1684–1688; SSS 3:519b–20a). Typeset in SSS 3:130–41. Partially typeset and annotated in SNKBT 90:387–411. The cover is reproduced as frontispiece 6 in SSS 3 (unnumbered p. 6); the illustrations are reproduced in SSS 3:632–35.

Amida no munewari 阿弥陀胸割 (1721)   A woodblock-printed *shōhon* in six acts, attributed to the chanter "Dayū" 太夫. Published by the Murataya 村田屋 publishing house of Edo in the first month of Kyōhō 6 (1721). Typeset in Hirotani Yūtarō, ed., *Tokugawa bungei ruijū* (Tokyo: Yokotani kokusho kankōkai, 1925), 8:98–105.

Goō-no-hime

My translation is based on the single surviving woodblock-printed *shōhon*, titled *Goō-no-hime* ごわうのひめ (牛王の姫) and published in six acts by Hachimonjiya Hachizaemon 八文字屋八左衛門 of Kyoto in the first month of Kanbun 13 (1673). Formerly owned by Yokoyama Shigeru (Akagi bunko archive); currently in the possession of Osaka University Library. Typeset and annotated in SNKBT 90:413–38. Photographically reproduced at the Akagi bunko *ko-jōruri* Web site of Osaka University Library.[6]

Karukaya

My translation is based on the annotated edition of the 1631 *Sekkyō Karukaya*, in SNKS *Sekkyō shū*, 11–77.

Some *Karukaya* texts that are available in photographic or modern typeset editions:

Sekkyō Karukaya せつきやうかるかや (late sixteenth century)   An illustrated and untitled *shahon* (*e-iri shahon* 絵入写本) dating from the end of the Muromachi period. Formerly owned by Yokoyama Shigeru (Akagi bunko archive); currently in the possession of the Suntory Museum. Typeset in SSS 1:402–35. Typeset and annotated in SNKBT 90:247–314. Nine of its pages are reproduced as a frontispiece to SSS 1 (unnumbered pp. 28–36). Preserves an especially old rendition of *Karukaya* but lacks the middle "Kōya chapter" (Kōya no maki).[7] Although not a *shōhon*, it is the oldest known *sekkyō* text.

Sekkyō Karukaya せつきやうかるかや (1631)   An illustrated *tanrokubon* in three volumes, published by Jōruriya Kiemon しやうるりや喜衛門 (Tsuruya Kiemon) of Kyoto in the fourth month of Kan'ei 8 (1631). The chanter is unknown; Yokoyama Shigeru, Muroki Yatarō, and Shinoda Jun'ichi suggest that it was Osaka Yoshichirō (SSS 2:505b; SNKS *Sekkyō shū*, 411; SNKBT 90:569). Typeset in SSS 2:3–34. Typeset and annotated in SNKS *Sekkyō shū*, 11–77, and Tōyō bunko 243:61–114. Photographically reproduced in TTZS 50:3–106. The cover and twenty of its pages are also reproduced as a frontispiece to SSS 2 (unnumbered pp. 6, 12–16). Facsimile reproduction by Yoneyamadō (1931); photographically reproduced in SKFS 13:191–302.

Karukaya Dōshin かるかや道心 (ca. 1661)   An illustrated woodblock-printed *shōhon* in six acts, published by Hangiya Hikoemon 板木屋彦右衛門 of Edo sometime in the first years of the Kanbun era (1661–1673). The original title slip (*daisen*) has been lost, but Yokoyama Shigeru suggests that the work was attributed to the chanter Tenma Hachidayū (SSS 2:311a; SSS 3:549b). Typeset in SSS 2:35–54. Illustrations reproduced in SSS 2:517–20.

Urokogataya *Karukaya Dōshin* かるかや道心   An illustrated woodblock-printed *shōhon* in six acts, attributed to the chanter Tenma Magoshirō. Subtitled *Shigeuji midai michiyuki* (*Shigeuji's and His Wife's Travel Passages*) and *Ishidōmaru Kōya-iri* (*Ishidōmaru's Admission to Mount Kōya*). Published by the Urokogataya 鱗形屋 publishing house of Edo. According to Yokoyama Shigeru, this is a Tenna era (1681–1684) re-release of the circa 1661 *Karukaya Dōshin* published by Hangiya Hikoemon and likely attributed to Tenma Hachidayū; Yokoyama speculates that after acquiring the blocks, the Urokogataya simply updated the names of the chanter and the publisher (SSS 3:549b). Photographically reproduced at the Akagi bunko *ko-jōruri* Web site of Osaka University Library.[8] The cover is also reproduced as frontispiece 4 in SSS 3 (unnumbered p. 4).

Urokogataya Magobei *Karukaya Dōshin* かるかや道心   An illustrated woodblock-printed *shōhon* in six acts, attributed to the chanter Tenma Hachidayū. Published by Urokogataya Magobei 鱗形屋孫兵衛 of Edo (Urokogataya publishing house). Photographically reproduced at the Akagi bunko *ko-jōruri* Web site of Osaka University Library.[9]

Oguri

My translation is based on the unannotated edition of the *Oguri nara ehon* (seventeenth-century Tenri University Library text) in SSS 2:351–83.

Some *Oguri* texts that are available in photographic or modern typeset editions:

Oguri おくり (ca. 1625)   An illustrated, incomplete, and untitled *kokatsuji tanrokubon* dating from the first years of the Kan'ei period (1624–1644). Only the third of three volumes survives, and it, too, is missing an indeterminate number of pages at its end. Shinoda Jun'ichi argues that it predates the circa 1634 *Sekkyō Oguri* (SSS 2:506a). Shinoda also suggests that it is not actually a *shōhon*, but Yokoyama Shigeru disagrees, maintaining that it is in fact the oldest *sekkyō shōhon* known to survive today (SSS 2:506b–8a). In the possession of the Jingū bunko archive. Typeset in SSS 2:405–18. Ten of its pages are reproduced as a frontispiece to SSS 2 (unnumbered pp. 1–5).

Sekkyō Oguri せつきやうおくり (ca. 1634)   A fragmentary woodblock-printed text (likely a *tanrokubon*) in three volumes, dating from the middle of the Kan'ei period (1624–1644). Only three sheets (two-and-a-half "double pages," or *chō* 丁) survive: the cover of volume 2, much of the upper half of the first double-page of volume 2, and much of the upper half of another double-page from early in volume 2. The fragments are discussed in SSS 2:500a–505b and are partially typeset in SSS 2:504a–5a. The cover and the first double-page are reproduced as a frontispiece to SSS 2 (unnumbered pp. 7, 17). The chanter is unknown; Yokoyama Shigeru and Shinoda Jun'ichi suggest that it was Osaka Yoshichirō (SSS 2:505b; SNKBT 90:569). Based on its fragments, the text seems to have been close in content to the *Oguri nara ehon* (SSS 2:505a). In the possession of Shinoda Jun'ichi.

Oguri emaki おくり絵巻   A fifteen-scroll *emaki* with illustrations by (or at least in the style of) Iwasa Matabei, dating from around the mid-seventeenth century (late Kan'ei through Meireki periods, ca. 1640–1658). The textual portions are believed to be derived from a *sekkyō shōhon*. The chanter is unknown; Muroki Yatarō suggests that it was either Osaka Yoshichirō or Sado Shichidayū (SNKS *Sekkyō shū*, 411). Typeset in SSS 1:345–401. Typeset and annotated in SNKS *Sekkyō shū*, 211–98; SNKBT 90:160–246; and Tōyō bunko 243:201–71. Nineteen of its illustrations are reproduced as a frontispiece to SSS 1 (unnumbered pp. 18–27). In the possession of the Museum of the Imperial Collections (Kunaichō sannomaru shōzōkan 宮内庁三の丸尚蔵館). Translated by Susan Matisoff in "*Oguri*: An Early Edo Tale of Suffering, Resurrection, Revenge, and Deification," *Monumenta Nipponica* 66, no. 1 (2011): 49–97.

Oguri nara ehon おぐり奈良絵本   An illustrated *nara ehon* in three volumes, dating from the early Edo period (seventeenth century). Particularly close in content to the incomplete, circa 1625 *Oguri*. It is either a transcription of an old *sekkyō* (*ko-sekkyō* 古説経) performance or a "readerly" (*yomihon* 読み本) adaptation of a *sekkyō shōhon*. Yokoyama Shigeru suggests that its textual portions may be derived from a copy of the circa 1634 *Sekkyō Oguri* or another, closely related Kan'ei-period *shōhon* (SSS 2:505b). Formerly owned by Yokoyama Shigeru (Akagi bunko archive); currently in the possession of the Tenri University Library. Typeset in SSS 2:351–83. Four of its pages are reproduced as a frontispiece to SSS 2 (unnumbered pp. 26–27).

Oguri Hangan おぐり判官 (1666)   An illustrated woodblock-printed *shōhon* in six acts, published by Yamamoto Kuhei 山本九兵衛 of Second Avenue, Kyoto, in the ninth month of Kanbun 6 (1666). The chanter is unknown. Described in SSS 2:316a–17a. Three of its nine illustrations are reproduced in SSS 2:525 and SNKS *Sekkyō shū*, 216–17, 223.

Oguri monogatari おぐり物語 (ca. 1673)   An illustrated and incomplete woodblock-printed text in three volumes (first volume missing). Apparently a "readerly" (*yomihon*) adaptation of a *sekkyō shōhon*. Published by Tsuruya Kiemon 鶴屋喜右衛門 of Edo in the late Kanbun or early Enpō period (early to mid-1670s).[10] Formerly owned by Yokoyama Shigeru (Akagi bunko archive). Typeset in SSS 2:384–404. Illustrations reproduced in SNKS *Sekkyō shū*, 228–29, 240–41, 250–51, 255, 257, 259, 265, 268–69, 272–73, 283, 287, 295, 297 (together with the textual portions of the *Oguri emaki*). Two of its illustrations are also reproduced as a frontispiece to SSS 2 (unnumbered pp. 24–25).

Oguri Hangan おぐり判官 (1675)   An illustrated woodblock-printed *shōhon* in six acts, published by Shōhon-ya Gohei 正本屋五兵衛 in Enpō 3 (1675).[11] The chanter is unknown. Yokoyama Shigeru suggests that it may have been Higurashi Kodayū and that the text may be a reprint of an older *sekkyō shōhon* from the Manji or very early Kanbun period (1658–1661 and 1661–1673). Yokoyama furthermore observes that the language of the 1675 *Oguri Hangan* seems to be older than that of the 1666 *Oguri Hangan* (SSS 2:314b–15b). Typeset in SSS 2:55–79. Cover and illustrations reproduced in SSS 2:521–24.

Oguri no Hangan おくりの判官 (ca. 1711–1736)   An unillustrated woodblock-printed *shōhon* in six acts, attributed to the chanter Sado Shichidayū Toyotaka. Published by Sōhei 惣兵衛 of Edo around the Shōtoku and Kyōhō periods (1711–1736). Typeset in SSS 2:80–107.

Sanshō Dayū

My translation is based on the annotated edition of the incomplete circa 1639 *Sanshō Dayū*, supplemented by the circa 1670 *Sanshō Dayū monogatari*, in SNKBT 90:318–85. I have also consulted Muroki Yatarō's annotated *Sanshō Dayū*, in SNKS *Sekkyō shū*, 81–152.[12]

Some *Sanshō Dayū* texts that are available in photographic or modern typeset editions:

Sanshō Dayū さんせう太夫 (ca. 1639)   An illustrated and incomplete *tanrokubon* in three volumes, attributed to the chanter Tenka-ichi Sekkyō Yoshichirō 天下一説経与七郎 (Osaka Yoshichirō). Published by Sōshiya Chōbei さうしや長兵衛 (Nagata Chōbei) of Kyoto in the late Kan'ei period (1624–1644) or, according to Muroki Yatarō, around 1639 (SNKS *Sekkyō shū*, 411). The single extant copy (Tenri University Library text) is missing several pages, including the first part of volume 1 and the last part of volume 3. Typeset in SSS 1:3–27. Typeset and annotated in SNKBT 90:318–85; SNKS *Sekkyō shū*, 81–152; and Tōyō bunko 243:3–57. Photographically reproduced in TTZS 50:109–68. Ten of its pages are also reproduced as a frontispiece to SSS 1 (unnumbered pp. 2–6).

Sekkyō Sanshō Dayū せつきやうさんせう太夫 (1656)   An illustrated woodblock-printed *shōhon* in three volumes, attributed to the chanter Tenka-ichi Sekkyō Sado Shichidayū 天下一説経佐渡七太夫 (Sado Shichidayū). Published by Sōshiya Kuhei さうしや九兵衛 (Yamamoto Kuhei) of Kyoto in the sixth month of Meireki 2 (1656). Typeset in SSS 1:28–45. Photographically reproduced in TTZS 50: 171–222. Thirteen of its pages are also reproduced as a frontispiece to SSS 1 (unnumbered pp. 8–11). According to Sakaguchi Hiroyuki, this text reads like a condensed version of the circa 1639 *Sanshō Dayū* (SNKBT 90:317b). Facsimile reproduction by Yoneyamadō (1932); photographically reproduced in SKFS 15:163–214.

Sanshō Dayū さんせう太夫 (1667)   An illustrated woodblock-printed *shōhon* in six acts, published by Yamamoto Kuhei 山本九兵衛 of Kyoto in the fifth month of Kanbun 7 (1667). Two volumes bound into one. Typeset in SSS 1:46–69. Illustrations reproduced in SSS 1:491–94.

Sanshō Dayū monogatari さんせう太夫物語 (ca. 1670)   An illustrated woodblock-printed text in three volumes. Published by Tsuruya Kiemon 鶴屋喜右衛門

of Edo in the mid- to late Kanbun period (1661–1673). Also known as the *sōshihon* 草子本, or "book text," because of its publication as a "readerly" (*yomihon*) edition, rather than a *shōhon*. Volumes 2 and 3 are typeset in SSS 1:319–44; the first few pages of volume 1 are typeset and annotated in SNKBT 90:318–23. Volumes 2 and 3 are photographically reproduced at the Akagi bunko *ko-jōruri* Web site of Osaka University Library.[13] Three of its pages are also reproduced as a frontispiece to SSS 1 (unnumbered pp. 15–17). According to Sakaguchi Hiroyuki, this text is particularly close in content to the circa 1639 *Sanshō Dayū* (SNKBT 90:317a).

Sanshō Dayū さんせう太夫 (around the Genroku period) A fragmentary woodblock-printed *shōhon* in six acts. Published in Edo around the Genroku era (1688–1704). Photographically reproduced at the Web site of the Maizuru City and Ritsumeikan University Art Research Center.[14]

Sanshō Dayū さんせう大夫 (1710) A fragmentary illustrated woodblock-printed *shōhon*, published in Edo in Hōei 7 (1710). Photographically reproduced at the Akagi bunko *ko-jōruri* Web site of Osaka University Library.[15]

Sanshō Dayū 山庄太輔 (1713) An unillustrated woodblock-printed *shōhon* in six acts, attributed to the chanter Sado Shichidayū Toyotaka. Published by San'emon 三右衛門 in the ninth month of Shōtoku 3 (1713). Typeset in SSS 1:70–94. The cover and three pages are reproduced in SSS 1:495.

Sayohime

Also known as *Matsura Chōja*, *Chikubushima no honji*, and *Tsubosaka monogatari*.

My translation is based on the annotated edition of the seventeenth-century Kyoto University *Sayohime nara ehon*, in Shimazu Hisamoto, ed., *Kinko shōsetsu shinsan* (1928; repr., Tokyo: Yūseidō, 1983), 125–58; and on the unannotated editions in SSS 3:462–88 and MJMS 4:422–47.

Some *Sayohime* texts that are available in photographic or modern typeset editions:

Sayohime no sōshi さよひめのさうし A single-volume unillustrated *shahon* dating from around the Keichō period (1596–1615). Formerly owned by Yokoyama

Shigeru (Akagi bunko archive). Typeset in SSS 3:447–61. The cover is reproduced as frontispiece 13 in SSS 3 (unnumbered p. 13).

Chikubushima no honji ちくふしまのほんし A single-volume illustrated *kokatsuji-ban tanrokubon* dating from around the Genna period (1615–1624). Typeset in SSS 3:489–94. Four of its pages are reproduced as frontispiece 44–45 in SSS 3 (unnumbered pp. 44–45). Facsimile reproduction by Nihon koten bungaku kankōkai (1973).

Sayohime さよひめ (Kyoto University) An illustrated *nara ehon* in three volumes, dating from the early Edo period (seventeenth century). A "readerly" (*yomihon*) adaptation of an early *sekkyō* version of the tale. Typeset in SSS 3:462–88; MJMS 4:422–47; and Kyoto daigaku bungakubu kokugogaku kokubungaku kenkyūshitsu, ed., *Kyoto daigaku-zō Muromachi monogatari* (Kyoto: Rinsen shoten, 2000), 6:425–52. Mostly typeset and annotated in Shimazu, ed., *Kinko shōsetsu shinsan*, 125–58.[16] Photographically reproduced in Kyoto daigaku bungakubu kokugogaku kokubungaku kenkyūshitsu, ed., *Kyoto daigaku-zō Muromachi monogatari*, 6:5–164.

Matsura Sayohime まつらさよひめ (Tōyō bunko) An illustrated and incomplete *nara ehon* in three volumes (second volume missing), dating from the early Edo period (seventeenth century). Based on its illustrations, Sakaguchi Hiroyuki tentatively dates it to around the Kanbun period (1661–1673; "Tōyō bunko-bon *Matsura Sayohime*: Shōkai to honkoku," *Jinbun kenkyū* [Osaka shiritsu daigaku bungakubu kiyō] 34, no. 4 [1982]: 162b, typeset pp. 161–81).

Matsura Chōja まつら長じや (1661) An illustrated woodblock-printed *shōhon* in six acts. Published by Yamamoto Kuhei 山本九兵衛 of Kyoto in the fifth month of Kanbun 1 (1661). The chanter is unknown; Muroki Yatarō suggests that it may have been Osaka Yoshichirō (SNKS *Sekkyō shū*, 389, unnumbered headnote). Typeset in SSS 1:163–80. Typeset and annotated in SNKS *Sekkyō shū*, 347–89. Illustrations reproduced in SSS 1:504–7.

Sayohime さよひめ (Museum of Applied Art, Frankfurt) An illustrated *nara ehon* in three volumes, dating from around the Kanbun period (1661–1673). In the possession of the Museum für Angewandte Kunst (Museum of Applied Art) in Frankfurt. Typeset, photographically reproduced, and translated into German in Katja Triplett, *Menschenopfer und Selbstopfer in den japanischen Legenden: Das Frankfurter Manuskript der Matsura Sayohime-Legende*, Religiöse Gegenwart Asiens / Studies in Modern Asian Religions, vol. 4 (Münster: LIT-Verlag, 2004).

Matsura Chōja まつら長者 (ca. 1704)　An illustrated woodblock-printed *shōhon* in six acts. Published by Urokogataya Magobei 鱗形屋孫兵衛 of Edo in the first years of the Hōei period (1704–1711). The chanter is unknown; Yokoyama Shigeru suggests that it may have been Tenma Hachidayū or someone in his lineage (SSS 1:464a). Typeset in SSS 1:181–95. Front and last pages and illustrations reproduced in SSS 1:507–10.

Tsubosaka monogatari 壺坂物語　A single small-scroll *emaki* dating from around the mid-Edo period (eighteenth century). Formerly in the collection of Tsukudo Reikan 筑土鈴寛. Typeset in MJMS 4:448–53.

Shintokumaru

My translation is based on the annotated edition of the 1648 *Sekkyō Shintokumaru*, supplemented by the final two pages of the Urokogataya *Shintokumaru*, in SNKS *Sekkyō shū*, 155–207.

Some *Shintokumaru* texts that are available in photographic or modern typeset editions:

Sekkyō Shintokumaru せつきやうしんとく丸 (1648)　An illustrated *tanrokubon* in three volumes, attributed to the chanter Tenka Musō Sado Shichidayū 天下無双佐渡七太夫 (Sado Shichidayū). Published by Kuhei 九兵衛 (Yamamoto Kuhei) of Second Avenue, Kyoto, in the third month of Shōhō 5 (1648). The single extant copy (Tenri University Library text) is missing one or more pages at the end of its third volume. Typeset in SSS 1:95–118. Typeset and annotated in SNKS *Sekkyō shū*, 155–207, and Tōyō bunko 243:117–59. Photographically reproduced in TTZS 50:223–84. Ten of its pages are also reproduced as a frontispiece to SSS 1 (unnumbered pp. 11–13). Facsimile reproduction by Yoneyamadō (1934); photographically reproduced in SKFS 14:257–318.

Shintokumaru しんとく丸 (1661)　A woodblock-printed *shōhon* in six acts, published by Yamamoto Kuhei 山本九兵衛 of Kyoto in the ninth month of Kanbun

1 (1661). Typeset in Hirotani Yūtarō, ed., *Tokugawa bungei ruijū* (Tokyo: Yokotani kokusho kankōkai, 1925), 8:45–58.

Urokogataya *Shintokumaru* しんとく丸 An illustrated woodblock-printed *shōhon* in six acts, subtitled *Nobuyoshi Kiyomizu mōde* (*Nobuyoshi's Pilgrimage to Kiyomizu*) and *Otohime michiyuki* (*Otohime's Travel Passage*). Attributed to the chanter Shichidayū (Sado Shichidayū). Published by Urokogataya Magobei 鱗形屋孫兵衛 of Edo around the Tenna and Jōkyō eras (1681–1688). Typeset in SSS 1:119–32. Partially reproduced in SSS 1:496–98. The cover of the Tokyo University Library copy is reproduced as a frontispiece to SSS 1 (unnumbered p. 14). Yokoyama Shigeru suggests that the illustrations were drawn by Sugimura Jihei 杉村治兵衛 (SSS 3:553a).

NOTES

1. http://ir.library.osaka-u.ac.jp/web/e-rare/akagi/.
2. Muroki Yatarō, "*Aigo-no-waka*," in *Nihon koten bungaku daijiten* (Tokyo: Iwanami shoten, 1983), 1:3d.
3. http://base1.nijl.ac.jp/iview/Frame.jsp?DB_ID=G0003917KTM&C_CODE=99-091.
4. Shinoda Jun'ichi, "*Amida no munewari*," in *Nihon koten bungaku daijiten* (Tokyo: Iwanami shoten, 1983), 1:80–81.
5. http://ir.library.osaka-u.ac.jp/web/e-rare/akagi/.
6. Ibid.
7. In the case of the SNKBT 90 recension, the editors interpolated the "Kōya chapter" from the 1631 *Sekkyō Karukaya*.
8. http://ir.library.osaka-u.ac.jp/web/e-rare/akagi/.
9. Ibid.
10. Not to be confused with Tsuruya Kiemon of Kyoto, also known as Jōruriya Kiemon.
11. Shōhon-ya Gohei was also the publisher of the 1678 *Sanshō Dayū*, discussed in SSS 1:446.
12. As does SNKBT 90, SNKS *Sekkyō shū* reproduces the circa 1639 *Sanshō Dayū* and supplements it with the circa 1670 *Sanshō Dayū monogatari* (vol. 3). However, at the time of SNKS *Sekkyō shū*'s publication, the first volume of *Sanshō Dayū monogatari* had not yet been found. SNKS *Sekkyō shū* therefore reproduces in its first four pages the 1656 *Sekkyō Sanshō Dayū* creatively supplemented with excerpts from the 1667 *Sanshō Dayū*.
13. http://ir.library.osaka-u.ac.jp/web/e-rare/akagi/.

14. http://www.arc.ritsumei.ac.jp/archive01/theater/html/maiduru/dgsansyo.htm.

15. http://ir.library.osaka-u.ac.jp/web/e-rare/akagi/.

16. In the *michiyuki* travel passage in volume 2, Shimazu inexplicably omits all the text between illustrations 9 and 10, corresponding to SSS 3:475a–76a and MJMS 4:434b–35b.

Glossary

EMAKI 絵巻   "Picture scrolls" with hand-drawn or hand-painted illustrations. They frequently include hand-written textual passages (*kotobagaki* 詞書) between their illustrated scenes, and they always unroll horizontally (as opposed to *kakejiku* 掛軸, or hanging scrolls, which unroll vertically).

KO-JŌRURI 古浄瑠璃   The seventeenth-century "old *jōruri*" puppet theater; a term traditionally used to designate early *jōruri* before the playwright Chikamatsu Monzaemon's *Shusse Kagekiyo* (*Kagekiyo Victorious*) of 1685. Includes the subgenre of *Kinpira jōruri* (fl. ca. 1657–1662).[1] *Ko-jōruri* survives in a limited number of seventeenth-century woodblock-printed *shōhon* "true texts."

KOKATSUJI-BAN 古活字版   A "movable-type edition," a kind of a woodblock-printed book (*hanpon* 版本) produced by using interchangeable wooden characters that could be arranged to form a recyclable printing block. All such books date from approximately the first fifty years of the seventeenth century.

NARA EHON 奈良絵本   So-called Nara picture books, although their connection to the city of Nara is tenuous at best. These are hand-copied books with colorful hand-painted illustrations, mass-produced from the late Muromachi through the mid-Edo periods (sixteenth through eighteenth centuries). The term is also sometimes used to designate a kind of picture scroll (*nara ehon emaki* 奈良絵本絵巻) from the same period.

OTOGIZŌSHI お伽草子 A generic designation for various types of short, usually anonymous works of prose fiction from around the Muromachi period (1336–1573). Some four hundred different examples are known to survive. Frequently illustrated, *otogizōshi* were produced in *shahon*, *nara ehon*, *emaki*, and woodblock-printed formats.

SEKKYŌ 説経 (or SEKKYŌ-BUSHI 説経節) The medieval and early Edo-period "sermon-ballad" storytelling genre. *Sekkyō* survives in a limited number of seventeenth- and early-eighteenth-century woodblock-printed *shōhon* "true texts," which date from an age in which *sekkyō* had begun to move into urban theaters and to be influenced by the *ko-jōruri* puppet theater.

SHAHON 写本 A "transcribed text," a term used to designate any kind of hand-copied manuscript, usually without illustrations.

SHŌHON 正本 Woodblock-printed "true texts" that purport to be faithful transcriptions of *sekkyō*, *jōruri*, and *nagauta* manuscripts employed by professional chanters. *Shōhon* often include illustrations and musical notations (*fushizuke* 節付け).

TANROKUBON 丹緑本 "Red and green books," a type of woodblock-printed book with distinctively red, green, yellow, and occasionally blue illustrations, mass-produced from around the early 1620s through the early 1660s (late Genna through Manji periods), although most prolifically in the Kan'ei period (1624–1644). Many of the early *shōhon* are also *tanrokubon*.

NOTE

1. Janice Shizue Kanemitsu, "Guts and Tears: Kinpira Jōruri and Its Textual Transformations," in *Publishing the Stage: Print and Performance in Early Modern Japan*, ed. Keller Kimbrough and Satoko Shimazaki (Boulder: University of Colorado Center for Asian Studies, 2011), 15–35.

Bibliography

Abe Yasurō 阿部泰郎 et al., eds. *Nikkō tenkaizō Jikidan innenshū: Honkoku to sakuin*. Kenkyū sōsho, no. 225. Osaka: Izumi shoin, 1998.
Arnzen, Michael A. "Who's Laughing Now? . . . The Postmodern Splatter Film." *Journal of Popular Film & Television* 21, no. 4 (1994): 176–84.
Asahara Yoshiko 麻原美子 and Kitahara Yasuo 北原保雄, eds. *Mai no hon*. Shin Nihon koten bungaku taikei, vol. 59. Tokyo: Iwanami shoten, 1994.
Asakura Haruhiko 朝倉治彦, ed. *Tōkaidō meishoki 2*. Tōyō bunko, vol. 361. Tokyo: Heibonsha, 1979.
Bridgstock, Martin. "The Twilit Fringe—Anthropology and Modern Horror Fiction." *Journal of Popular Culture* 23, no. 3 (1989): 115–23.
Dunn, C. J. *The Early Japanese Puppet Drama*. London: Luzac, 1966.
Edo meishoki. Kinsei bungaku shiryō ruijū: Kohan chishi hen, vol. 8. Tokyo: Benseisha, 1977.
Franks, Amy Christine. "Another *Tale of the Heike*: An Examination of the Engyōbon *Heike monogatari*." Ph.D. diss., Yale University, 2009.
Freud, Sigmund. *Three Essays on the Theory of Sexuality* (1905), translated by James Strachey. In *The Essentials of Psycho-Analysis*, edited by Anna Freud, 277–375. Harmondsworth: Penguin, 1986.
Glassman, Hank, and Keller Kimbrough. "Editors' Introduction: Vernacular Buddhism and Medieval Japanese Literature." *Japanese Journal of Religious Studies* 36, no. 2 (2009): 201–8.

Goodwin, Janet R. *Selling Songs and Smiles: The Sex Trade in Heian and Kamakura Japan.* Honolulu: University of Hawaiʻi Press, 2007.

Hirotani Yūtarō 廣谷雄太郎, ed. *Tokugawa bungei ruijū.* Vol. 8. Tokyo: Yokotani kokusho kankōkai, 1925.

Hirukawa Yoshiko 肥留川嘉子. *Sekkyō no bungakuteki kenkyū.* Osaka: Izumi shoin, 1986.

———. *Sekkyō to bukyoku: Bungakuteki kenkyū.* Osaka: Izumi shoin, 2002.

Hokekyō jikidanshō. 3 vols. Kyoto: Rinsen shoten, 1979.

Ishii, Nobuko. "Sekkyō-bushi." *Monumenta Nipponica* 44, no. 3 (1989): 283–307.

Ishikawa Tōru 石川透. *Nara ehon, emaki no tenkai.* Tokyo: Miyai shoten, 2009.

Kanemitsu, Janice Shizue. "Guts and Tears: Kinpira Jōruri and Its Textual Transformations." In *Publishing the Stage: Print and Performance in Early Modern Japan,* ed. Keller Kimbrough and Satoko Shimazaki, 15–35. Boulder: University of Colorado Center for Asian Studies, 2011.

Keene, Donald. "The Hippolytus Triangle, East and West." *Yearbook of Comparative and General Literature* 11 (1962): 162–71.

———. *World Within Walls: Japanese Literature of the Pre-modern Era, 1600–1867.* New York: Holt, Rinehart and Winston, 1976.

Kikuchi Hitoshi 菊地仁. "Sekkyō *Karukaya* to '*Kōya no maki.*'" *Denshō bungaku kenkyū* 21 (1978): 23–35.

Kimbrough, Keller, and Satoko Shimazaki, eds. *Publishing the Stage: Print and Performance in Early Modern Japan.* Boulder: University of Colorado Center for Asian Studies, 2011.

Kimbrough, R. Keller, trans. *Chūjōhime* and *Shintokumaru.* In *Traditional Japanese Literature: An Anthology, Beginnings to 1600,* edited by Haruo Shirane, 1138–50, 1160–81. New York: Columbia University Press, 2007.

———. *Preachers, Poets, Women, and the Way: Izumi Shikibu and the Buddhist Literature of Medieval Japan.* Ann Arbor: University of Michigan Center for Japanese Studies, 2008.

———. "Tourists in Paradise: Writing the Pure Land in Medieval Japanese Fiction." *Japanese Journal of Religious Studies* 33, no. 2 (2006): 269–96.

Kita, Sandy. *The Last Tosa: Iwasa Katsumochi Matabei, Bridge to Ukiyo-e.* Honolulu: University of Hawaiʻi Press, 1999.

Kitahara Yasuo 北原保雄 and Ogawa Eiichi 小川栄一, eds. *Engyō-bon Heike monogatari: Honbun hen.* Vol. 2. Tokyo: Benseisha, 1990.

Kokusho kankōkai 国書刊行会, ed. *Shin gunsho ruijū.* Vol. 9. Tokyo: Daiichi shobō, 1976.

Kuroki Kanzō 黒木勘蔵. *Jōruri-shi.* Tokyo: Seijisha, 1943.

Kyō suzume. Kinsei bungaku shiryō ruijū: Kohan chishi hen, vol. 4. Tokyo: Benseisha, 1979.

Kyoto daigaku bungakubu kokugogaku kokubungaku kenkyūshitsu 京都大学文学部国語学国文学研究室, ed. *Kyoto daigaku-zō Muromachi monogatari.* Vol. 6. Kyoto: Rinsen shoten, 2000.

Matisoff, Susan. "Barred from Paradise? Mount Kōya and the *Karukaya* Legend." In *Engendering Faith: Women and Buddhism in Premodern Japan*, edited by Barbara Ruch, 463–500. Ann Arbor: University of Michigan Center for Japanese Studies, 2002.

———. "Deciphering the Code of Love: *Yamato kotoba* in Literature and Life." In *Currents in Japanese Culture: Translations and Transformations*, edited by Amy Vladeck Heinrich, 117–34. New York: Columbia University Press, 1997.

———. "Holy Horrors: The Sermon-Ballads of Medieval and Early Modern Japan." In *Flowing Traces: Buddhism in the Literary and Visual Arts of Japan*, edited by James Sanford, William LaFleur, and Masatoshi Nagatomi, 234–61. Princeton, N.J.: Princeton University Press, 1992.

———. *The Legend of Semimaru, Blind Musician of Japan*. New York: Columbia University Press, 1978.

———. "The Log Cabin Emperor: Marginality and the Legend of Oguri Hangan." *Cahiers d'Extrême Asie* 13 (2002): 361–77.

———. "*Oguri*: An Early Edo Tale of Suffering, Resurrection, Revenge, and Deification." *Monumenta Nipponica* 66, no. 1 (2011): 49–97.

———. "Reflections of Terute: Searching for a Hidden Shaman-Entertainer." *Women and Performance: A Journal of Feminist Theory* 12, no. 1 (2001): 113–34.

McKelway, Matthew Philip. *Capitalscapes: Folding Screens and Political Imagination in Late Medieval Kyoto*. Honolulu: University of Hawai'i Press, 2006.

Minobe Shigekatsu 美濃部重克. "*Monokusa Tarō no kōshōteki shikumi shōkō*." In *Ronsan: Setsuwa to setsuwa bungaku*, edited by Mitani Eiichi 三谷栄一 et al., 417–30. Tokyo: Kasama shoin, 1979.

Moerman, D. Max. *Localizing Paradise: Kumano Pilgrimage and the Religious Landscape of Premodern Japan*. Cambridge, Mass.: Harvard University Asia Center, 2005.

Morrison, Barbara S. "Body Rhetoric: Women en Route to Salvation in *Oguri* and *Pilgrim's Progress*." Ph.D. diss., University of North Dakota, 2006.

———. "Feminist Voices: Representations of Female Agency and the Figure of Terute in the Sermon Ballad, *Oguri*." *Utsunomiya daigaku kokusaigakubu kenkyūronshū* 24 (2007): 125–35.

Muroki Yatarō 室木弥太郎. "*Aigo-no-waka*." In *Nihon koten bungaku daijiten*, 1:3. Tokyo: Iwanami shoten, 1983.

———. "Kaisetsu." In *Sekkyō shū*, Shinchō Nihon koten shūsei, 393–423. Tokyo: Shinchōsha, 1977.

———. *Zōtei katarimono (mai, sekkyō, ko-jōruri) no kenkyū*. 2nd rev. ed. Tokyo: Kazama shobō, 1992.

Nishida Kōzō 西田耕三. "Sekkyō jōruri to ko-jōruri: Toshika, gekika." *Kokubungaku: Kaishaku to kanshō* 70, no. 12 (2005): 112–20.

Nishino Haruo 西野春雄, ed. *Yōkyoku hyakuban*. Shin Nihon koten bungaku taikei, vol. 57. Tokyo: Iwanami shoten, 1998.

Ōshima Tatehiko 大島建彦 and Watari Kōichi 渡浩一, eds. *Muromachi monogatari sōshi shū*. Shinpen Nihon koten bungaku zenshū, vol. 63. Tokyo: Shōgakukan, 2002.

Saitō Ken'ichi 斉藤研一. *Kodomo no chūsei-shi*. Tokyo: Yoshikawa kōbunkan, 2003.

Sakaguchi Hiroyuki 阪口弘之. "Sekkyō *Karukaya* to Kōya denshō." *Kokugo to kokubungaku* 71, no. 10 (1994): 1–18.

——. "Tōyō bunko-bon *Matsura Sayohime*: Shōkai to honkoku." *Jinbun kenkyū* (Osaka shiritsu daigaku bungakubu kiyō) 34, no. 4 (1982): 161–81.

Shimazu Hisamoto 島津久基, ed. *Kinko shōsetsu shinsan*. Tokyo: Chūkōkan, 1928. Reprint, Tokyo: Yūseidō, 1983.

Shinno Toshikazu 真野俊和. "Kōbō Daishi no haha: Akoya-gozen no denshō to Shikoku reijō engi." In *Kōbō Daishi shinkō*, edited by Hinonishi Shinjō 日野西真定, 89–113. Tokyo: Yūzankaku shuppan, 1988.

Shinoda Jun'ichi 信多純一. "*Amida no munewari*." In *Nihon koten bungaku daijiten*, 1:80–81. Tokyo: Iwanami shoten, 1983.

——. "*Amida no munewari* fukugen kō." In *Kinsei bungaku: Sakka to sakuhin*, edited by Nakamura Yukihiko hakushi kanreki kinen ronbunshū kankōkai 中村幸彦博士還暦記念論文集刊行会, 410–32. Tokyo: Chūōkōronsha, 1973.

——. "Kinsei shoki no katarimono." In *Ko-jōruri, sekkyō shū*, 551–81. Shin Nihon koten bungaku taikei, vol. 90. Tokyo: Iwanami shoten, 1999.

——. "Tenma Hachidayū zakkō." In *Sekkyō shōhon shū*, edited by Yokoyama Shigeru 横山重, 3:590–601. Tokyo: Kadokawa shoten, 1968.

Shinpan Shikidō ōkagami kankōkai 新版色道大鏡刊行会, ed. *Shinpan Shikidō ōkagami*. Tokyo: Yagi shoten, 2006.

Sorimachi, Shigeo. *Catalogue of Japanese Illustrated Books and Manuscripts in the Spencer Collection of the New York Public Library*. Tokyo: Kōbunsō, 1978.

Tokuda Kazuo 徳田和夫, ed. *Otogizōshi jiten*. Tokyo: Tōkyōdō shuppan, 2002.

——. *Otogizōshi kenkyū*. Tokyo: Miyai shoten, 1988.

Triplett, Katja. *Menschenopfer und Selbstopfer in den japanischen Legenden: Das Frankfurter Manuskript der Matsura Sayohime-Legende*. Religiöse Gegenwart Asiens / Studies in Modern Asian Religions, vol. 4. Münster: LIT-Verlag, 2004.

Tsuji Eiko 辻英子. *Zaigai Nihon emaki no kenkyū to shiryō*. Kasama sōsho, no. 328. Tokyo: Kasama shoin, 1999.

Wakatsuki Yasuji 若月保治. *Ningyō jōruri-shi kenkyū*. Tokyo: Sakurai shoten, 1943.

Warner, Marina. *From the Beast to the Blonde: On Fairy Tales and Their Tellers*. New York: Farrar, Straus & Giroux, 1994.

Watson, Burton, trans. *The Lotus Sutra*. New York: Columbia University Press, 1993.

Yasuda Fukiko 安田富貴子. *Ko-jōruri: Tayū no zuryō to sono jidai*. Tokyo: Yagi shoten, 1998.

Yokoyama Shigeru 横山重. "Takadachi." In *Ko-jōruri shōhon shū*, 1:323–29. Tokyo: Kadokawa shoten, 1964.

Yoshida Kōichi 吉田幸一, ed. *Sekkyō jōruri shū 2*. Koten bunko, vol. 145. Tokyo: Koten bunko, 1959.